The Strip-Built Sea Kayak

The Strip-Built Sea Kayak

Three Rugged, Beautiful Boats You Can Build

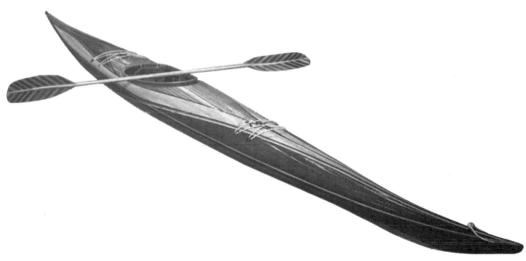

Nick Schade

Ragged Mountain Press
Camden, Maine

New York • San Francisco • Washington, D.C. • Auckland • Bogotá
Caracas • Lisbon • London • Madrid • Mexico City • Milan • Montreal
New Delhi • San Juan • Singapore • Sydney • Tokyo • Toronto

International Marine/
Ragged Mountain Press

A Division of The McGraw·Hill Companies

6 8 10 9 7 5

Copyright © 1998 Ragged Mountain Press

Library of Congress Cataloging-in-Publication Data
Schade, Nick. 1995–Present
    The strip-built sea kayak : three rugged, beautiful boats you can
build / Nick Schade.
        p.   cm.
    Includes bibliographical references (p. 194 cm.   ) and index.
    ISBN: 0-07-057989-X (acid-free paper)
    1. Kayaks—Design and construction—Amateurs' manuals.   I. Title.
VM353.S3   1997
623.8'29—dc21   97-19039
                                                                         CIP

Questions regarding the content of this book should be addressed to:
Ragged Mountain Press
P.O. Box 220
Camden, ME 04843

Questions regarding the ordering of this book should be addressed to:
The McGraw-Hill Companies
Customer Service Department
P.O. Box 547
Blacklick, OH 43004
Retail customers: 1-800-262-4729
Bookstores: 1-800-233-4726
Visit us on the World Wide Web at www.books.mcgraw-hill.com

A portion of the profits from the sale of each Ragged Mountain Press book
is donated to an environmental cause.

The Strip-Built Sea Kayak is printed on 60-pound Finch Opaque, an acid-free paper.

Printed by Quebecor Printing Company, Fairfield, PA
Design by Chris McLarty, Silverline Studio
Photos and illustrations by the author
Production management by Janet Robbins
Page layout by Publishers Design and Production Services, Inc.
Production assistance by Shannon Thomas
Edited by Jonathan Eaton, Tom McCarthy, John Vigor

Dedication

In memory of my wife Cathy. I would not have
started this project without her encouragement.
The memory of that encouragement let me finish it.

Contents

Contents

The Strip-Built Sea Kayak

Acknowledgments

I would like to thank all those who helped me expand this book beyond what I could have accomplished on my own: my brother, Eric, for his collaboration as we learned together how to make strip-built kayaks and what we could do with the strips; also for his input on the Artistic Creation section of this book (Chapter 8) and his review of the manuscript; Michael Vermouth, of the Newfound Woodworks, and Chris Hardy, of Marine CAM Services, for their material support in the making of some of the boats used in the photographs; Jay Babina for his contribution of techniques; and the members of the Internet's kayak community for their insight into all kinds of things. My thanks to Jon Eaton, of International Marine and Ragged Mountain Press, for his editing, encouragement, and especially his patience and understanding as I went through some hard times.

Finally, I must thank my parents for their help: my mother was my photographic consultant and also helped me negotiate some of the vagaries of the publishing industry; my father provided his simple interest; my father-in-law, Peter Stern, with his editing, is, as much as anyone, responsible for making my original book proposal something that Ragged Mountain Press would be interested in. This book would have been better had he survived to provide that editing on the finished result; and my mother-in-law, Helen, for keeping me as her son after the loss of her daughter.

After the loss of Cathy during the writing of this book, there were innumerable people who helped me in ways they probably don't understand. It is the simplest things that help the most. I thank you all.

The Strip-Built Sea Kayak

Introduction

Strip-building is the art of taking stacks of thin strips of wood and converting them into beautiful and durable watercraft. It has been a popular method of making canoes for years, and now you can use it to create rugged sea kayaks, too. Despite the complex shape of a kayak, building with strips is not as difficult as you might imagine. You don't need extraordinary skills or knowledge, and you won't have to invest a small fortune in specialized tools. You can believe me when I say it's easily within the ability of the average do-it-yourselfer.

I started paddling as a kid, mainly in my parents' canoe and a kayak my father made from a kit, so when I got out of college I wanted a boat of my own. I had read about the idea of a "sea kayak," but I'd never seen a real one. It sounded like the ideal vessel, because although I had enjoyed paddling my father's little kayak, it wasn't fit for the sea, which was really where I wanted to be. The problem was, as a typical college student I didn't have enough money to buy a sea kayak.

I remembered, though, that a couple of years previously, my father had bought a book called *Building a Strip Canoe*, by Gil Gilpatrick. My brother had used it to build a canoe of his own, and I'd helped him. He didn't have much faith that the canoe would be any good, but it seemed like a fun thing to try. Wonder of wonders, the canoe worked out

Strip-building a kayak means taking a pile of narrow strips of wood and wrapping them around a temporary form. The strips can be laid in almost any direction as long as you cover the forms with wood.

The wood strips are covered with fiberglass and resin to create a durable and beautiful craft that is also a work of art.

great—in fact, all these years later he still has it. I figured that I could probably make a decent kayak using this strip method. I did some research. I studied everything I could find about sea kayaks and I decided what qualities my boat would need. Then, on my parents' dining-room floor, I drew up plans for a kayak. I subsequently built it in the basement of my brother's house.

When it was finished, I tried it out on the waters of the Maine coast. After a couple of trips, I was hooked. My brother tried it, and he was hooked. He took my forms and built a kayak of his own. Then a friend tried his kayak and he, too, was soon building one for himself.

That first boat wasn't perfect, of course, but it was fun to build and it taught me a lot about kayaking. Inevitably, I had the urge to build another kayak. I am now deeply addicted to both sea kayaking and kayak building.

I build my own boats for hard use. I also want kayaks that perform well in a wide variety of conditions, from backwaters to surf, so I have refined my designs to the highest performance standards. Three of the best are featured in this book.

For the beginner, I've included a design that has served me well for 10 years. It's a stable, comfortable, easy-to-build kayak. Thanks to the simplicity of its lines, the design is very adaptable. You can modify it to build a custom craft of your own, from a small paddle boat to a roomy two-person kayak.

The second boat is a high-performance design suitable for intermediate and skilled kayakers wanting a boat for day use and overnight trips. This design is more of a challenge to build than the first one. It's influenced by the kayaks of Greenland, and would look good even if it were made of plastic and painted white. Made of wood, it's nothing less than spectacular.

The third boat fills the desire of many builders—a boat they can share with a friend. Although it's based on the high-performance lines of the second design, this boat is a comfortable tandem.

To complement the plans for these three designs, this book features comprehensive descriptions of the building process. I find it very frustrating when books leave out crucial details, so I made myself a promise: A complete novice will be able to construct a finished kayak after reading nothing but this book. And to help transform that promise into reality I describe alternate methods for those few of you who might feel the initial description is beyond your ability.

Furthermore, if you're an experimenter, I encourage you to take risks.

Much of the pleasure of building a wooden kayak lies in the beauty of the finished product. As if the wood alone weren't attractive enough, the thin flexible strips provide a unique opportunity for you to get artistically creative. Different kinds of wood produce natural contrasts that enhance the inherent grace and style of the kayak, so if you have an artistic bent I offer some techniques to get you started on a kayak that is more than just a nice boat.

I've also included in this book a discussion of the design considerations that will help you choose the right kayak for your particular purposes, either from my designs in this book or from other sources. I don't dwell on technical terms but I do give practical advice on what you should look for.

As for the tools required to strip-build a kayak, well, they're pretty basic. You'll find many of them in your toolbox already, but I have to add that the exact right tools will greatly ease the building process. You'll find information here about what's important to look for when you select new tools and how to get the most out of tools you already have.

One of the most frustrating tasks when building a boat is finding sources of the specialized materials. As usual, however, they're not hard to acquire when you know where to look. I provide a list of reliable sources and offer suggestions on where to find other suppliers.

Incidentally, talking about frustration, I urge you not to sweat the details. The reason for building the boat is to get out on the water. It's sometimes difficult to remember while you're building that what you need is not a perfectly constructed example of naval architecture but a reasonably solid kayak that floats. There are no mistakes that you can't fix with a bit of patience and a little elbow grease, so don't let the small stuff get in the way of the finished product. I want to get you afloat as soon as possible. I am addicted to building boats and paddling the boats I build. I want to spread the disease.

Finally, a word of assurance: If you need more information to boost your confidence, or a little moral support, or more inspiration to get you started or to help you finish, there's free help on the Internet. Go to http://www.guillemot-kayaks.com/. You will find reports about building and paddling kayaks, a bulletin board for discussing building techniques, links to more information, and updates to this book.

Strip-Building in a Nutshell

Here's a step-by-step overview of the strip-building process. The numbers following each step are page numbers where the step is described in more detail. While building a kayak may at first appear complicated and huge, it can easily be broken down into a series of small, manageable tasks. None of these steps is beyond the capability of anyone who has ever picked up a hand tool.

Getting Ready

1. Cut ¼-inch strips off a ¾-inch cedar, redwood, or pine plank. (64)
2. **Optional**: Mill a "cove" and "bead" on each edge of the strips. (65)
3. Obtain a fairly straight 2 × 4.
4. Draw the building forms at full size. (51)
5. Glue the drawings to a sheet of plywood (or particleboard). (66)
6. Cut out the forms from the plywood. (67)
7. Thread the forms onto the 2 × 4. (73)
8. Check alignment of the forms and secure them in place. (74)

Stripping the Boat

9. With the boat upside-down, staple a strip along one sheerline. (77)
10. Double-check the strip's alignment. (79)
11. Trim the strip's ends. (79)
12. Repeat steps 11 and 12 on the other side.
13. Apply carpenter's glue to the top of the strip installed in the previous step. (79)
14. Lay a strip on the glue and staple it tightly in place. (79)
15. Trim the ends of this strip and install a strip on the other side. (79)
16. Repeat steps 13 through 15 until the strips have extended up the side and just start covering the bottom.
17. Install strips down either side of the keel, tapering the ends to fit the existing strips. (86)
18. Fit strips into the remaining gaps. Alternate between strips following the sheerline and strips following the keel line. (92)
19. Flip the boat over into a cradle. (93)

20. Install the first deck strip next to the first hull strip. Do not glue this strip to the hull, just staple it in place. (94)
21. Install strips on either side of the centerline in a similar manner to step 17.
22. Strip in the rest of the deck in a similar manner to step 18. Do not strip all the way over the cockpit.
23. Cut out the cockpit hole. (94)
24. Install the coaming strips. (97)
25. Remove all the staples from the deck and hull. (101)
26. Scrape off any glue drips. (102)
27. Plane the wood fair and smooth. (102)
28. Sand the wood. (104)

Fiberglassing

29. Temporarily remove the deck from the forms. (107)
30. With the hull side up, drape fiberglass over it. (108)
31. Trim the fiberglass close to the sheer line. (109)
32. Smooth the fiberglass with a brush. (109)
33. Mix up a small amount of resin. (109)
34. Pour the resin onto the middle of the hull and spread it with a squeegee. (109)
35. Mix more resin and spread as needed. Use a brush to apply resin to dry spots. (112)
36. Scrape off the excess resin with the squeegee. (112)
37. Let the resin partially cure. (113)
38. Apply fill coat of resin to the whole surface and let it cure. (113)
39. Remove the hull from the forms and return the deck to the forms. (113)
40. Repeat steps 30 through 39 for the deck.
41. Plane and sand the inside of the hull. (114)
42. Fiberglass and resin the inside as you did the outside. (114)
43. Trim off the bottom of the coaming inside the deck. (114)
44. Plane, sand and fiberglass the inside of the deck. (115)
45. Glue multiple laminations of hardwood around the coaming to create the lip. (116)
46. Cut off the excess coaming above the lip, and sand smooth. (118)
47. Fiberglass over the coaming lip. (118)
48. Install the cheek plates on the inside of the cockpit. (123)

49. Roughen the cured resin along the sheer line of the deck and hull with sandpaper.
50. Align the deck and hull together, securing with packing tape as you go. (124)
51. Turn the boat onto one side and measure out some fiberglass tape for the inside seam. (125)
52. Soak the tape in resin until it is completely saturated, then squeeze out excess. (126)
53. Roll tape along the inside seam as far as you can reach by hand and push it the rest of the way with a stick. (126)
54. Smooth the inside seam with a brush on the end of the stick. (126)
55. After the first side cures repeat steps 51 through 54 for the other side.
56. Remove the packing tape on the outside. (126)
57. Sand the outside seam smooth.
58. Lay fiberglass tape on the outside seam and resin it in place. (126)

Finishing the Boat

59. Sand the entire outside of the boat with 80-grit sandpaper. (129)
60. Apply an additional fill coat of resin in two stages to cover the deck and hull. (129)
61. Sand with progressively finer paper up to 220-grit. Repeat step 61 if necessary. (130)

62. Pour a small amount of filled resin into each end. (127)
63. Varnish the boat. (129)
64. Sand with fine sandpaper. (130)
65. Repeat 63 and 64 until bored.
66. Drill holes to install footbraces. (147)
67. Install the seat, backrest, footbraces, and other outfitting. (143)
68. Find a suitable body of water.
69. Paddle.
70. Repeat steps 68 and 69 until you're ready to build another.
71. Go back to step 1.

I rarely build a kayak the same way twice, so it would be a lot for me to ask of you to follow this schedule to the letter. Use it as a basis for determining your upcoming tasks. Don't get hung up on fears that taking some of the steps out of order will ruin the boat. With my first boat I was so impatient that I put the boat in the water (step 69) before I installed the cockpit coaming (step 25). Obviously, I had to rearrange the steps a bit, and I may have made my task more difficult in the end, but the boat came out great.

Part I

The Background

A packet freighter steaming Down East from Kittery, Maine, need travel only about 250 miles to reach Eastport, yet the true length of Maine's coastline between these two points is about 3,500 miles. Kayaks are designed to take advantage of this seeming contradiction. They can get in among the rocks the freighter must steer clear of, and explore miles of shoreline and thousands of little islands and inlets inaccessible to the freighter. To a kayaker, those rocks and islands are not dangers to navigation, but objects of beauty to be observed up close.

At the edge of the ocean, where the water invades the land at every tide, there is almost no limiting boundary. How much you see is defined by how closely you approach. Kayaks permit you to get as close as you want.

The kayak is as much at home bouncing in the waves off a headland, with surf booming ashore, as it is negotiating a narrow tidal estuary. The same boat can be used to cross a small quiet lake or an exposed ocean bay.

Figure 1-2. A kayak can safely take a paddler to remote parts of the shoreline. Here, the author's brother paddles a Great Auk off the coast of Maine.

But where do you get such a craft? One good way is to build one. There are many sound, logical reasons for building your own kayak. Commercially built boats are expensive. It's cheaper to build your own. In any case, often you can't find the right boat for your particular needs. Or, maybe you simply want a better boat than you now have. These are all very logical reasons for building your own.

But I urge you to forget logic. Concentrate on the fun. It's fun to build your own boat. It's fun paddling a boat you built yourself. It's fun saying, "I built it myself," when people come by to admire it. Building a kayak is a project you should do for the fun of it. Logical, analytical reasons are good, but they are secondary.

Let me say straight away that building a kayak is not a project you should undertake merely to save money. If all you want is an inexpensive boat, and you have no interest

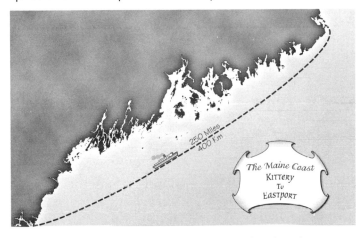

Figure 1-1. The coast of Maine accessible to a kayak is about 3,500 miles long, even though a ship can navigate the whole coast while traveling only 250 miles.

in the building process itself, save yourself a lot of frustration: Buy a used kayak or an inexpensive plastic one. You will be happier.

If, on the other hand, the idea of spending time fiddling with wood appeals to you, a kayak is a gratifying project even if you don't want to paddle. Building your own boat has an appeal that not many other projects provide. The finished boat can transport you to places that are inaccessible any other way. I'll agree that building a chair can be a challenging project, with beautiful and practical results, but when you've finished it, all you can do is sit in it. When you build a kayak, the limits of your travel are set only by your own ambition and imagination. Kayaks have crossed the North Sea and rounded Cape Horn. Kayaks have traversed the Atlantic and reached Hawaii from the Americas. In fact, the kayak was evolved by the Aleuts and Inuits of the Arctic to serve as their primary transportation and to survive in some of the toughest sea conditions in the world. All this in a boat that is also great fun on a quiet protected lake.

Why Use Wood?

With all the modern high-technology materials available for kayak construction, why choose wood? People come up to my boat and remark, "I would be afraid to put it in the water." To them, it obviously looks fragile. But they're wrong. That would be a severe liability for a boat. You can hardly call something a boat if you can't put it in the water! I certainly wouldn't want a kayak that I had to baby. I want to be able to squeeze into those little cracks between two rocks that lead to the places where no other boat would venture. If my kayak could not endure the miscalculation that lands it on top of the rocks instead of between them, I would choose some material other than wood. Believe me, wood and fiberglass can handle the abuse.

Figure 1-3. *Although a strip-built wooden kayak looks deceptively delicate, it will safely take you to places where few other boats would dare go.*

Wood is nature's own composite material. It consists of tubes of cellulose fiber glued together with lignin. Weight for weight, it is stiffer than steel and is less prone to fatigue than most of today's high-tech material. Wood is still used in the construction of cutting-edge racing sailboats and power boats. It is used in the rotor blades of the latest wind-powered generators. Large structural beams for modern commercial construction are laminated from wood.

When you combine wood with modern materials and adhesives, you create a composite material that retains wood's excellent stiffness and fatigue resistance while remaining light and resistant to rot. Two "slices" of fiberglass on either side of a wood sandwich act like an I-beam. The fiberglass sheathing, bonded to the wood with epoxy resin, acts like the two horizontal webs of the I-beam, absorbing much of the tension and compression created when a force is applied. The vertical section of steel is there to act as a lightweight separator between the webs. The greater the separation, the stiffer the beam. Likewise, the wood keeps the layers of glass separated, and the thicker the wood, the stiffer the skin of the kayak.

In theory, you could replace the wood with plastic foam. The decks and even the hulls of some larger boats are built this way. But foam

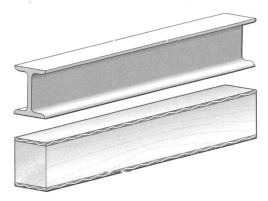

Figure 1-4. *The composite construction of a strip-built boat is similar to that of an I-beam. The wood acts like the vertical web of the steel beam, and the covering of fiberglass acts like the webs at the top and bottom of the beam. The result is a stiff, strong, and very light material.*

doesn't have wood's inherent stiffness or resistance to compression, and regardless of the other benefits of using wood for a small kayak, there is one advantage that is unrivaled. Wood is beautiful. The coating of fiberglass and epoxy enhance this beauty. The epoxy looks like rich, deep varnish; so much so, that a strip-built kayak will be the center of attention in any crowd.

Admittedly, foam won't rot, but neither will wood once it's encapsulated in the epoxy and fiberglass. Water can't reach it to promote rot. With very little care, a strip-built kayak will last indefinitely. Take my word for it, rot is not a concern.

Why Use Strips?

It's hard to go wrong with wood. It's strong and beautiful, any way you use it. Plywood makes a good building material and it's actually stronger than the wood used in strip-built boats, so it can be thinner and lighter. The best ply-

wood is rich with color and interesting grain. But the shapes you can achieve with plywood are limited because flat panels do not easily conform to compound curves. If you are planning to build a traditional Greenland-style kayak, but don't want to use the traditional skin-on-frame technique, plywood is the material of choice. Then again, plywood suitable for a good kayak can be expensive and hard to obtain. Furthermore, although plywood kayaks are easy to build, it's also easy to make a catastrophic mistake.

Luckily, wood suitable for a strip-built kayak is available at any good lumberyard, and while wood seems to be getting more expensive all the time, the amount you need is small. As far as boatbuilding skills go, the strip-building technique is very forgiving. Major mistakes are very rare, even among beginners, and you can ignore minor mistakes because they won't detract from the usability of the boat. Virtually any kayak design can be built using the strip technique, but beyond that, it enables you to upgrade your work from a mere boat to a work of art. The constant variations natural to wood can be used to enhance the design, and by selecting a variety of different wood species, the skin of the boat becomes a canvas on which you can let your imagination run free.

I get great pleasure from converting a pile of nondescript strips of wood into a fine, fun, functional craft. It's gratifying to watch the transformation. It's like reading a good novel: you want to keep going to see what the next page will reveal. While other methods of building kayaks are quicker, none provide the same satisfaction of a task well done.

Building with strips is the premier technique for easily creating fine, high-performance kayaks of distinctive beauty. After once building a kayak this way, few people ever go back to any other method.

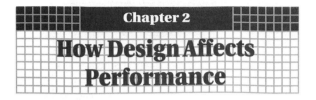

Chapter 2
How Design Affects Performance

The kayak was originally developed by Inuit and Aleut people who depended for their livelihoods on being able to survive the treacherous conditions of the Arctic Ocean. Survival time for someone immersed in those waters is measured in minutes, so the Eskimo hunters could not risk their lives in boats that dumped them in the water too often.

Why didn't they build big, stable boats that would be virtually impossible to tip over? There were many reasons. For one thing, these hunters lived beyond the easy reach of good lumber. They were dependent on driftwood. Then, too, they needed hunting vessels that were fast, quiet, and very maneuverable. The craft that evolved naturally from these requirements was a small, narrow boat, built of driftwood covered with animal skin. It sacrificed inherent stability for speed and agility, but in the hands of an experienced paddler it was very safe. When a skilled paddler used body balance to compensate for lack of stability, the kayak could handle conditions that would sink bigger vessels.

Over generations, the Inuit and Aleut hunters evolved finely honed designs superbly suited to a wide variety of conditions. In fact, one of the beauties of the kayak is that as long as you stick to the general principles of the design, you can make a lot of changes and still end up with an excellent boat. While it is possible to make a bad design, you need to really screw up to do it. Most of the changes will merely enhance certain desired characteristics and detract from others.

The basic design is so distinctive that most of today's kayaks would be recognized immediately by Stone Age hunters. There were, however, two ancestral strains, the West Greenland Inuit kayak and the Aleut baidarka.

The West Greenland kayak is generally *hard-chined*, with an *upswept sheerline*, a relatively flat deck and fairly long *overhangs*.

The Aleut designs have *round bottoms* or *multiple chines*, a straighter sheerline, *V-shaped decks* and relatively short overhangs. The word baidarka (Russian for "small boat") has become synonymous with some Aleut-designed kayaks. (See Figure 2-2 and the glossary, Appendix 7, for explanations of the terms italicized above.)

It would be difficult to trace one of today's kayaks back to either ancestor because modern naval architecture has interbred them. There are now round-bottomed kayaks with long over-hangs, and hard-chined designs with no over-hang, so it's probably a mistake to try to classify a modern design along the original family lines. Learning that a design is a "Greenland" kayak will tell you very little about the performance of the boat. What's more important are some of the particulars of the design, such as its length and width at the waterline, and the shape of the hull.

When you get down to the interesting business of analyzing boat designs, you run across a lot of nuances and subtleties. Conventional wisdom says longer boats go faster, wider boats are harder to tip

Figure 2-1. *The original kayaks were developed by the Aleut and Inuit peoples commonly known as Eskimos. While both are kayaks, the Aleut variety is now known by the Russian word "baidarka." The kayaks of today are all based on these Eskimo designs formerly made of sealskin and driftwood.*

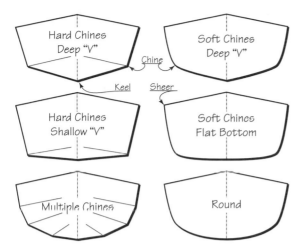

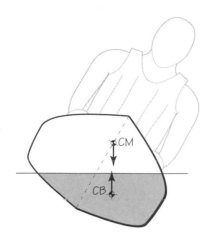

Figure 2-2. *The cross-sectional shapes of kayaks cover a wide spectrum. The shape is usually described by certain key features: "V" and "chines." V is the angle made by the bottom at the keel. A deep V will rise quickly from the keel, where a shallow V will come up at less of angle. The extreme version of shallow V is a flat bottom. Chines define any change in the angle of the hull as it moves from the keel to the sheer, for example where the bottom joins the sides. Chines can be "hard," with a sharp angle, or "soft," with a more gradual curve. Some boats with multiple chines, a series of discreet steps, can behave like a round-bottomed boat.*

Figure 2-3. *The stability of any boat is dependent on the interaction of the center of mass (CM), and the center of buoyancy (CB). As long as they are lined up vertically, the boat is balanced. The stability of a boat depends on the relative length of the moment arms of the CM and CB (their horizontal distance from where the centerline crosses the waterline). Here the CM is farther from the centerline than the CB and the paddler is about to get wet.*

over and harder to push through the water, and flat bottoms are more stable than round ones. And, as is generally the case with conventional wisdom, the rules are right. The trouble is that they're too simplistic to really help you evaluate a design. Let's have a look at some basic design factors and their effects.

Stability

The passerby watches you unload your kayak and says, "Oooh, aren't you worried you're going to tip over in that thing?" I've heard it many times. Kayaks are long and narrow, and look tippy. For someone new to kayaking, stability is often the biggest concern.

Yes, a wider boat will be more stable than a narrow boat with the same cross-sectional shape, but this simplistic rule of thumb does

not adequately explain how stability works. Stability is a function of the relation between the center of buoyancy (CB) of the kayak and the center of mass (CM) of the kayak and kayaker combined, as shown in Figure 2-3. As long as the two centers are in line vertically, the boat will stay upright. If the CM is closer to the centerline than the CB is, the boat will tend to rotate upright and is stable. If the CM moves out beyond the CB, the boat will want to continue tipping and can be called unstable. The angle at which the kayak becomes unstable depends on the shape of the hull and the height of the CM.

Boat designers talk in terms of "righting moments" when they discuss stability. A "moment" refers to a force acting at a distance from an axis, such as a lever pushing around a fulcrum. The moment is the distance from the fulcrum times the force applied. In a kayak, the righting moment is the distance of the CB from the centerline times the weight of the water displaced. When a boat is floating upright and level, the righting moment is zero because the CB is at the center line.

In English units, the righting moment is typically measured in foot-pounds. So we can say that a 2-pound force applied at the end of a 1-foot lever (2 foot-pounds) is the same as a 1-pound force applied at a distance of 2 feet. The implication of this for kayaks is that a narrow boat can be as stable as a wide boat if it's designed correctly.

The force that counteracts the righting moment is the heeling moment, which is the amount of force being applied to tipping. When a paddler is floating level in a kayak, the heeling moment is zero because the CM is over the centerline. Typically, the heeling moment is a function of the CM of the paddler, whereas the righting moment is usually a function of the boat's CB. The heeling moment comes into play when you're paddling in waves.

As Archimedes showed, a boat will always displace a weight of water equal to the weight of the boat and its contents, so the buoyancy at the CB and the mass at the CM will always be equal. Therefore, the force parts of the moment equation will be equal, and all you need to do is look at the distances or lengths of the levers creating the moments. Now let's look at some factors that affect the lengths of those levers.

Hull Shape

A boat will feel stable as long as the righting moment grows faster than the heeling moment. When the heeling moment starts growing faster, the boat may still be stable but it will start to feel more and more tippy. The boat will capsize when the heeling moment is greater than the righting moment. How fast the righting moment grows is a function of the hull shape.

You can determine a lot about a boat's stability by looking at its cross-sectional shape. Try to imagine how the distribution of volume will be changed by tipping the boat. From Figure 2-4 you can see that flatter shapes are more stable because the CB moves more quickly towards the

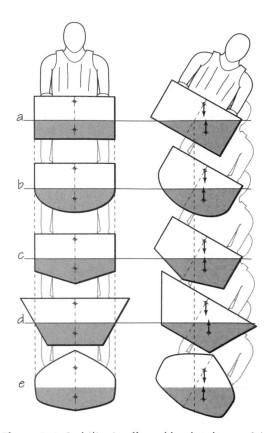

Figure 2-4. *Stability is affected by the shape of the hull. Here are five hulls with different cross sections, all with the buoyancy area below the waterline. All are the same width at the upright waterline, yet they each show different stability characteristics. When tipped, the rectangular shape (a) quickly gains buoyancy on the right side. This places the CB out beyond the CM, so this hull will return to the upright position. The round-bottomed hull (b) does not move the CB as quickly, so this paddler will get wet. The V-bottomed hull (c) is almost a cross between (a) and (b), and the CB and CM are lined up. This paddler is balanced. If he tips more to the right he will go over and if he tips a little to the left he will come upright. Hull (d) has a lot of flare. As a result the boat gets wider as it is leaned and the CB moves quickly to the right causing a strong force to right the boat. Hull (e) is a real kayak, similar to the Guillemot in this book. It is V-bottomed, similar to (c), but with some roundness like (b). As a result its stability is somewhere between the two. Notice also that the deck is starting to get wet. This means that the boat will start getting narrower and become less stable.*

side of lean than it does with rounder shapes. In the rectangular hull the bottom lifts up quickly, taking buoyancy away from the high side while the low side makes up for it by sinking.

Imagine a boat with two hulls, a catamaran. With a small angle of heel, one hull will come out of the water. The CB moves abruptly over to the remaining hull. It is hard to make the boat heel initially, but it gets progressively easier as the CM gets closer to being over the hull in the water.

Now imagine sitting on a log. It doesn't care which way up it floats. It has no inherent stability at all. In fact, if you stand on it, you have to run to keep from swimming. So what's the difference between the log and the catamaran? When you tilt the catamaran, the CB moves over to one side. When you run on the log, the CB stays in one place and you need to work hard to keep your CM directly over it, or you'll get dropped in the drink.

The rounded bottom in the figure looks about the same tipped as it does level. As a result, the CB does not move much. A V-shaped hull can be visualized as a cross between the round hull and the flat-bottomed hull. The deeper the V, the more it acts like a rounded bottom.

Initial stability, or how tippy the boat feels when it's floating upright, is dependent primarily on the width. Any boat of the same width will feel about the same to start with. As the lean gets greater, the bottom shape will begin to be felt. The final stability is often a function of the shape of the boat above the waterline. Like the flared hull second from bottom in Figure 2-4, a boat that widens above the waterline will have stability held in reserve and may actually be more stable on its side than upright. The opposite effect occurs with low decks.

All of the above holds true as a kayak's width is changed. A boat with a given cross section becomes more stable as it's made wider. And yet, as the Eskimos discovered centuries ago, the most stable design is not necessarily the best because the hull shape affects other aspects of performance as well.

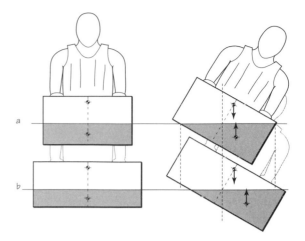

Figure 2-5. *Given two hulls of the same shape, the wider one will be more stable. Here the left side of the wide hull lifts out of the water more quickly than does the left side of the other hull, while it sinks more volume on the right side. This moves the CB farther to the right, and the wider hull will want to come upright.*

Lowering Your Weight

How fast the heeling moment moves is a function of how high the center of mass is. With the CM low, the boat can lean a lot and the CM does not move very far. The CM is the center of your weight and the boat's weight combined, of course, and mostly your weight, so if you stand up in the boat and move a little off balance, your CM moves beyond the point of no return. Splash! But, as you'll notice in Figure 2-6, just lowering the seat half an inch will dramatically improve the stability of the boat. A narrower boat often creates a lower CM because it sinks lower, and if you're sitting on the bottom of the boat, your CM gets lowered, too. In this way, a narrower boat doesn't become unstable as easily as you might imagine.

Incidentally, all my illustrations show the paddler sitting bolt upright, even though this is not how you should sit in a kayak. The drawings merely demonstrate the principles, using worst-case examples. Good paddlers will stay loose at the hips, always adjusting their position to keep

Figure 2-6. *The black and the gray outlines of this paddler represent small differences in the height of the seat. As the paddler is lowered, the CM is lowered also, making the boat more stable. At this angle, the gray paddler will capsize, but the black one will return upright.*

their center of mass over the center of buoyancy of the kayak. While this may sound like a lot of work, it's not. Imagine you're walking around the side of a steep hill. You don't walk perpendicular to the slope. You stay vertical, with your CM straight above your feet, and you do this without thinking about it. You'll do the same thing in a kayak. It soon comes naturally.

Stability and Waves

Strange as it may seem, there are times when rock-solid stability becomes a liability. The same stability that keeps you upright may flip you over on some waves that come at you broadside-on. Swells or rounded waves from the side are not a problem because the kayak will just bob up and down, but it is harder to deal with wind-driven waves that are cresting and breaking with whitecaps.

Figure 2-7 shows two kayaks beam-on to the face of a breaking wave, one narrow and "tippy," the other wide and "stable." The stability of the wider boat has created a heeling force that is tipping the kayak. While it looks pretty dire, it's not because the boat is leaned over so

much, but because of another factor peculiar to wave behavior. Let me explain. The oncoming wave is pushing on the boat in several ways. One of the forces is accelerating the boat to the left. The center of mass does not distinguish between the force of gravity and the force of acceleration, and as a result "down" feels like a direction perpendicular to the face of the wave, even when the wave is tilted. What's going to upset the boat is the force of the water inside the approaching wave.

The water inside the wave is rotating up and over into the crest, as depicted by the arrows in Figure 2-7. This flow pushes upward against the low side of the boat and destabilizes it. It's that motion of the water inside the wave, more than the external wave shape, that's trying to flip the boat over.

But all is not lost. By leaning the boat toward the wave, the paddler can present the water with less bottom area to push on, so the rotation of the water is less likely to produce a corresponding rotation of the kayak and paddler. And here's the important point: Because it's "less stable," the narrower kayak is easier to tilt toward the oncoming wave. The kayaker in the "more stable" boat can do the same thing, but it will be slower and take more effort.

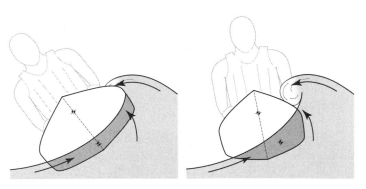

Figure 2-7. *If you talk to enough experienced kayakers, you will eventually hear one say, "Narrower boats are more stable in waves." That's not really true, but it's close. Capsizes happen not because the wave is inclined but because the water at the surface of the wave is rotating, as shown by the arrows in these diagrams. If you can quickly lean the kayak into the wave, the rotating water has less bottom surface area to push against. And a narrow hull is quicker and easier to tilt than a wide one.*

To give you an idea of how important it is to be able to tilt the kayak quickly and easily, you should know that in stormy weather you often need to get the waves to break into your lap. It's this ability to easily lean the boat into waves that makes a "less stable" kayak safer and more comfortable in rough conditions; but be aware that it requires some skill on the part of the paddler. I've been putting stability in quotation marks in the above discussion because it's all relative; to put it in perspective, you should realize that in skilled hands a kayak can stay upright in conditions that would overturn most other boats.

Much of the fun you get from a high-performance kayak comes from the ability to control the boat easily with skillful paddling. This improved control comes at a price, of course—you have to pay more attention. You can't relax as much in a high-performance boat. But remember that "high performance" depends on the performance characteristics you desire. The kayak for a day of surfing is not necessarily the best one for a day of fishing.

The Importance of Speed

Having spent some time discussing what makes a boat stable, we now come to the question of what is the best design. That's hard to answer because it's dependent on many variables. Stability, as I've already pointed out, is a relative term. What is rock-steady for an adventurous paddler heading out to play in surf may be a treacherous pencil to someone looking for a relaxing exploration of the local lake. There are factors other than stability that must be considered. Speed and maneuverability each impose requirements on the shape of the hull that will in turn affect stability. Let's take a look at each in order.

Even though you might not want to race, speed is still an important consideration. The ability of a kayak to go fast is an indication of its efficiency. A more efficient boat will be easier to paddle and you won't get tired quickly. But besides this, there are times when you want to go fast even if you don't race. Perhaps there's a storm coming and you need to get off the water fast, or maybe you've been caught in a strong current and are being swept somewhere undesirable. Speed concerns both safety and efficiency.

That said, the fastest boat is not necessarily the most efficient or the best for your needs. The energy needed to paddle different boats at different speeds varies widely. A boat that is fast and efficient at top speed may be harder to paddle at low speed than a second boat that will not reach that same top speed no matter how hard you try. That's exactly why you should choose a design that fits the kind of paddling you'll be doing. Most people don't want to race, but they do need to be able to paddle for a long time without tiring, and they'd like to be able to put on the occasional burst of speed.

The Effect of Length on Speed

A good way to judge the efficiency of a boat is to look at its wake. The waves produced by the hull's passage through the water contain energy. Where does this energy come from? You. That's why you don't want your kayak to make waves. To illustrate my point, take a kayak out and try surfing on a powerboat's wake. You can often keep up with a twin-engined speedboat without paddling at all. The powerboat is wasting energy by making waves, and you are recycling some of that energy, using it to make you surf. I've often wondered how many kayaks could be pulled along by a powerboat wake. It wouldn't slow down the powerboat at all because that energy is already lost, yet a whole flock of kayaks could ride along with no additional power. Powerboats can afford to be this wasteful because they just pour in more gas when they run out. Kayakers might not find it so easy to refuel. Chocolate-chip cookies help, but are usually in limited supply.

Generally, the longer the boat, the more speed it's capable of attaining. The term "hull speed" is defined as a function of length, although it's a bit of a misnomer. It doesn't mean that a kayak can't go faster than hull speed. There is just a hump that must be climbed over, literally.

As a boat moves through the water it makes waves, as shown in Figure 2-8. The faster the boat moves, the longer the distance between the tops of the waves. Eventually the waves are about as long as the boat. When this happens, the top of the wave is at or near the bow and the trough of the wave is near the stern. In essence, the boat is being paddled uphill, which is very strenuous for the paddler. The fact is that when you reach hull speed, paddling harder does not make you go much faster, it just makes a bigger wave. I'll say it another way because it's important: your energy is wasted making bigger waves.

In theory, your boat *can* exceed hull speed. Powerful speedboats do it all the time. It's called planing. But the simple fact is that the average human can't produce enough power to make the average kayak plane consistently. You'll only exhaust yourself trying.

By the way, when we talk about length affecting speed, we refer to waterline length, not overall length. After all, it's only the part of the kayak that's in the water that makes the wave. Therefore, it is the length of the waterline that determines the hull speed. Figure 2-9 shows how two kayaks of the same overall length can have different waterline lengths. From this we can deduce that a 17-foot kayak with long overhangs will have a lower hull speed than a 16-foot kayak with a near-plumb bow and stern.

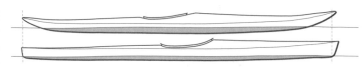

Figure 2-9. *It's waterline length that determines maximum hull speed, not overall length. As shown here, the Guillemot (top) and the Great Auk (bottom) are the same overall length. But the Guillemot has a much shorter waterline length and will probably have a lower hull speed.*

The Effect of Shape on Speed

The length of the waterline, by itself, doesn't totally govern a boat's potential speed. The shape of the waterline matters, too. Some boats have a very "fine" entry, that is, the bows start off narrow and stay narrow for a while, then the width gradually expands to the full beam. Generally, the stern will be similar in form to the bows, gradually tapering from the full beam down to a narrow section and a fine exit. These fine ends do not have much effect on the water at first. It is when the shape starts accelerating the water out to the side that the waves are formed. In other words, when a kayak has fine ends the effective waterline length, as far as wave generation is concerned, is even shorter than the real waterline length. So a 17-foot kayak with fine ends may have a lower hull speed than a 16-foot boat with full ends.

Now the fullest possible ends would produce a rectangular waterline, and while this would result in the maximum hull speed, which would seem desirable, it actually produces its own problems. As I've already mentioned, the widening hull will accelerate the water out to the side. As the boat passes through the water it must move the water out of the way and then let it back into place. But water has a lot of inertia and doesn't like being moved suddenly. The trouble with a rectangular hull is that it just barges bluntly into the water. It makes no effort to ease the flow of water around the boat. It pushes a big wave in front of itself as the water scrambles to get out of the way. At the

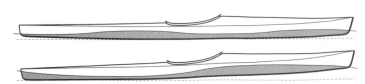

Figure 2-8. *The waves created by moving kayaks at cruising speed (top) and hull speed (bottom). Other things being equal, longer boats have higher top speeds.*

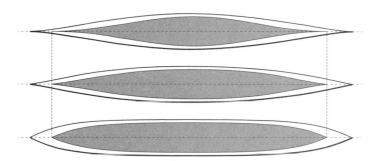

Figure 2-10. *The shape of the waterline also affects speed. The top hull here has a distinct hollow in the waterline fore and aft. This smoothly accelerates the water out and around the boat but reduces the effective length of its waterline and lowers its hull speed. The bottom hull makes maximum use of its length and will have a higher hull speed, but will need more power to attain it. It may also be harder to paddle at lower speeds. The middle hull is a compromise offering low-speed efficiency and a satisfactory top speed.*

stern the water quickly rushes back into place. It probably can't get back fast enough, and a depression forms that pulls more waves after it. The rectangular hull builds up pressure in front and suction behind, two forces that slow down the boat with drag.

Of course, all hulls will suffer from these forces to some extent, but if the water is slowly accelerated outward, then smoothly decelerated as it approaches the widest part of the boat, then easily accelerated back inward, and finally decelerated gradually back into its original position, the drag on the hull will be lessened. This requires a fine entry and exit. It also requires fair lines. The shape of the hull affects the size of the waves produced by the passage of the boat. A smooth shape with no sudden curves or bumps will produce smaller waves and therefore cause less drag.

It's all very well to talk about fine entries and exits, but how do you determine degrees of fineness? Designers often use a term called the prismatic coefficient. It's determined by calculating the volume of the immersed hull and dividing it by the volume of a similar prism, which is a rectangle the length of the waterline with a cross-section the same as the hull's midship section, as shown in Figure 2-11. A fine

hull has a prismatic coefficient of about 0.45, while a boat with fuller ends may have a prismatic coefficient of about 0.6. If you look back at Figure 2-10, you'll now understand that the top hull is fine, and will have a lower prismatic coefficient than the bottom hull, which is full. The full hull will be capable of higher speeds, but the fine hull will be more efficient at lower speeds.

But now we have two conflicting ideals, a long effective waterline and a fine entry. What's the best compromise? Maximum hull speed only makes a difference when you are trying to push the boat as fast as possible. Most of the time you'll probably be easing along well below hull speed, and then the efficiency of the hull form will determine how easily the boat is moved. Therefore, you don't want a design that sacrifices efficiency at cruising speed for a maximum hull speed that will be used only in a sprint. Most of the time, you want fine ends.

Let me throw one more conflicting factor into the mix. You also want as little wetted-surface area as possible. One of the most important forms of drag comes from friction. Now you might be surprised to hear it, but the drag of water moving past the skin of a boat can be a significant factor in slowing it down. The best way to lessen this skin friction is to minimize

Figure 2-11. *The prismatic coefficient describes the "fineness" of the hull. It's calculated by dividing the displacement of the hull into the displacement of a prism with the same shape as the widest point in the hull and the same length as the hull.*

the area that the water rubs against. So bear in mind that a long boat with a potentially high hull speed and an efficient shape for displacing water can still be slow if it has too much wetted surface area.

Maneuverability and Tracking

You are paddling close to shore when suddenly you see a large wave rolling in. If you continue on your present course you will almost certainly be swept onto the rocks as the wave breaks. What do you do? Well, you could get swept ashore and test just how strong your boat really is, or you could turn quickly into the oncoming wave and paddle out beyond it. This requires maneuverability.

Now you are safely away from the shore, crossing a sound to the next island. The wind picks up and is blowing in one ear and out the other. You don't want to expend all your effort in just keeping the kayak going straight as you have five more miles to paddle. This requires the ability to track, or maintain a straight course.

Generally, the shorter a boat is, the easier it is to maneuver. And, generally, the longer the kayak is, the better it tends to track. Naturally, most people want a maneuverable boat that tracks well. This is possible.

Since most of the resistance to turning comes from the ends of the boat where the water has the most leverage, maneuverability can be improved by keeping the boat shallow at the ends. This is where the term "rocker" comes into play. It is a loosely defined term that indicates how much upward curve the keel has, like the rockers on a rocking chair. A boat with a lot of rocker (a keel that curves relatively sharply upward at the ends) can be turned more easily than a similar boat with a straight keel. See Figure 2-12.

A boat that tracks well will not easily be pushed off course by wind or waves. But good tracking depends on the shape and area of the hull above water as well as below. Luckily, the whole boat tends to be exposed to the same weather, and a wind pushing on the side of the bow will also push on the side of the stern. The different shapes of the two ends will produce different forces, but these forces can be balanced by hull shape in the water. In theory, the resistance of the bow to being pushed sideways should balance the resistance of the stern to being pushed sideways. In practice, you want the stern to be less easily pushed. This can be accomplished with a rudder or a skeg, or by having less rocker in the stern than at the bow. The location of the center of lateral area (CLA) will give an indication of where the balance point is.

The CLA should be behind the longitudinal center of buoyancy (LCB). The LCB is the fore-and-aft location of the center of buoyancy, that is, its position along the length of the kayak. This will always be at the same place as the center of mass. Since most of the mass of the boat is the paddler, the LCB will be right in front of the paddler's torso. A boat with a CLA that matches the LCB will generally center on the paddler when it rotates. Moving the CLA behind the paddler is like fletching an arrow. The feathers on the back of an arrow help it

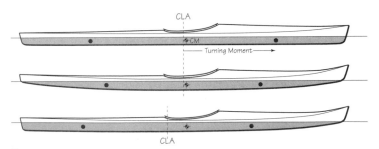

Figure 2-12. Three hulls with different amounts of keel rocker. The top hull has an almost straight keel with no rocker. The center hull shows a lot of rocker, reducing the water's "grip" on the ends. The bottom hull is a compromise, with forward rocker lifting the bow out of the water to help maneuverability, and no rocker aft, to help tracking. These pictures are exaggerated for clarity.

go straight. But beware: Moving the CLA too far behind the LCB will make the boat hard to steer. Incidentally, a rudder can move the point of rotation pretty far back, but that's canceled out by the rudder's ability to make the boat turn. Another way to look at the relationship of the CLA to the LCB is to split the underwater profile at the LCB and look at the centers of area of the bow and stern profiles separately. The distance of the centers of area from the center of buoyancy will give an indication of the ease of turning each half. A boat with the centers of area further out will be harder to turn. A boat with the center of area further out in the stern than in the bow will tend to track straighter.

It's simpler to calculate the CLA when a hull's cross-sectional shapes are similar at the bow and stern. Because water finds it easier to flow around some shapes than others, the relative shapes of each end will change the performance, too. Rounded or U-shaped sections slide sideways through the water more easily than angular or V-shaped sections. Therefore a V-shaped hull will tend to be less maneuverable than one that's U-shaped, but a U-shaped hull with a V-shaped stern will track better.

Another term naval architects often refer to is the block coefficient. It's a factor that gives you a mental picture of the sectional shape of the hull. It's like the prismatic coefficient, but it's actually the ratio of the displacement divided by the displacement of a block as long as the waterline, as wide as the boat at the waterline, and with the same draft as the boat. Generally, a kayak with a lower block coefficient will be less maneuverable, but will track better.

Volume, or Interior Size

The bigger the boat is, the more stuff you can bring with you, but to be realistic, you don't need that much space, even for long trips. Backpackers carry everything they need right there on their backs. Even the smallest sea kayak has more room in it than a backpack has. Most kayaks will provide more volume than you need, even if you don't pack efficiently. The long and

short of it is that you don't need to pay much attention to volume. Usually, other considerations will come first. If you want to carry a lot of gear, you need a kayak that can perform well with a heavier load, generally a longer or wider boat. Although designs that describe themselves as "high-volume" are not telling you much about their ability to carry a load, it's a fact that a high-volume kayak will probably rise up over waves more easily. More volume in the bow provides extra buoyancy to raise the bow when it meets a wave. Of course, this assumes that the "high volume" the design boasts of is located where it's needed. Volume concentrated back by the cockpit won't provide this benefit.

Choosing the Right Boat

The first step in choosing a boat is to determine why you want it. What will you do with it? Where will you paddle it? If you live near the open ocean, your needs are different from those of a friend who lives near a bunch of small ponds. If you've been kayaking for a while, this decision will be easier. If you're not experienced, you need to do some thinking, and your decision will also be influenced by your woodworking skills, or lack of them.

So sit down and make a list of what you want to do with your kayak. This list will help you decide what characteristics are important, what kind of kayak you need. Your list will determine the design you want, and later it will help you decide what materials you should use. Try to list the characteristics of the area where you intend to paddle, and what you want to do there.

Long, open-ocean crossings will require a fast kayak that tracks well. Exploring small lakes is more fun with a lightweight, easy-to-maneuver design. Navigating through marshlands needs excellent maneuverability, too. Photography or fishing is easier from a stable platform. You need more volume for camping trips than for day trips. Surfing calls for a lightweight design with a flat bottom. The possibilities are almost endless, but here are some considerations that will help you choose the best boat for your purposes:

For a large lake or the sea. You need a kayak somewhat bigger than average. A slightly bigger boat will often perform better in the conditions a large body of water produces.

For a small pond, river, or lake. Usually, a sheltered body of water calls for a small boat that will get into the snug hideaways more easily. A light boat will be easier to carry to the next pond.

For dealing with waves. A narrower, "less stable" boat will often be more comfortable in waves. Rocker also will improve handling over waves.

For calm waters. Since there are few waves trying to push you over, you can sit and relax. And you might as well do it in a boat you don't need to worry about flipping over, so go for a wide boat. A smaller boat will be easier to handle and lighter to carry.

For exposed waters. You need a low-profile, fast boat that doesn't catch much wind, one that will get you out of trouble quickly if necessary. This boat will be long and fairly narrow.

For long-distance trips. Get a fast, efficient boat. If you're going to be paddling all day, you want to do it with the least amount of effort. Since you probably will not be paddling at full speed, you need a boat that will reach a reasonably fast speed with ease, rather than a boat that will reach the highest potential speed for its size, but only with a lot of effort. Your long-distance boat should be moderately long, narrow, and straight-tracking.

For narrow, winding waterways. A short, maneuverable boat does best in constricted waters. It will be fast and efficient when navigating narrow, twisting streams and passages.

For camping trips. You need extra displacement to carry a lot of gear. A long boat, rather than a wide one, will generally be more efficient, but don't get too long. Top speed is not that important. The added cargo weight also calls for a stronger boat. Stability is not a big concern because the weight of the gear will help stabilize the boat.

For day trips. Short trips don't tire you as much as long ones do, so a little efficiency can be sacrificed for other benefits. Your boat can be wider and more stable. If you are just going out to play, good maneuverability will add greatly to your fun.

For exploring. Since you never know what conditions you may run into, you need a "general purpose" kayak with good maneuverability and decent speed. A moderately long boat with some rocker should work well.

For racing. Here, you want flat-out speed. Your boat needs to be light, long, and narrow, with the minimum of wetted surface area. A boat that's too long will just add unnecessary wetted surface area and weight. Figure out how fast you need to go to win, and design the boat around that speed. You can sacrifice strength for light weight in this case.

For rock-strewn waters. Get yourself a strong, maneuverable boat that will swerve around rocks appearing in your way. You'll need a heavier-than-normal lay-up.

For sandy or muddy waters. Colliding with a pile of mud or soft sand may be messy, but it won't do much damage to your boat. Your kayak can be built a little lighter than average.

It's important to remember that you won't find a design that's ideal for everything. Kayaks are versatile boats, however, and if you choose the best design for one purpose you will still be able to use it for vastly different conditions. There are some trade-offs, such as maneuverability versus speed, that will require a compromise, but you don't have to go to extremes to choose your ideal boat.

Now, after providing all the above information about the different performances of different designs, I'm going to say, "Don't get bogged down in the details." Let me repeat myself: Kayaks are versatile craft and you will enjoy whatever design you build. A design originally intended for lakes can safely be used on the open ocean as long as you stay within your paddling skills. Furthermore, if you're lucky, you'll be able to find some fault in your kayak that will give you an excuse to build another.

Some Proven Designs

Kayak designers like strip-building because it's so versatile. With small strips of wood you can build almost any kayak design imaginable, so strip-building is the method of choice for prototypes of kayaks that will eventually be manufactured in fiberglass and other materials. It's also a good way for a home builder to get a strong, beautiful craft.

A kayak manufacturer will typically strip-build a prototype of a new design and use it for sea trials and testing. If the prototype meets with approval, a mold will be made from that boat. If

Figure 2-14. The traditional Aleut baidarka has an interesting stern treatment that Rob Macks was able to reproduce with strips on his North Star.

the prototype is too beaten up, or if some design changes are required, a "plug" will be strip-built. This plug is simply a mold that is used to make another mold. The second mold is used to make the actual boats. In this way, most of the fiberglass and Kevlar kayaks on the market started out as strip-built boats.

The technique can be used to produce smoothly rounded or hard-chined hulls. Highly contoured decks and transomed sterns are equally achievable. No other method of constructing a small boat gives the builder a wider choice of shapes. Over the years, people have built kayaks ranging from the small Wee Lassie, with a simple canoe shape, to reproductions of the complex Aleut designs. If you cut the strips small enough, there are no shapes you can't produce. See Figures 2-15 and 2-16.

Figure 2-13. This North Star kayak built by Rob Macks, of Laughing Loon Kayaks, is an interpretation of the Aleut baidarka. It shows the freedom of design possible with strip building. Note the traditional bifid bow—but built of solid wood and strips instead of sealskin over a wood frame.

Figure 2-15. "Mac" McCarthy's Wee Lassie is a minimalist kayak. A small open boat like this, propelled with a kayak paddles is typically called a double-paddle canoe.

Look for a design that fits your needs and desires. For some people, building a boat is the only way to get the one they want. If the boat you want isn't here and you can't find any source for it, feel free to design your own. If you don't feel capable of design work, hire a designer to help you out.

Three special designs. I design kayaks for my own use. I want boats that look good and perform to the highest standards, as well as kayaks that use to the fullest extent the design freedom available to the stripbuilder. From my designs I have selected three that meet a wide variety of requirements:

The Great Auk

The Great Auk kayak is named after a now-extinct species of water bird, *Pinguinus impennis*. In the North Atlantic, the great auk filled the same ecological niche as the penguin did in the Antarctic. It was a flightless bird renowned for its swimming ability. The 24-inch to 30-inch birds would migrate up and down the northern shores of the North Atlantic. With their feet far back on their bodies, they were easy prey for hunters when they came ashore to nest. They were killed for meat, feathers, and oil until their extermination on June 3, 1844. The last-known breeding pair were "collected" for an Icelander named Carl Siemsen who was seeking specimens. The great auk has since become a symbol, focusing attention on man's destruction of the environment.

As a kayak, the Great Auk is a fast, stable, comfortable boat for novices and intermediate paddlers. It is well suited to camping and has room for plenty of gear. The simplicity of the lines make this boat easy to build and you can tailor it to a variety of needs. Simple adjustment of the forms can create a small paddle boat or a long tandem kayak. As drawn, the boat is 17 feet long and 24 inches wide. The plumb bow and stern give this design a long waterline at over 16 feet 7

Figure 2-16. The author's brother, Eric Schade, built this customized double for their parents, who cannot paddle as far as they used to. It has a battery-powered motor. The diagonal deck pattern is discussed in Chapter 8.

inches. With a little flare to the sides, the Great Auk shows a 22¾ inch beam to the water, providing good stability. The flared bow provides lift over waves for a dry ride. She is drawn with a wide and long cockpit for people who want room to move. If you need a little better performance, you should cut a smaller, snugger cockpit.

The simple lines of the Great Auk make this design the easiest boat in this book to build and the most easily modified. This basic design has been used to build an 18-footer, a 10-footer, and a tandem kayak, just by adjusting the form spacing.

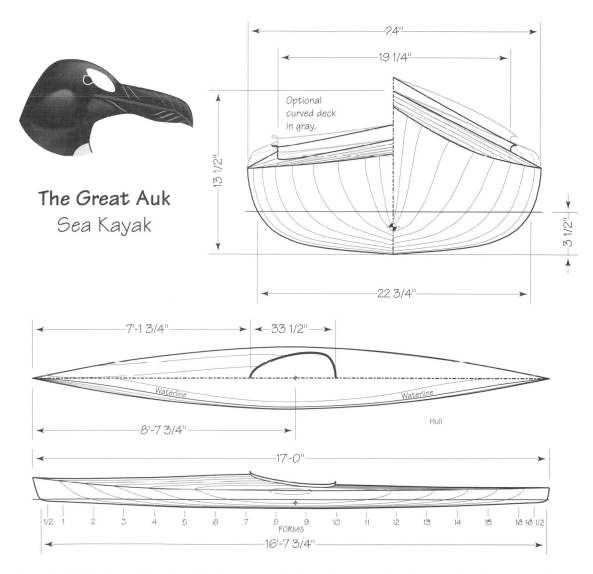

The Great Auk
Sea Kayak

Figure 2-17. The lines of the Great Auk kayak, next to its extinct namesake. The gray lines in the end view show an optional rounded sheer that can be built using the numbers in the offset table. See Chapter 4, Figure 4-5.

Figure 2-18. The author paddles an early version of the Great Auk, a fast, stable kayak suitable for the beginning kayaker or a paddler wanting a lot of space for gear when camping.

The Guillemot

Around my favorite paddling area in Maine you often see a black, robin-sized bird with white wing patches buzzing in inquisitive circles around your kayak. This is the black guillemot, *Cepphus grylle.* In English, it's pronounced GIL-uh-mot, with a hard "g." Like the great auk, this diving bird is a member of the alcid family which includes a variety of skilled swimmers such as the puffin and the razor-billed auk. Their wings are adapted to flying underwater, and

they need to flap pretty fast to stay in the air.

You'll often see the guillemot paddling around the surf zone, poking its head underwater occasionally to see if lunch is swimming by, or to plan its route should it need to make a quick underwater getaway. It often swims in places I'd enjoy exploring, so I designed the Guillemot kayak to go exactly where the bird goes.

The Guillemot is a beautiful, high-performance design for intermediate and skilled kayakers. The distinctive lines perform well in a variety of conditions. This boat is fun to build, using the flexibility of the strip-building technique to the utmost. At 17 feet long, and 21 inches wide, it's a good boat for day trips and short camping trips. The long overhangs give it a waterline of 14 feet 8 inches—shorter than the Great Auk's, but providing better maneuverability. With a waterline beam of 20¾ inches the Guillemot is easy to lean without feeling too tender (tippy). The fairly flat bottom surfs easily, while the swept bow rides over waves nicely. The low profile of the deck presents little area for the wind to push against. The rounded transition from deck to hull across the sheer makes it very easy to roll.

The Guillemot has a more complex shape than the Great Auk and is therefore more difficult to build. As you might imagine, the sweep of the bow and stern uses the flexibility of the strips to their limits. Although slight adjustments in the forms can result in usable designs, the Guillemot should be modified only with care. But achieving its designed shape is well worth the effort—you could build this boat from anything and it would still be beautiful. Just imagine what wood does for it.

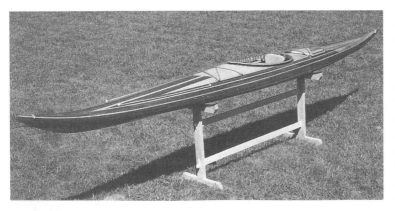

Figure 2-19. The Guillemot, a sleek stylish kayak suitable for ambitious beginners, intermediates, and skilled paddlers. This low-profile kayak comes alive in rough conditions and is easy to handle in sheltered estuaries.

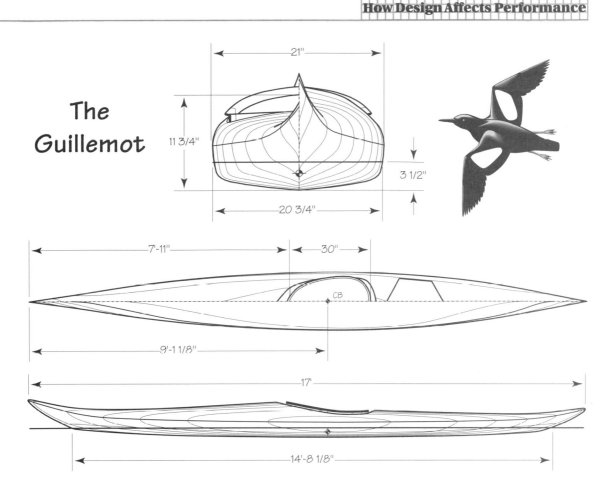

Figure 2-20. *The lines of the Guillemot, alongside its namesake.*

The Guillemot's final design evolved after several years designing and building slightly different versions. This version was drawn up for an article in *Sea Kayaker* magazine, and has somewhat simpler lines than earlier versions, which makes it easier to build. I've also produced several variations of the basic design, including a small play boat and a long expedition version. For more information on these and other designs please see Appendix 3.

The Guillemot Double

A kayak is almost by definition a one-person boat. The original kayakers would probably have called a tandem kayak an umiak, meaning a larger boat traditionally paddled by women. In this age of political correctness, it's probably best that we avoid that designation. A two-person kayak is a good way to extend your range of operation because two paddlers in a tandem can generally travel farther and faster than the same two in singles. It's also a practical solution to the problem of teaching friends how to paddle. You can be there to show them.

The Guillemot Double offers two people a nice way to get out on the water. Originally based on the lines of the Guillemot, this kayak is comfortable, stable, and fast. At 20 feet long and 28 inches wide, the Double is spacious, able to accommodate the weight of two passengers plus their cargo. Its stability makes it suitable for beginners and intermediate paddlers. The cockpits are spaced far apart, so the paddlers need not worry about keeping in sync. Paddling in sync is more efficient and comfortable, but at times it's convenient for one paddler to be able to stop without interfering with the other. The stern paddler in the Guillemot Double can stop, and the bow paddler need never know!

The flare of the bow, combined with the high volume, provides a comfortable ride through waves. The plumb section of the stern provides a good mounting point for a rudder. The Guillemot Double

Figure 2-21. The Guillemot Double is a roomy stable boat that will keep a pair of paddlers happy and comfortable. It carries enough gear for several days of camping.

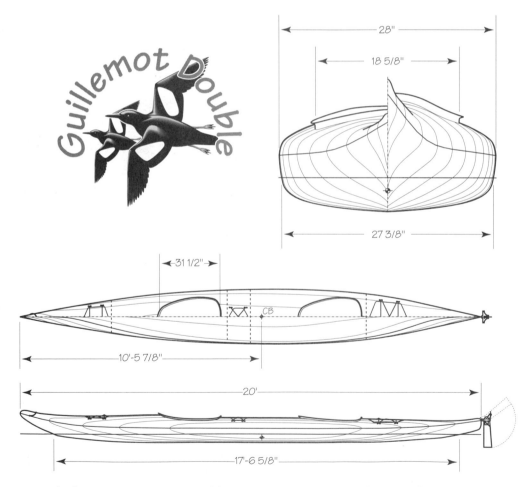

Figure 2-22. The lines of the Guillemot Double. The 27³/₈-inch waterline beam prevents your being thrown off balance when your partner moves suddenly, and the distance between cockpits is sufficient to prevent your partner clocking you in the back of the head with a paddle, even if you deserve it.

has a shape similar to that of the Guillemot, in fact, but it's easier to build because the length softens the bends, although the hollow at the bow and stern requires some patience to achieve.

A final word about making your choice: It will always be hard to decide what boat to build, so I'd like to urge you not to take my arbitrary classifications of "beginner" or "skilled" too seriously. Even if you've never paddled a kayak before, you can still paddle the Guillemot single. You'll quickly become accustomed to handling it.

To end this chapter, here's a table listing all the details of the three designs we've discussed above. If you'd like to do your own analysis of the designs in this book, here are the particulars of the kayaks.

Kayak Particulars

	Great Auk	Guillemot Double	Guillemot	
Length Over All (LOA)	17	20	17	ft
Beam	24	28	21	in
Height	14.5	16.7	13.7	in
Volume	13.8	24.8	12.3	ft³
Length water line (LWL)	16	17	14	ft
	7.7	6.8	8.6	in
Maximum cross section	61.2	94.6	61.1	sq in
Hull draught	3.5	4.4	3.7	in
Beam at the waterline	22.7	27.2	20.7	in
Displacement at DWL	215	410	215	lbs
LCB aft of forward WL	8.4	9.0	7.8	ft
LCB as percent of LWL	50.6	51.2	53.1	%
VCB below DWL	1.3	1.7	1.4	in
Waterplane area	18.3	26.0	17.0	sq ft
Lateral plane area	3.5	5.4	3.5	sq ft
Center of lateral area aft of forward WL	8.4	8.7	7.6	ft
Wetted surface area	20.4	29.6	19.7	sq ft
Total surface area	57.7	79.5	47.3	sq ft
Prismatic coefficient	0.475	0.555	0.542	
Block coefficient	0.365	0.439	0.438	

Figure 2-23. Vital statistics of the three kayaks featured in this chapter.

hree vital factors contribute to the success of any building project: skill, tools, and materials. Skill is the hardest for you to acquire. It comes only with experience, and I'm afraid that reading a book does not contribute directly to skill. What this book *can* do, however, is increase your knowledge, so your skills develop more rapidly. And, right from the start, you have full control over the tools you use and the materials you obtain.

Let's face it, the best tools and materials can be expensive. In most cases it's false economy to cut corners, but, on the other hand, you don't always need to buy the most expensive stuff. Evaluate your goals. The tools and materials needed to build a kayak suitable for display in a museum are different from those needed for a quick-and-dirty kayak that will get you out on the water as speedily and cheaply as possible. And what you're willing to invest will depend on whether you're building one boat or planning on making a dozen. Just remember that "better" usually translates into "easier."

plement them, they'll still do most of the work. There may be other tools that are marginally superior for some small task or other, but you can do without them.

With the exception of the table saw, which I recommend you borrow or hire, not buy, none of the tools required for strip-building is expensive. You can buy the best and still afford to build the boat. And you'll enjoy the building process more because a good tool works better and lasts longer. If you can buy a woodworking plane for the price of a meal at a family restaurant, why buy one for the cost of a meal at a fast-food place? You're only saving enough to buy another hamburger or two. A good tool will serve you better and last longer than any hamburger.

Sharpness is the most important attribute of any edge tool, and if you're ever having trouble making the tool work the way you think it should, try sharpening it in the way discussed later in this chapter. Sharpening is not a once-a-year project. Learn how to sharpen your tools

Tools

Good tools will add skill to any hand, and conversely, using an inappropriate tool can make the simplest task exasperating. The right tools for strip-building a kayak are simple. Most of the work can be done with a block plane, a jackknife, a razor saw, and a stapler. If you cut your own strips, you will need a large power saw for a day or two. Fiberglassing demands a few cheap brushes, and sanding calls for a sanding block. These few tools can do all the work, and even if you sup-

Figure 3-1. *The primary tools used for strip-building. Most of the work is done with a jackknife and a block plane. A small handsaw can be used to cut the strips. The small round file is used to make a cove.*

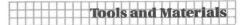
and do it often—honing the edge of your plane every day before you start work is not unreasonable. A touch-up does not take long and makes your tools work better. And a word to the wise: Most tools straight out of the box are not sharp enough to use.

Planes

Planes are wonderful tools. They have a satisfying heft, which gives you confidence that you can really accomplish something. When your plane is tuned up right, with a sharp blade set to cut lightly, the shavings of wood can be as light and transparent as tracing paper. It can be worth fixing a piece of pine in a vise just to pull curls off with a newly sharpened plane. Nothing does the job of smoothing wood better.

The block plane. This is my favorite tool, a small, one-handed plane with the blade set at a relatively low angle. Officially, a block plane is a plane set up with the bevel on the blade facing up, instead of facing down as it is in a jack plane. The block plane normally would be used mostly for smoothing end grain, but in strip-building it's used for everything.

A good block plane will have an easily adjustable blade depth, a lever to adjust the blade alignment, and an adjustable throat. These adjustments are important. The depth adjustment is used to account for different wood characteristics and how much wood you want to remove. Wood with smooth, straight grain will plane easily and the blade can be set deep without fear of wood tearing out, creating a rough surface. You can also set the blade deeper when you are roughing out a shape and just want to remove a lot of wood quickly.

The blade-alignment lever helps you set the blade flat and even with the bottom of the plane. It can be difficult to true up the blade after sharpening, but the lever makes it easy.

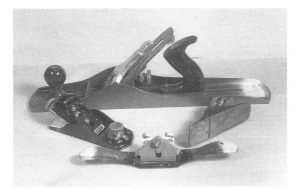

Figure 3-2. *A sharp plane is a joy to use. Here are the planes I find useful. At the top of the picture is a big jack plane used for smoothing large flat areas. At left center is the block plane, the workhorse of strip-building. At right center is a modified block plane with the bottom rounded to smooth hollows. At the bottom of the picture is a spokeshave, a versatile tool for fairing the hull.*

The throat adjustment is a big help. Some wood with curved grain can be very difficult to deal with. The throat adjustment will limit the amount of tear-out. By closing the throat so there is just enough room for the shaving to rise up the blade, a sharp plane can cut against the grain without tear-out. Most good block planes will have a knob and lever at the front that permit throat adjustment.

Of course, you generally want to plane with the grain. The grain should rise up to the surface as you push the plane forward. Think of dragging a hoe down a shingled roof, as opposed

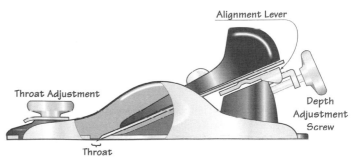

Figure 3-3. *A good block plane will have an adjustable throat and an easily adjusted depth. The alignment lever gives you an easy way to square the blade with the bottom.*

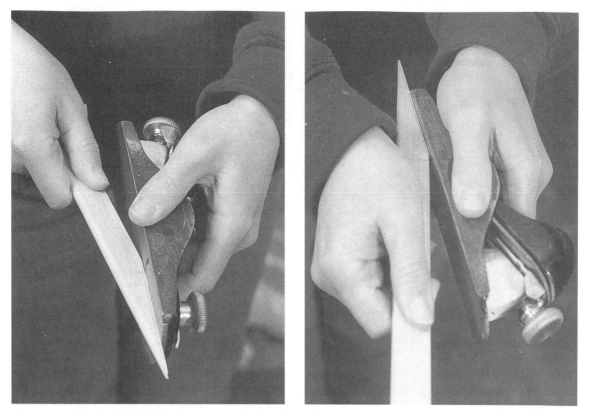

Figure 3-4. *Block planes are small enough to be used in one hand. It is often convenient to be able pull the tool toward you (right) as well as push it away (left).*

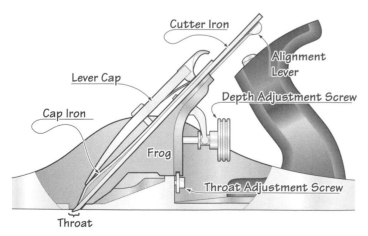

Figure 3-5. *A jack plane is more complicated than a block plane. The cap iron needs to adjusted close to the end of the blade (within about $1/16$ inch). For difficult grain you may want to close up the throat but you'll have to loosen the screws holding down the frog before you can make this adjustment.*

Labels in Figure 3-5: Cutter Iron, Alignment Lever, Lever Cap, Depth Adjustment Screw, Cap Iron, Frog, Throat Adjustment Screw, Throat

to pulling it up. When you pull down, the hoe will slide easily over the shingles. If you pull up, you'll tear out all the shingles and make a mess. The same thing happens with a plane, but closing the throat limits the damage to the wood, which is very helpful when you can't figure out which way the grain is going, or when it changes along the length of the strip.

The jack plane. A large jack plane or jointer plane comes in handy for smoothing and fairing large flat areas. The longer the plane, the better it will be for fairing, but you won't be able to use it in all the places you can get a shorter plane into. It's probably not worth your going out and buying a plane especially for this project, but an 18-inch plane comes in handy for a variety of tasks, including building paddles.

A good jack plane will have much the same adjustments as a block plane, including a depth-adjustment screw and a blade-alignment lever. The throat adjustment will not be as easy as the block plane's because the adjustment screw is less conveniently placed and there are bolts down through the frog that must be loosened before the adjustment screw is operative.

The spokeshave. A spokeshave is essentially a plane with handles on either side of the blade instead of in line with it. With this orientation, it has a very short, flat "foot" section, so it may not appear to be very good for fairing, but in fact it has many uses. Because you hold the spokeshave in line with the blade, you have precise control over the angle of the blade. Spokeshaves were designed to shape and smooth wagon-wheel spokes, which are round in cross-section and straight in length. On a kayak, you find the same arrangement in the keel and chines.

Because of the spokeshave's short foot, it's useful for smoothing concave sections. By setting the blade deeper, you can reach into regions inaccessible to a block plane.

A good spokeshave will have two depth-adjustment screws, one on each side of the blade. This gives you control over the depth on both sides of the tool. Sometimes you'll want to set one side deep for quick cutting and the other side shallow for fine smoothing.

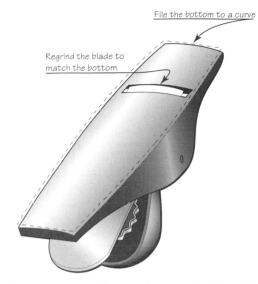

File the bottom to a curve

Regrind the blade to match the bottom

Figure 3-7. _By grinding the bottom of a cheap block plane you can make a tool that will do a better job of fairing concave areas than a spokeshave will._

A curved plane. There are some parts of a kayak that none of the above planes can reach, namely the deepest concave areas, and this is where it's useful to have a plane with a curved bottom. Unlike the planes already mentioned, which most good hardware stores will have, this one may be hard to find.

If you can't find it, you can make it. I have a small, cheap block plane that has been modified for this job. Just grind the foot of it so that it is convex (about a 4- to 5-inch radius). A belt sander or a metal file will do the job of shaping the cast iron. Then grind the blade to match the curve of the plane.

The Jackknife

If you don't have one already, this is your excuse to get a good-quality jackknife. While you're fitting the strips, there will be many places where you'll want to remove a section of wood quickly. A few quick swipes with a jackknife will usually get you most of the way there.

Depth Adjustment Screws

Figure 3-6. _Spokeshaves are very good for smoothing parts of the kayak that are hard to reach with other planes. The short foot lets you work in concave sections. But note that those without adjustment screws are hard to set up correctly._

The reason I recommend a jackknife instead of a utility knife is that it can be resharpened. Replacing the blades on a utility knife accomplishes the same thing, but if you're going to have sharpening stones for your planes, as you should, you might as well use them for your knife as well. It can also be useful to have some other tools available on a jackknife. For example, if you need to remove a staple quickly, it's easier to open up the screwdriver on your knife than it is to search around for your staple puller.

Scrapers

A sharp scraper can be used in many places instead of sandpaper and it will also get into places that a plane can't reach. But I mostly use my scraper to remove beads of glue before I start planing.

Scrapers come in two varieties: cabinet scraper and paint scraper. You can use either one. The cabinet scraper is a piece of flexible sheet steel with a fine edge. A paint scraper is thicker and mounted in a handle. I use a paint scraper to knock down the texture at the edge of a piece of fiberglass. The cabinet scraper gives a smooth final finish and can be used on some woods instead of fine sandpaper. The cabinet scraper works best on hardwood, so you may not find much use for it on softwood strips, but it can be useful for smoothing cured epoxy.

Sandpaper

Like any other cutting tool, sandpaper becomes dull with use. While this is not a big revelation, the consequence of dull sandpaper is not just slower sanding. Dull sandpaper also results in a poorer finish.

Because the grain of wood varies in hardness, dull sandpaper will continue to cut the softer part of the grain after it can no longer cut the harder grain. The result is a wavy surface instead of the nice flat finish you get with fresh, sharp sandpaper.

Use a good-quality aluminum oxide paper; it stays sharp longer than flint or garnet because as you use it the aluminum oxide crystals break to expose new, sharp edges. But eventually it, too, will become dulled.

The fairing sander. Many people are tempted to use power tools when it comes to sanding, and while I must admit they have their uses, I prefer sanding by hand most of the time because it raises less dust, is quieter, and is often faster. Sanding by hand certainly does require more physical effort, but not as much as you might think if you use the right tool. And the right tool is the fairing sander.

You may be able to buy a fairing sander somewhere, but it's probably just as easy to make your own. You need a piece of ¼-inch plywood that's half the width of a sheet of sandpaper and twice as long. Screw on some handles at each end. Glue two halves of a sheet of sandpaper to it, using feathering-sander adhesive or contact cement, and go to it. You can rip the paper off to replace it, but it comes off more easily if you first warm it with a hair drier, a heat gun, or an iron.

The fairing sander is a whole-body tool. By that, I mean you really get your whole body behind it and use long, smooth strokes. This makes much quicker work of the job than a sanding block does, and it's superior to a power sander.

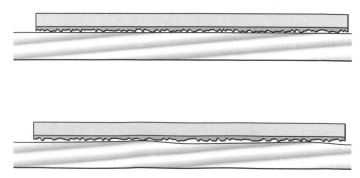

Figure 3-8. Sharp new sandpaper (top) will create a smooth, even surface. Dull sandpaper (bottom) cuts faster into the soft wood of the grain, creating hollows.

Sanding blocks. Anything from a block of pine with sandpaper wrapped around it to a specially made rubber block can function as a sanding block. The rubber blocks have a handy system for holding the paper, but they also waste a lot of it. I made a curved block by cutting one side of a thick piece of pine to a gradually changing curve. This is good for getting to the inside of the boat and other hollow areas. See Figures 3-9 and 3-10.

The random orbital sander. If you are going to get a power sander, the tool to get is a random orbital. This is not the old "oscillating" sander which, after you'd spent 10 minutes installing the paper, vibrated your hand without doing much sanding. The random orbital is more voracious. It will remove a lot of material without producing swirl marks in the wood.

There are two types of random orbital: a palm sander and a two-handed tool with the motor coming out at a right angle to the sanding pad. I use the latter because it's more powerful, but the palm version also works well.

Files

A ¼-inch-diameter round file is useful for cutting a cove in a strip of wood. The easiest way to find one of these is to ask for a chain-saw file. This kind of file is not the best for use on softwood, but it works. It will tend to become clogged with wood dust, so use a wire brush to clean it out.

A "four-in-hand" file, or shoemaker's rasp, with one flat side and one rounded side and two different coarsenesses on each side can be useful for removing a lot of wood quickly in a hard-to-reach area. You can use it to file the taper on the end forms, with a little effort, or you can clean up around the coaming. While it's not a mandatory tool, you wouldn't be sorry if you bought one.

Saws

The razor saw. There are two types of razor saws, the Japanese kind, and the modelmaker's variety. The Japanese saw is an elegant tool that cuts on the pull stroke, which is easier than pushing. The modelmaker's version is small and rather ugly—see Figure 3-1. It usually has simple triangular teeth that cut in both directions. I prefer the modelmaker's saw because it is small and easy to handle, lightweight, and cheap. Usually the blades are replaceable. The Japanese razor saw is a better tool, one that will last longer and

Figure 3-9. You can do all your sanding with this fairing sander, or "long board," and a small sanding block made of rubber or wood.

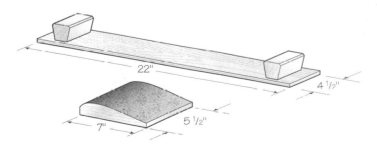

Figure 3-10. Dimensions for a fairing sander made from ¼-inch-thick plywood, and a curved wooden sanding block.

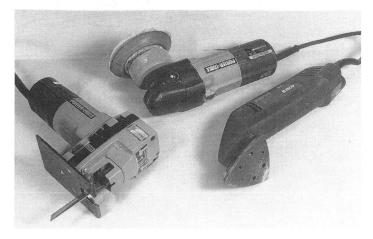

Figure 3-11. *Some of the small power tools that speed up the job. A jigsaw (left) can be used to cut out forms and remove material for the cockpit and hatches. A random orbital sander (center) is excellent for sanding wood and smoothing fiberglass. A detail sander (right) is occasionally useful for tight spots, but I've gone a lot of years without one.*

cut more easily, but I've been happy with the cheap modelmaker's saw. The primary advantage of a razor saw is that it makes a very smooth cut and is easy to control. A good middle ground between the modelmaker's saw and the Japanese saw is a dovetail saw. It's cheaper than the Japanese saw and more rugged than the modelmaker's.

The jigsaw. If you're going to cut your own forms and don't have a bandsaw, use a jigsaw like the one in Figure 3-11. The best jigsaws have variable speeds, a dust blower, and an orbiting blade. Incidentally, different materials are best cut at different speeds. Thicker and harder materials are generally better cut at slower speeds. The dust blower clears the sawdust away from the blade so you can see where you are cutting. You usually still need to supplement this with the occasional puff from your own lungs, but the blower helps. The orbiting blade causes the blade to go back and forward as it goes up and down. In thicker material, this allows the sawdust to fall clear of the blade on the downstroke. Since the teeth of the blade are oriented for cutting on the

upstroke, the blade will stay sharp longer.

But don't worry if your jigsaw doesn't have all these features; it will still work. Do put in a fresh blade before starting, however, because it's much easier to control a sharp blade than it is a dull one.

If you have a bandsaw, well great, you can do most of the form-cutting with it. Cutting out the hole for the strongback is easier with a jigsaw, though. A scroll saw is also a good tool for cutting out the forms, and you can cut the strongback hole with it if you need to.

The table saw. I do not recommend you go out and buy a table saw just for this project. You need it only to cut the strips, and you can probably cut all of them in a day. If you don't have a table saw, try to borrow one from a friend for a day or so.

Most of the wood used for strips is soft and relatively easy to cut, so you don't need a powerful saw. However, you'll be cutting a lot of strips and a less powerful saw may eventually overheat. A long fence makes it easier to keep the board straight—see Figure 5-5. I set up a fence made of pine boards that extends 10 feet out on either end of the saw.

Cutting the strips with a standard "combination" blade results in a lot of wasted wood because of the thickness of the blade. Get a thinner blade that leaves a narrower kerf. For example, if your table saw uses a 10-inch blade, you may want to use a $7\frac{1}{2}$-inch blade because its kerf is thinner.

Again, a sharper blade is better. It will put less strain on your saw, cutting will go faster, and you won't have to push the board so hard. You may be able to find someone to sharpen an old blade, but if you buy a new one, choose a carbide blade as it will stay sharp longer.

The bandsaw. Instead of a table saw, you can use a bandsaw. A bandsaw leaves a thinner kerf so it wastes less wood when cutting strips. Unfortunately, it also will produce a rougher cut, although this isn't really a problem because you will plane all the strips smooth after they're on the boat. It can be a little tricky to set up a bandsaw to cut strips, though, because it won't necessarily cut parallel to the fence. To find out which direction it's biased toward, draw a line on a piece of scrap wood, parallel to the straight side. Now take it to the bandsaw and try to saw along this line freehand. You'll soon discover the way you have to turn the wood to get a straight cut. Leave the wood in this position as you turn off the saw and mark a line on the table, parallel to the straight side of the scrap wood. Set up your fence parallel to this line.

The bandsaw is also a good replacement for the jigsaw when it comes time to cut the forms. It is easier to move the forms on the table of the bandsaw than it is to move the jigsaw on the forms. I am usually more accurate when cutting with the bandsaw.

Feather Boards

I guess you could classify feather boards more as safety devices than as tools. They keep the work tight up against the fence, and down against the table of a saw, router, or shaper, so you don't have to put your fingers in harm's way. They are very simple to make: you just cut slots in a piece of wood. A length of plywood makes a nice one with a bunch of 2-inch-long slots cut diagonally every $1/2$ inch on one edge. You can make one from a piece of pine by trimming the end of a board at a diagonal and cutting slots parallel with the grain every $1/4$ inch or so.

Clamped in place on the table, these boards do make it easier and safer to cut strips all by yourself. They're like an extra pair of hands to help keep the board aligned as you push it through the saw. If you're using a feather board to hold your work against the fence as you cut strips, you'll need to move it after every cut, as the board gets narrower. Figures 5-6 and 5-8, Chapter 5, show feather boards in use.

The Router or Shaper

If you choose to mill your own cove-and-bead strips, as discussed in Chapter 5, you will need a router in a router table, or a shaper. A hand-held router without a table will not do. A shaper is essentially the same thing as a router table, but it's usually more powerful. Not that cutting a cove or bead needs much power. Nevertheless, the router you use should be rated for con-

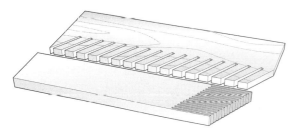

Figure 3-12. Two kinds of feather boards. The upper one is cut from a piece of plywood with diagonal slots that let the $1/2$-inch-wide fingers flex and spring. The lower version has slots cut in the end of a board. The end is cut diagonally and the fingers may be about $1/4$ inch wide. These boards are clamped to the table saw or router table so as to exert pressure on the wood to stop it drifting away from the fence, yet still allow it to slide easily.

Figure 3-13. Special router bits for cove-and-bead strips are made by several manufacturers. But if you have a shaper, you can purchase blades of larger diameter that will cut better. From left, cove cutter, and bead cutter on $1/2$-inch shafts for router, a pair of shaper cutters, and a pair of router cutters with $1/4$-inch shafts.

tinuous duty. It will be running a long time. The best router bits use a ¹/₂-inch shank, so the router needs to be able to accept that size.

Special bits. Several manufacturers now supply router bits specifically for making cove-and-bead strips. These are worth getting because the thin edges of the cove are very delicate. They're likely to split off while you're cutting the cove if you're not careful. But the bigger the radius of the cutter, the less likely the wood is to split. A shaper also offers the advantage of larger-radius cutters. You may be able to find a standard half-round (core-box) router bit of the right size, but it will probably make a mess of your edges.

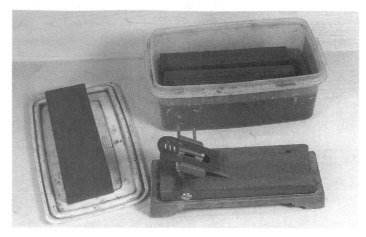

Figure 3-14. A good set of sharpening stones is essential to keep your edge tools working their best. I have four waterstones that I keep in a plastic container full of water. Here my block plane blade is set up in a sharpening jig. The jig holds the blade at the proper angle, which speeds up the task.

Sharpening Tools

One thing that can hardly be overstated is the importance of keeping your tools sharp. Sharp tools are easier to control. If you're concerned that you might remove wood too fast with a sharp tool and end up beyond where you want to be, don't worry. Because a sharp tool will cut with less applied pressure, you can take off just the amount you want. A dull tool needs more pressure, so it's easier to slip and mess up a piece.

The whetstone. There are a lot of good sharpening stones available today. Each has its own advantages but you generally want a fairly coarse stone to grind out the nicks in the blade, and a finer stone to give a sharp edge. To sharpen plane blades you want a 6-inch or longer stone. Either waterstones or oilstones will work, but you don't want to mix them. A waterstone should not get any oil on it.

Sharpening jigs. You can now get jigs for sharpening planes and chisels. These jigs consist of a clamp to hold the blade, and a wheel so you can move it. These jigs hold the blade at a constant angle while sharpening, which helps produce a good edge quickly.

Clamps

One of the nice things about clamps is that they never need sharpening. This is lucky because boatbuilding can require a lot of clamps. It's impossible to have too many, nor can you have too many different kinds. The task for which you will need the most clamps is laminating the cockpit coaming.

The most useful ones are spring clamps. They're basically oversized clothespins, and they're good at quickly holding a part while you align it for a cut. Because you only need one hand, you can hold the work with one hand while you clamp it with the other.

The standard C-clamp is good if you need to apply a lot of pressure. For a strip-built boat this doesn't happen often, but C-clamps are useful for making the cockpit coaming.

Bar clamps, particularly the quick-adjusting variety, help when you need to clamp across a long distance, as you do when making a paddle. In fact, making a paddle requires at least four bar or pipe clamps.

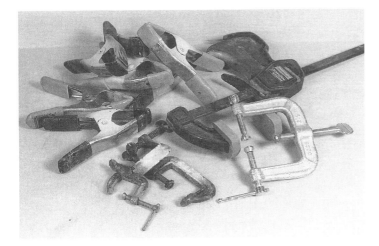

Figure 3-15. *A variety of clamps used in boatbuilding. It's impossible to have too many.*

Stapling

A standard staple gun is going to be in your hand a lot, but a good one doesn't cost a lot. Make sure you can take it apart to clean it if it jams, though, because when you're stapling the glued strips you're going to get glue in the stapler. The stapler will usually be held together

with pins with C-clips on the end. The C-clips are removable so you can disassemble the tool and wash out accumulated crud. If you can't get your stapler apart, try soaking it in hot water. After it has soaked, operate it a few times to remove the crud from the interior works, then dry it and spray it with light oil. Just be sure to wipe off the excess oil before using it on your wood.

Staple remover. After putting all the staples in, you'll need to take them out again. This can be a drag, but a good staple remover makes the task go as quickly as possible. There are several choices. The standard staple remover is like a curved screwdriver with the end slightly forked. This is worked under the staple and the staple is levered up. An alternative do-it-yourself tool is a "church-key" type of can opener. Sharpen the point so it is easier to get under the staple. Thirdly, you can use a pair of diagonal cutters. With these you can grasp one leg of the staple and pry it up, then pull the staple straight up.

If you want a more specialized tool, look in a stationer's store for a heavy-duty paper staple-puller. Not the small one that looks like a saber-toothed tiger's mouth, because it will mar the wood, but the heavy-duty version that has a lever attached to a large flat pad. The lever has a tab that is slipped under the staple, and pushing down on the lever pulls the staple while the metal pad protects the wood. When I first used this tool, I thought there must be something wrong with it. It worked too well. It was just too good at the task. I have yet to find its weakness. I'll keep looking.

Some people advocate stapling through plastic strips, so that when you're done, you pull on the plastic and all the staples come zipping

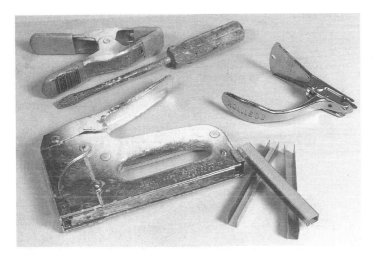

Figure 3-16. *Tools for applying and removing staples. Counterclockwise, from bottom left: a standard utility stapler with spare staples; a heavy-duty office staple remover; a screwdriver used to remove staples; and a spring clamp for holding stubborn strips.*

out. This works fairly well, assuming you use plastic thick enough not to rip, in which case you'll have a boat full of staples with little bits of plastic stuck under them. I don't feel it's worth it.

Tools to Use with Epoxy

Most kinds of epoxy can be purchased with calibrated "ketchup" pumps. One stroke on the resin pump and one stroke on the hardener will produce the correct mix. It's worth purchasing the pumps but be aware that they're not 100 percent accurate. They make the measuring easier, however, and most of the time they work perfectly.

The pumps are no different from the kind on a picnic ketchup or mustard dispenser, but epoxy is harder to pump than ketchup is, and sometimes they burp. For this reason it's good practice to pump into a calibrated measuring cup—this way you can double-check the dosage. It's important to get the ratio correct because epoxy fails most often when ratios of resin to hardener are inaccurate. The simplest measuring cup is a paper cup marked with the amounts for each pump. Don't use kitchen measuring cups because the epoxy will ruin them. Disposable medicine cups hold about 2 ounces of liquid, and you can use them to mix up small batches.

Several tools are suitable for applying epoxy. My two primary tools are a squeegee and a disposable brush. The squeegee is a thin rectangular piece of moderately flexible plastic. This can quickly move the epoxy around in a smooth thin layer. If you wipe it off after use, you can reuse it without having to peel off hardened epoxy.

Disposable brushes will apply epoxy in places that are hard to reach with the squeegee and allow you to place resin where you need it before spreading it with the squeegee. These brushes have natural bristles that are not affected by

the resin. I also use a foam paint roller for covering large flat areas.

A specialized tool that I use sometimes is a fiberglassing bubble roller. It looks like a small paint roller and is made out of aluminum or plastic with a series of ribs and slots that press down on the epoxy-soaked fiberglass so air bubbles can rise and escape.

Brushes

A fine natural-bristle brush is usually considered the best for applying varnish, but they can be awfully expensive, and no matter how well you clean them, they eventually start causing problems. I don't like cleaning brushes, so I use the disposable foam brushes with wooden handles. These brushes are nearly as good as a fine bristle brush, and they're cheaper and more convenient. The 2-inch-wide size is typically about right. Smaller brushes take longer to do a job, and bigger brushes hold too much varnish.

Miscellaneous tools

- Drill
- Drill bits
- Screwdriver
- Hammer

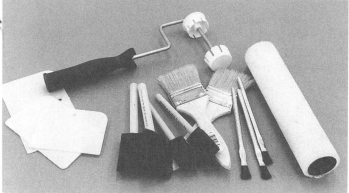

Figure 3-17. The best application tools, from left: plastic squeegees to spread epoxy; gray foam brushes to apply varnish; cheap bristle brushes to apply epoxy in smaller areas; acid brushes for gluing small pieces; and a fine bristle paint roller for applying expoxy over large areas.

- Scissors
- Paint roller
- Tape measure
- Square
- Chalk line
- Safety glasses
- Respirator
- Dust mask
- Gloves
- Coping saw
- Sanding blocks
- Paint strainer

Materials

The success of the whole project depends on the materials. The best materials cost more, but you can get away with lesser quality if you're willing to compromise. The trade-off is a less durable, less attractive kayak, but this boat will be just as much fun to use. So, if you need to save money, use the cheaper materials without shame, but still aim for the best quality you can afford. You'll put a lot of effort into the building and it would be a shame to shorten the boat's life unnecessarily. The amounts of materials you require are relatively small, so you can often buy the best without breaking the bank.

Wood

Most of the wood I use is available from a local lumberyard as raw lumber. If you don't have a decent local lumberyard, there are companies that will ship to your home. Pre-milled strips can also be shipped from a number of sources. Kits including all the required wood may also be ordered from the author. See the Material and Tool Sources appendix for mail-order sources.

If any of the woods listed below are not available where you live, look for straight-grained, knot-free, low-density softwood. Rot resistance is not required, because the wood will be encapsulated in epoxy and fiberglass, and small knots are not a problem. Wood with larger knots can be used but it will be harder to bend without breaking and more difficult to plane smooth. The knots can look attractive when the boat is done, however, so look for tight knots. Loose knots often have a black ring around them.

In my experience, you can often get wood with knots and still cut a lot of nice clear strips. Shuffle through the pile and choose the boards with the fewest knots, and knots located so there are still long sections of clear wood. Knots smaller than 1/8 inch will not be a problem. After cutting your strips, sort through the pile

Figure 3-18. *Small knots like the one shown here (left) may break (right) while you are bending strips into place on the boat. Break any knots in advance, so they don't surprise you later.*

and look for knots and for grain that cuts across the strip instead of running lengthwise. Break the strip at the blemish. You'll still be able to use the shorter sections, and you won't be surprised by a fault in the middle of the strip you've just glued and stapled in place.

The strips you use to build your kayak can be either flat-grained (sometimes called plain-sawed or slash-grained) or vertical-grained (also known as quarter-sawed or edge-grained). The best wood available at the lumberyard will be vertical-grained, but the problem for us is that when you cut a vertical-grained board into strips for your boat, you'll end up with flat-grained wood. Figure 3-19 illustrates this. So try to find boards with a lot of flat grain from which to make vertical-grained strips, which are easier to sand and plane.

It's okay to use flat-grained strips, but if you do, you'll find the softer parts between the annual rings abrading faster during sanding. This will raise the grain at the rings and give you a rippled surface—a problem you can combat by using sharp tools and sandpaper.

Cedar. The ideal wood for strip-building boats is found in the cedar family. Most cedars are light, flexible, and strong, all necessary requirements for a rugged, lightweight boat. Cedar suitable for building a kayak comes in a number of varieties: western red, Atlantic white, Port Orford, Alaskan white, and others. It does not include

eastern red, the aromatic "cedar chest" wood. This typically is not straight-grained enough and is full of knots.

Usually the name will tell you something about the color of the wood. Western red, which is the most readily available cedar, typically is a slightly reddish tan. However, it can vary from a dark chocolate brown to a pale, almost white, tan.

As their names imply, Atlantic white and northern white cedar are both nearly white. Northern white cedar is considered by many to be the premier wood for strip-building. It is lightweight, flexible, and strong. It works easily and produces a beautiful boat. Of course, others prefer western red for all the same reasons.

Redwood. Somewhat denser than the cedars, redwood is also more brittle, which makes it harder to work with when creating tight bends. It has a nice reddish hue and tends to be darker than cedar. It makes a good wood for accent strips or darker hulls.

Pine. One big advantage pine has over other woods is that it's easy to find. Any lumberyard will have clear pine suitable for a strip-built boat. Being denser than cedar or redwood, it isn't the best wood for our purposes, but it still works well. Pine actually comes in many different varieties, but you probably won't be able to tell which is which at the lumberyard. Whatever kind of pine you select will have a yellowish-white color that makes a nice contrast with western red cedar or redwood.

Other woods. There are many other woods you can use. Sometimes you'll find spruce 2 × 4s, free of knots and with straight grain, that you can cut up for strips. You can use fir for decking. Mahogany is pricey and dense, but will produce a beautiful-looking boat. Cypress is available in some regions and is said to be good for strip-building. Feel free to experiment with different kinds of wood.

If you have some choice when you are purchasing your wood, you might want to glance at

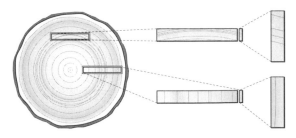

Figure 3-19. *Flat-sawed wood (top) and quarter-sawed wood (bottom). As you cut thin strips from the boards, however, you reverse the grain. So, to get quarter-sawed strips for your kayak you need to start with a flat-sawed plank.*

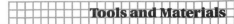

the accompanying table listing the mechanical properties of woods. Notice that western red cedar is lighter than redwood (specific gravity 0.32 versus 0.35) and has more impact resistance. Cedar has similar strength when bending, but is weaker in compression, shear, and tension. Since most of the loads on the wood when it is sandwiched in fiberglass will be compression, shear, and tension, someone wanting a stronger boat may go for redwood if they are willing to pay the weight penalty. Don't let the table scare you away from using any of the woods listed, however. They're all good. Simply use the table to optimize or maximize some characteristic.

Length of strips. You don't need full-length strips. If, for example, you're building a 19-foot boat, you don't need 20-foot strips. You can get by with 6-foot strips, which is just as well because long, clear wood is getting harder to come by.

Much of it comes from old-growth forests, and as these forests get cut down this lumber will disappear. Meanwhile, it will get more and more expensive, so it will be easier and cheaper for you to buy shorter pieces and join them together to make the length you need.

Not only do you save money and valuable wood by using shorter strips; also, it's often easier to use short strips. Long strips can be fragile and hard to handle. For example, if you're fitting both ends of a strip into a space, you need to be careful to get the length correct. By using shorter strips you can fit one strip in one end and another strip in the other, then cut them to length in the middle where it is easier. In the few instances when it is actually easier to use a long strip, it's easy enough to scarf a couple strips together.

Width of strips. The width of the strips is usually determined by the thickness of the board

Mechanical properties of some woods typically used in strip-building[1]

Species Name:	Specific Gravity[2] (Dry)	Static Bending			Impact Bending— Height of Drop Causing Complete Failure	Compression Parallel to Grain— Maximum Crushing Strength	Compression Perpendicular to Grain— Fiber Stress at Proportional Limit	Shear Parallel to Grain— Maximum Shearing Strength	Tension Perpendicular to Grain— Maximum Tensile Strength	Side Hardness— Load Perpendicular to Grain
		Modulus of Rupture	Modulus of Elasticity	Work to Maximum Load						
		Psi	Million Psi	In–Lbs/in³	In	——————————— Psi ———————————				Lbs
Cedar:										
Alaska	.44	11,100	1.42	10.4	29	6,310	620	1,130	360	580
Atlantic White	.32	6,800	.93	4.1	13	4,700	410	800	220	350
Northern White	.31	6,500	.80	4.8	12	3,960	310	850	240	320
Port-Orford	.43	12,700	1.70	9.1	28	6,250	720	1,370	400	630
Western Red	.32	7,500	1.11	5.8	17	4,560	460	990	220	350
Douglas Fir	.48	12,400	1.95	9.9	31	7,230	800	1,130	340	710
Mahogany, Hon.	.45[3]	9,000	1.34	9.1	–	4,340	–	1,230	–	740
Pine:										
Long Leaf	.59	14,500	1.98	11.8	34	8,470	960	1,510	470	870
Sugar	.36	8,200	1.19	5.5	18	4,460	500	1,130	350	380
Western White	.38	9,700	1.46	8.8	23	5,040	470	1,040	–	420
Redwood	.35	7,900	1.10	5.2	15	5,220	520	1,110	250	420
Sitka Spruce	.40	10,200	1.57	9.4	25	5,610	580	1,150	370	510
Spanish Cedar	.41[3]	11,500	1.44	9.4	–	6,210	–	1,100	–	600

[1] Extracted from the Forest Products Laboratory's "The Encyclopedia of Wood – Revised Edition"

[2] Specific Gravity is the density relative to water where the specific gravity of water is 1.

[3] Specific gravity calculated: Volume wet, weight dry.

Figure 3-20. *Use this table to evaluate the strengths and weaknesses of your chosen material for strips. See text.*

that the strips are ripped from. It used to be that, if you bought a 1-inch-thick board, the actual thickness was ³/₄ inch. The ¹/₄ inch disappeared in planing the raw board smooth at the mill. Now, when you buy cedar or redwood, it will often be ⁹/₁₆-inch thick instead of ³/₄-inch when you get it. It's not that the mill planed it even smoother. In an effort to make more money, the mills are just cutting the boards thinner. This means that your strips are going to be narrower. Aside from feeling ripped off, you shouldn't regard this as a problem.

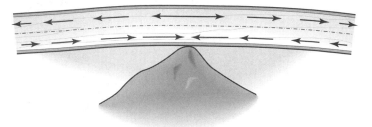

Figure 3-21. When your kayak hits a rock, a bending force is transferred through the skin. The wood nearest the rock is compressed, but it will absorb the compression forces as long as the hard epoxy-and-fiberglass shell protects it from point damage. The fiberglass on the far side (top) is put under tension, which it is designed to handle well. See text.

The wood will still work—you'll just need more strips. In fact, the narrower strips will actually be easier to bend into place than ³/₄-inch-wide strips would be.

If you buy pre-cut strips, or a kit, the strips will typically still be the full ³/₄ inch. The mills making the strips can still order the thicker stock, even if the average Joe can't find it. Note however, that if you are building with cove-and-bead strips, the effective width of your strip is less because the cove cuts ¹/₈ inch into one side.

When you're stripping around tight curves it's easier to use narrower strips. If you're cutting your own wood, it's often easiest to cut one of the full-width strips in half. If you are using the ⁹/₁₆-inch wood, that means you'll end up with quite narrow strips, especially after the saw kerf is subtracted. The alternative is to cut some strips a little wider before halving them, but that way, you'll end up with more waste.

Thickness of strips. One way to save weight is to use thinner wood. The typical thickness of ¹/₄ inch can be reduced to ³/₁₆ inch, and if you're concerned about every pound, this is a logical method of weight reduction. However, everything is a trade-off. If you use thinner wood, you'll weaken the skin of the boat.

Although the wood by itself is fragile, when you sandwich it between layers of fiberglass and epoxy you create a very strong structure. Like an I-beam with horizontal webs held apart

by a lightweight thin section, the wood acts as a core that separates the stress-absorbing fiberglass.

When the glass-wood-glass sandwich is bent, the material on the inside of the curve is compressed and the material on the outside is stretched. See Figure 3-21. Most of the tension of the stretching is taken by the material on the outside of the curve—the fiberglass and epoxy. With thicker material in the middle, the fiberglass must be stretched more to achieve the same bend. Since it requires more work to stretch more, the resulting sandwich will be stiffer. Now, stiffer is not necessarily stronger, but a stiffer material will spread the force of impact over a wider area, and so lessen the chance of major structural damage.

Instead of reducing weight by making the wood thinner, you could reduce the thickness of the glass and epoxy. This can save almost as much weight, with less loss of stiffness. Thinner glass also weakens the whole structure, but that is the trade-off. By retaining wood thickness and reducing fiberglass thickness, you can at least maintain most of the skin stiffness, which will distribute forces better.

How strong is strong enough? It depends on what the boat is being used for. A boat used for playing in surf-washed rock gardens must be stronger than a kayak used on the open sea. A boat used to cross wave-swept bays needs to be stronger than a kayak that stays in sheltered

Relative Weights of Boats[1]
Built with Different Thickness
of Wood and Fiberglass

Wood Thickness	1/4"	3/16"	1/4"	3/16"
Glass Thickness	6 oz	6 oz	4 oz	4 oz
Wood Weight[2]	20.8	15.6	20.8	15.6
Glass Weight[3]	6.3	6.3	4.2	4.2
Resin Weight	9.4	9.4	8.1	8.1
Total (lbs)	36.5	31.3	33.1	27.9
Stiffness[4]	451	293	333	191

[1] 50 sq ft surface area
[2] Western red cedar with a density of 20 lbs/ft[3]
[3] One layer inside and out with additional layer on the bottom
[4] Pounds per inch of deflection at failure. Derived from data in "Epoxyworks", Number 10, Winter 1998, Gougeon Brothers.

Figure 3-22. It may be false economy to save weight by skimping on wood, which weakens the boat. Thinner glass saves a lot of weight, but does not affect the skin stiffness much. Using 1/4-inch wood with 4-ounce glass will save almost as much weight as 3/16-inch strips and 6-ounce glass while still maintaining more stiffness. The trade-off is that the thinner glass will be more prone to point damage. These calculations are based on the Guillemot design and the weights do not include any outfitting such as seats, so final weights will tend to be a few pounds heavier. Stiffness numbers are based on date, published by Gougeon Brothers, from 3-point bending load testing of 12-inch × 12-inch western red cedar panels. See text.

water. A kayak used by a 250-pound paddler in harsh conditions must be stronger than a boat used by a 120-pound flat-water racer. Anything from 5/16-inch-thick wood strips with two layers of 10-ounce glass, to 1/8-inch-thick wood covered with one layer of 2-ounce glass, may be reasonable, depending on the given situation.

Cove-and-bead strips. If boats were built with straight lines they'd look awful, but building them would certainly be a lot easier. Fortunately, from an aesthetic viewpoint, there are very few straight lines on a boat. This does make

building a kayak more difficult, but there are ways to ease the task.

As Figure 3-23 shows, if you use square strips, you'll get gaps between the outer edges as you progress around the tight curves of the boat. One solution is to bevel the edge of the strips. Using a block plane, you can quickly run a bevel down the length of the strip.

There is a quicker solution than beveling. It requires more preparatory work, but it saves time in the long run. If you round one edge of your strip and hollow out the other edge to match, you can make strips that naturally nestle together with very small gaps. These are cove-and-bead strips. See Figure 3-24.

Because they don't need a bevel to fit together, they lie more fairly on the forms and need less sanding, which helps you get the boat together faster. You can either make your own beads and coves with a router, or you can buy the strips already prepared. Pre-made cove-and-bead strips will cost extra, but as there is a lot of effort required to make them yourself, the additional cost may be worth it in the long run. You'll find a list of suppliers of cove-and-bead strips in Appendix 2 at the end of the book. Some lumberyards will be willing to cut strips for you, and some cabinetmakers may be able to perform this service, too.

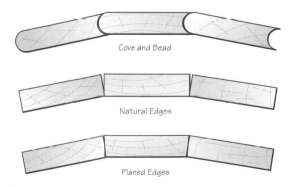

Cove and Bead

Natural Edges

Planed Edges

Figure 3-23. Cove-and-bead strips (top) make the tightest joints with the least effort. Naturally square edges (center) leave gaps on a tight radius, but they can be eliminated (bottom) with a few strokes of a plane. See text.

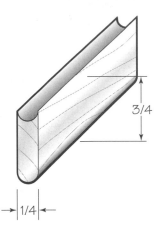

Figure 3-24. *Dimensions of a typical cove-and-bead strip, in inches. The strip has a hollow cove along one edge and a matching rounded bead along the other. The diameter of the cove and the bead is the same as the thickness of the wood, in this case, ¹/₄ inch.*

While cove-and-bead strips make the stripping go quicker, there's one thing you need to watch out for: they're more delicate. You need to be careful not to break off the fine edges of the cove. They can also make some of the joints between strips more complicated. For example, where the end of one strip joins to the side of another strip, you may need to add or remove a cove or bead. Removing the cove and bead is easy: you just cut them off. Adding a bead is not too hard, either, because you can do it with a hand plane. But adding a cove can be difficult. Still, a file will do the job.

Hardwood

While most of a strip-built kayak is made with softwood, there are a few places that need hardwood. The coaming, the stem, and the stern may all incorporate hardwood. All these places have sharp bends around which the wood is laminated, and that calls for material that bends easily without breaking. One of the best woods for this purpose is ash, a hard, light-colored wood that flexes easily without steaming. I have bent ¹/₈-inch-thick ash around a 2-inch radius without cracking it, and I'm glad to say that none of the curves on a kayak are quite that tight.

If some contrasting wood is required, cherry makes a good choice. I've also used mahogany but, unfortunately, mahogany doesn't like being bent around tight corners. Sandwiching it behind another wood that bends more easily is a good way to eliminate most cracks, but it may be difficult to work with. In any case, thinner strips of wood will be easier to bend.

Some people feel they should use hardwood for the whole boat. Well, you can if you want to, but please realize that hardwood is generally heavier and harder to work than softwood. It won't bend as easily and it may be hard to plane. If you understand this, and still feel it's worth it, go ahead; you can make a beautiful boat. Again, consider using thinner strips to make the boat lighter and the strips easier to bend.

Glue for the Strips

Your first thought may be to use epoxy or some other waterproof glue between the strips. This isn't necessary, because the wood is going to be encapsulated in resin and fiberglass, so it won't get wet. And if it's not going to get wet, why use an expensive and hard-to-prepare, harmful-to-your-health waterproof glue when an easy and inexpensive glue will do just as well? Standard white glue (polyvinyl acetate) such as Elmer's is very strong. As the ads say, it's "stronger than the wood itself." This is plenty strong enough. The only problem is that plain white glue can be hard to sand. The yellow carpenter's glue (aliphatic resin) is easier to work with as far as I'm concerned, and it's what I recommend. It dries harder and sands without gumming the paper too much.

You can now buy waterproof yellow glue, such as TiteBond II. It's easy to use, but once again, it's not necessary, so save a couple of bucks and don't bother with it on a strip-built boat. Of course, when it comes to gluing a paddle together, that's a different matter. I often use epoxy for gluing my paddles, but one of the new waterproof yellow glues would work as well.

Sometimes you need to tack something on quickly or temporarily, and the stuff to use then is

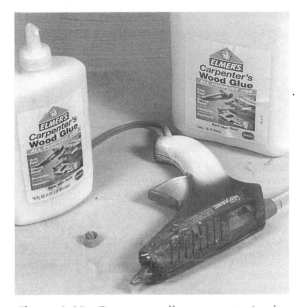

Figure 3-25. Common yellow carpenter's glue (aliphatic resin) is used between the strips. Buy a large jug and pour it into a smaller dispenser. Waterproof glue isn't needed here because all the wood will be encapsulated and sealed in epoxy. Hot-melt glue comes in handy for quick tacking.

hot-melt glue. It comes in sticks that are pushed through a heating applicator. It's not very strong but it bonds as soon as it cools, and when the strength of the glue joint is not critical it's a good solution. Some people build the whole boat with hot-melt between the strips, but because it sets up so fast you have to rush to assemble the strips before the glue dries. You need to make very sure you put the strip in the right place initially because as soon as the wood touches it the hot-melt glue cools.

Epoxy vs. Polyester Resin

Epoxy comes in the form of two liquids that harden through chemical reaction when they're mixed together. Similarly, polyester resin is a liquid that solidifies when methyl ethyl ketone (MEK) catalyst is added to it.

After they've been mixed, but before they've had a chance to harden, these resins are painted onto fiberglass cloth to create a glass-reinforced plastic (GRP). Polyester resin is readily available in automobile body shops and hardware stores at fairly low prices. Epoxy resin is much more expensive than polyester and harder to get but it's worth it. It's stronger, bonds better to the wood, and will last longer than polyester. Polyester is sometimes harder, but it's more brittle and less impact-resistant than epoxy.

If you want my advice, I'd have to say it doesn't pay to cut corners on the resin. You'll be spending a long time building the boat. You might as well do it right the first time, and that means epoxy. If you're really hard up for money, go ahead, use polyester resin. It will do a decent job and with proper care it can last a long time. My brother made his first canoe with polyester and it has been stored outside for years. I have to admit it's doing just fine. Just avoid the auto body or hardware store variety of polyester resin as it has additives that may cause problems if it has been sitting around a long time. Get your polyester from a marine supplier. See the sources of materials and tools listed in Appendix 2 for mail orders. Again, get the best stuff you can afford. Throughout this book, I'll be focusing mostly on epoxy but there's not much difference in the way you use polyester. Whichever

Figure 3-26. It pays to keep your epoxy organized in one place. A scrap piece of plywood protects the workbench from inevitable drips.

you use, however, be sure to take proper safety precautions. You'll find the safety information in Appendix 6.

Many epoxies suffer from "amine blush," a coating that develops on the surface of the cured resin when it hardens in the presence of humidity. This coating will cause problems for later coats of epoxy or varnish, so you should wash any epoxy coating that is older than a day or two. Use soapy water and one of those green plastic pot-scrubbing pads (Scotch-Brite). Some newer epoxy formulations don't suffer from amine blush but you'll have to read the individual manufacturer's literature to find out.

Look for a low-viscosity resin, that is, a thin one that will easily soak into the fiberglass cloth. A thick, high-viscosity resin needs to be worked more to wet out the fiberglass cloth, which forces air into the weave and may result in a clouded finish. If you want, you can thin a high-viscosity resin with solvent to help it penetrate the wood and to create a good bond for the fiberglass. In general, however, the lower-viscosity stuff is easier to work with. Incidentally, it pays to shop around for your epoxy. There are lesser-known manufacturers, such as MAS from Phoenix Resins, who produce a blush-free epoxy with excellent material and handling properties. See Appendix 2.

Most polyester resin will also get a coating when it cures. The curing reaction is inhibited by air, therefore many polyester resins contain a wax that rises to the surface, protecting it from the air and letting the skin cure to a hard finish. Before you add any more coatings, wash this wax off with ammonia and water.

Polyester designed for laminating doesn't have the wax, so the surface stays tacky for a long time and bonds better to the next coat of resin. You'll have trouble sanding that kind of finish, of course, but you can freely add more coats of resin. You can buy a wax additive that you mix in with the last coat only, so that it sets up hard, ready for sanding and painting or varnishing.

Both epoxy and polyester resin are damaged by ultra-violet light. If the boat is going to be stored outside, or spend a long time in the sun, it should be shielded from ultra-violet rays. Varnish with built-in ultra-violet protection will do it. More on varnish later.

Fiberglass

Fiberglass is just that: fibers of glass. It's often just called glass. Fiberglass is not, as commonly thought, that stinky liquid you get at the auto body shop. That is polyester resin, the stuff mentioned above. Fiberglass is made of glass fibers that are woven, stitched, or glued to make various fabrics with different properties. The cloth most often used in strip-built boats is the woven variety that looks and feels a bit like silk. In its raw form it's white, and the obvious question is: "How does it become clear?" Well, it's actually clear to begin with, and the white appearance comes from reflections on the surface of the fibers, and refraction inside them. Once the fibers have been wetted out with resin, the reflections and refractions disappear, as does the cloth itself. All you see then is the wood beneath it.

Fiberglass cloth is available in a variety of weights. The most typical weight for a kayak is 6 ounces per square yard, but it's available from 24-ounce down to 1-ounce. For lighter kayaks,

Figure 3-27. *Boatbuilders have many varieties of cloth available to them. From left: Strands of fiberglass woven roving can be pulled out and used; distinctively colored and costly, golden-yellow Kevlar is light and very strong; biaxial fiberglass cloth is strong, but like Kevlar, expensive; 6-ounce fiberglass cloth, the strip-built standard.*

4-ounce cloth is a good weight. The heavier varieties are unnecessary. You could use even lighter fiberglass than 4-ounce for very light boats and on paddles.

There are two varieties of fiberglass fibers: E-glass, and S-glass. These designations just indicate the kind of glass used to make the fibers and the meaning of "E" and "S" is not really relevant here. E-glass is the more common and is what is mostly used for in boatbuilding. S-glass is stronger and more expensive. Someone trying for the best strength-to-weight ratio may want to try S-glass, but it's overkill for most boats.

As I mentioned above, the fiberglass fibers can be made into several different kinds of cloth. The typical cloth is woven, but there are several varieties of non-woven cloth. The disadvantage of woven material is that the weaving process crimps the fibers as they pass up and down through the weave, and each of these little bends stresses the glass and builds in curves that detract from the cloth's straight-line strength. To put it another way, the fibers are usually not oriented in the strongest direction because the weaving causes the fibers to curve up and down.

Non-woven cloth overcomes this problem by keeping the fibers straight.

There are two varieties of non-woven cloths, the directional cloths and mat. We won't consider mat here because it is poorly suited to strip-building and is generally not compatible with epoxy. The directional cloths may be single uni-directional, with all the fibers oriented in the same direction in one layer, or they may have several unidirectional layers, with each layer designed to take maximum strain from a different direction. Because these cloths do not have a weft to hold them together, they are bound with a light knit fiber.

Because unidirectional cloth only provides reinforcement in one direction, along the direction of the fibers, it's of limited use for kayaks, although it can be used to make reinforcing ribs or to strengthen locations that are subject to forces primarily from one direction, such as behind the cockpit where you sit before climbing into the boat.

Biaxial cloth, therefore, is generally more useful, and normal woven fabric is essentially biaxial because the fibers are oriented in two layers, each layer running at right angles to the other. The layers may run lengthwise and across the fabric, or each layer may run at 45 degrees to the length of the cloth, which is called a "double bias". Either of these biaxial types would be useful for a kayak. Triaxial cloth, true to its name, has fibers running in three directions but it's probably overkill for a kayak.

With the exception of mat, the non-woven fabrics are appealing because they are stronger and produce a higher glass-to-resin ratio, which will be lighter. The more glass and less resin, the stronger the material for the same weight. The additional strength and weight savings are often worth the higher cost on other boats, but in the case of kayak-building there is a snag. Unfortunately, the thread used in the knit of non-woven fabrics is often something other than glass and it will show up in the finished boat as a line through the otherwise clear fiberglass.

Since woven cloth works well, the additional strength of a non-woven cloth is usually not worth the degraded aesthetics, at least on the outside of the boat. People seeking to make an especially strong boat may want to look into using non-woven fabrics on the inside where looks don't matter so much.

Interestingly, the inside is often where the most strength is needed. It's the inside that's subjected to tension forces when the hull strikes a rock, and most of the fabrics perform best in tension rather than compression. The fabric on the outside primarily provides protection from abrasion, while the fabric on the inside of the hull provides much of the strength against impacts. It's a convenient coincidence that the aesthetics of the inside are less important, so you may use materials there that are stronger, even if they're ugly.

As I mentioned above, one non-woven fiberglass product that should be avoided is mat, which consists of chopped strands of fiberglass bonded together lightly in random directions. Mat is used in some fiberglass boats as a quick way of adding thickness to a layup and for adding strength between layers of fabric. It absorbs a lot of resin and is not very strong by itself. The bonding agent in most mat is designed to be dissolved by polyester resin and using epoxy resin with mat will usually result in a big mess and wasted material.

Kevlar

Kevlar is the brand name of an aramid fiber developed by DuPont. Kevlar cloth has a golden tan color, so you can't call it ugly, exactly, but it isn't as good-looking as wood. It's best known for its use in bullet-proof vests, where the fact that it's very strong in tension, and not brittle in compression, stops the bullet. It's very hard to cut, requiring extremely sharp scissors that have never touched fiberglass. It is also difficult to wet out with resin, because the color makes it hard to see air bubbles. It's much lighter than fiberglass, but most of the weight savings may be lost because it absorbs more resin. It's also much more expensive than fiberglass, so for all these reasons, I would limit its use to the inside of the hull. The deck doesn't need the strength, so why waste the money there? Even on the hull, Kevlar should be considered only for kayaks that really need extra strength and light weight. And beware: don't ever put Kevlar in any location that you will later need to sand smooth. Let me tell you, this stuff does not sand. It instantly gets fuzzy, and the nap that forms eliminates any hope of sanding any further. It's like trying to sand a carpet: The exposed flexible fibers prevent the sandpaper from reaching the hard surface below.

Graphite

Graphite, or carbon fiber, is considered the ultimate high-tech material. It is stiff, strong, and light. It has high tensile and compressive strength. It's also brittle, so it's rarely used alone. Like Kevlar and S-glass, graphite is probably overkill for most strip-built applications. It's available woven in with other materials such as glass and Kevlar. A few yarns of graphite woven in with fiberglass provide much of the stiffness of pure graphite without the brittleness, and cost less. Graphite should only be considered when the utmost stiffness is required.

Polypropylene

Polypropylene cloth is available as a woven fabric or a knit. It's not as strong as fiberglass, being flexible and easily stretched. It should not be considered as a reinforcement, but it has good abrasion resistance. Like Kevlar, it fuzzes up when sanded. Laid up over a layer of fiberglass on the outside of the boat, polypropylene can provide good protection for a boat that will see a lot of abrasion. Unfortunately, polypropylene isn't as clear as fiberglass, but it's still quite translucent. A slight weave pattern may be visible, but it's not very noticeable.

Knitted polypropylene absorbs a lot of resin and may not be clear but you could place small patches where the kayak's hull is likely to be scratched most, such as on the keel at the bow and stern. Once again, just remember that polypropylene cannot be sanded.

Other Fabrics

There are many other fabrics you can use in making kayaks. Nylon, polyester, Dynel, and Spectra are all good for some aspects of kayak building. Feel free to do research and experiments, but in the end you'll probably come to the same conclusion as the rest of us: Woven E-glass is darned good and there's little reason to use anything else.

Fillers

There are some places on the boat where you may need a little putty to fill in a crack or a corner. This putty might serve structural purposes or it might be just cosmetic. Whatever it's for, I use some stuff I call "dookie schmutz." I didn't make up the term, but it sure fits. You can make dookie schmutz by adding various fillers to the resin (either polyester or epoxy) you're using, and the amount of filler depends on how thick a putty you need for the job. Thickness is usually defined in terms of food products such as catsup or peanut butter. Catsup thickness (or runniness) is often used for gluing, while peanut butter thickness is used for fillets and filling gaps.

Colloidal silica. Cab-O-Sil is an ingredient in many varieties of dookie schmutz. Cab-O-Sil is actually the brand name of one of the more commonly available brands of colloidal, or "fumed," silica and is made by the Cabot Corporation. Colloidal silica is a thixotropic powder that is used to control viscosity. "Thixotropic" has a technical definition we won't get into, but for our purposes it means the resin doesn't sag. Putties made with other fillers will tend to slump and flow unless you add some colloidal silica to keep the material where you want it. You can also use common flour from your kitchen as a thixotropic agent in resin as well, and it's definitely cheaper.

Wood flour. If you buy a sander, get one with a dust collector, because it's a good source of filler material for your resin. You can use wood flour and resin to make fillets or fill gaps between strips.

It would be very convenient if you could use the wood dust you collect to make matching dookie schmutz. Unfortunately, when you mix wood dust with resin it will no longer match the color of the wood it came from. It will always be darker, so you may want to add some lighter-colored material before applying it to your boat. The quartz microballons mentioned below make a nice pure white and you can mix them with the wood flour to lighten its color.

The pile under your table saw is also a source of filler. The coarse sawdust will make a rough-textured dookie schmutz, but in some interior applications, this may not be a problem. The price is certainly right.

Microballoons. There are two kinds of microballoon fillers available to mix with your resin. Both consist of microscopically small hollow spheres. You can use them to make a smooth, lightweight dookie schmutz with good compressive strength. Quartz microballoons alone create a bright white putty, while the phenolic variety create a reddish brown. For our purposes, they can be used interchangeably. Dookie schmutz made with phenolic microballoons alone is similar in color to redwood.

Milled glass fiber. Sometimes you need a little liquid glass. A dookie schmutz made with chopped up pieces of glass is a strong putty that can be used where tensile strength is needed. Glass fibers can be bought ready-cut in several lengths. If you use $1/4$-inch fibers, your dookie schmutz will be rough and strong. The $1/32$-inch fibers will give you a smoother but rather weaker filler.

Graphite powder. Mixed to a paint-like consistency, graphite powder and resin can be applied to the bottom of a boat. This black coating provides protection against marring, and when you sand it smooth it provides a slippery surface for boats that want to go fast. The bottom of a kayak covered with epoxy and graphite won't show scratches easily so it won't look much worse after a year of use; but then again, it won't look any better, either. It'll still be an unattractive black.

Varnished fiberglass and wood will show some ugly scratches after a year of use, but since the hull started out looking great, a few scratches won't detract much from its good looks. Still, since the graphite powder does offer extra protection, it may be a good idea to use it on a boat that will be abused or has been abused already.

Sometimes black epoxy is just the right stuff for accenting your trim. Graphite makes a nice rich black. Another source of black coloring is waste toner from a copying machine or laser printer.

All the above fillers can be mixed and matched to make the ideal dookie schmutz for your application. It's handy to have a variety of fillers around that you can mix with your resin at a moment's notice to take care of tasks that arise, and it's fun to experiment with them. A word of warning, though: Most of the fillers are fine dusts that you should avoid breathing. Wear a dust mask when you're using them. Incidentally, there are many other fillers you can substitute for some of those mentioned above. Look around your house for ideas. Even dryer lint has its uses.

Varnish

Both epoxy resin and polyester resin will be degraded by exposure to ultra-violet rays, so you'll need to protect the resin to keep it from becoming cloudy. The best protection is spar varnish, the traditional clear covering for wooden masts and other spars on sailboats. Most hardware stores will stock a decent spar varnish. Look for something for use outdoors with UV protection.

You'll notice that most varnishes will say: "Not to be used below the waterline." Ignore this advice. It's all right to use this kind of varnish everywhere on a kayak. On a boat that's left in the water all season, a varnished hull will have problems, but since a kayak is out of the water much of the time there won't be any problem using it below the waterline.

Most polyurethane varnishes are unsuitable for strip-built boats. Unless they are specifically formulated for outdoor use, they will quickly weather away, leaving the resin unprotected. There are two-part polyurethanes that are specifically designed for boats, and while they're excellent, they're also extremely dangerous to work with and very expensive.

There is a drive in the paint industry to create low-VOC (volatile organic compound) coatings, so as to do away with the dangerous fumes of paints with oil-based solvents. As a result, there are several water-based varnish substitutes now available that can be thinned and cleaned up with water. The low-VOC products I have tried were nice, and didn't have the bad smell of older coatings, but at this stage of their development I don't intend to make a permanent change. I plan to stick with old-fashioned spar varnish. These coatings are constantly being improved, however, and are worth investigating.

The shape of a boat is traditionally recorded with the help of what's called a table of offsets, and lofting is simply the art of converting the table of offsets back to the original shapes. The offsets, which are measurements from an arbitrary baseline, provide the curved outlines from which you can build the boat, but for some people, lofting the boat can be one of the most intimidating hurdles in the building process.

Let me put you at ease straight away. The lofting skills required for a boat the size of a kayak are minimal. When you're lofting, you're drawing full-sized slices of the boat, and obviously that's quite a stunt if it's a big boat. But since a kayak is not that big, the task does not require you to clear out the loft of your workshop.

Another reason for lofting is to discover if there are any errors in the offset tables, and to make sure the curves of the hull are fair, that is, free of unsightly bumps and hollows.

With a small kayak, the chances for errors in the offsets are similarly small because whereas the offset table for a large boat is traditionally derived from a small-scale half-model or drawing, a kayak is small enough to allow everything to be done full-size. This reduces the chances that measurement errors will be introduced. The kayaks featured in this book were designed on a computer that drew up the tables directly, and that suggests an obvious way to convert the tables back into lines.

Most spreadsheet software contains a graphing tool that allows you to type the offsets into a spreadsheet, plot the lines, and then transfer them to a drawing program for output. We'll delve deeper in this later, but first you need to understand what's actually in an offset table.

If you'll look at Figure 4-5 on page 52 for a moment, you'll notice that the offset tables in this book comprise three major sections. The upper two sections contain buttock measurements for the deck and hull, and the lower section contains waterline measurements. There is also a small additional section showing the location of the sheerline. (The sheerline is the curved line you see when you stand side-on to a boat and sight it from bow to stern. It's where the deck meets the hull.) The numbers across the top of the table indicate the locations of forms.

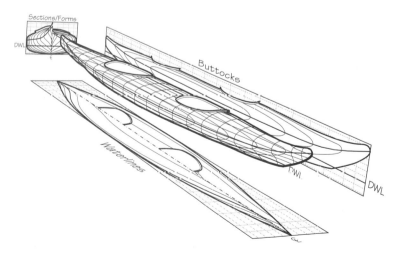

Figure 4-1. *The three-dimensional shape of a boat is defined by three sets of contour or "slice" lines: the waterlines, the buttocks, and the sections. The plan view, looking down on the boat from directly above, shows the waterlines, which resemble elevation contours on a hiking map. The buttock lines, shown here in the profile drawing, are longitudinal slices through the hull at various distances from the centerline. The sections, or forms, are crosswise slices spaced down the length of the boat.*

(The forms are usually called sections, but for our purposes "forms" makes more sense.) So what does all this mean?

Offsets for the Hull Forms

The hull forms are like slices of baloney cut at intervals from the sausage that is the kayak. In the case of the boats in this book, the chosen interval between forms is 1 foot, except at either end where it is 6 inches. The slicing starts from the bow, so the designated "long position" is the distance of the form from the bow of the finished boat. In the table of offsets for the Great Auk (Figure 4-5), for example, the first form is ½ foot (6 inches) from the bow (measured from the outside terminus of the strips, not from the end of the end form). The second form is 1 foot from the bow, the third 2 feet, and so on. The reason I use the word forms rather than sections is because they will be traced on plywood and cut out, becoming the cross-sectional shapes over which you will form the boat.

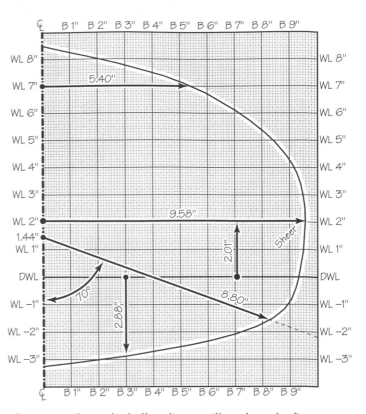

Figure 4-2. This is the hull outline you'll get from the figures provided in column 7 of the table of offsets in Figure 4-9. It's actually half of Form 7 for the Guillemot. Offsets are horizontal distances from the centerline (CL). Heights are vertical distances measured up (or down for negative numbers) from the datum waterline (DWL). The offset table will provide measurements for every place the outline of the form crosses an inch line. When you've finished this half-outline, you make a mirror image to complete the form shape. See text.

The buttocks and waterlines are lengthwise slices through the boat, the buttocks being vertical slices, and the waterlines horizontal slices. For example, a 3-inch buttock line represents a vertical slice drawn 3 inches out from the fore-and-aft centerline (CL) of the boat, and a 7-inch waterline represents a horizontal slice through the boat at a height of 7 inches above the datum waterline, sometimes called the design waterline (DWL). Looking in three dimensions, the zero point is the extreme bow of the boat on the centerline at the DWL.

It's a little confusing, but in the buttock sections of the table the numbers represent heights and depths from the datum waterline, even

though a buttock line is a horizontal offset from the centerline. That is because the first column of the table tells you how far from the centerline the buttock line is, and all the following columns give the height at which the form intersects that buttock line.

Let's take a moment to look at the offset table for the Guillemot, Figure 4-9. In the middle section that deals with hull buttocks, find the 3-inch row, at left, and follow it out toward the right until you come to the form marked 7. There you'll see the number -2.88. Note the minus sign. Now look at Figure 4-2 and find the horizontal datum waterline, marked DWL. Run your eye across to the right until it meets the 3-inch buttock line, marked B 3" and then, from that spot, measure down (down because it's minus) 2.88 inches along the B 3" line and make a dot there. This locates a specific point on the perimeter of your building form.

Now look at the offsets of the waterlines in Figure 4-9, the section below the hull buttocks. Find the 7-inch waterline and run your eye across to the number 7 form. You'll see there the number 5.40. Now go back to Figure 4-2 and note that the centerline of your form is at the left edge. Measure 5.40 inches out from the centerline, along waterline WL 7", and make another dot at that spot.

If you repeat this process for every buttock line and every waterline, you'll end up with a series of dots that outline the form. With the addition of the sheer data, which puts a mark 2.01 inches above the DWL and 9.58 inches over from the centerline, you can connect the dots to produce a drawing of the particular form that's located 7 feet from the bow of the boat. The Guillemot design also includes a diagonal measurement that locates another point on the chine. The diagonal starts 1.44 inches up from the waterline, and is angled 70 degrees up from straight down, as indicated in Figure 4-2. Measuring 8.80 inches along the diagonal line gives you the position of another dot for your outline, and the more dots you have, especially on the sharpest bends, the easier it will be to join them into fair curves.

The best way to do this without a computer is to use graph paper with $1/10$-inch grids. You don't need to draw the whole form right away, only one half, so the sheet need be no bigger than half the boat's width. Near one edge, draw a centerline (CL), and several inches up from the bottom mark the datum waterline (DWL), as I've done in Figure 4-2. If the offset table includes diagonals, mark them in now as well. Incidentally, plan to use one sheet of graph paper for each form's outline. You can, in fact, draw them all on one sheet, but you'll be less confused at first if you keep each form on a separate sheet.

By the way, you'll note that the offset measurements are given to $1/100$ inch, and while you

could try to find a ruler with $1/100$-inch gradations, it isn't really necessary. You can do it by eye accurately enough if you remember that $1/100$ inch is one-tenth of one $1/10$-inch square. If the offset is 1.36 inches, for example, place a mark slightly more than halfway between 1.3 and 1.4.

Proceed to mark all the offsets for the form, and depict the sheerline clearly on the drawing because it will come in handy when you start laying strips.

After you've plotted all your dots, you need to connect them. A naval architect would probably use a French curve or a spline to make sure the connecting lines are smooth. The French curve can be tedious to use, though; a spline or flexible ruler is easier. A spline is anything that bends in a nice smooth manner, such as a wooden batten. You'll also find several different flexible rulers in drafting stores.

But I have to tell you that the effort to draw a precision curve is probably not worth the trouble. You can actually get away with just connecting the points with straight lines because the offsets are pretty close together. You'll soon discover, when you're building the boat, that the wooden strips act as their own splines. Their natural tendency to bend smoothly will compensate for small problems in your draftsmanship. Alternatively, you can reach a happy medium between straight lines and splined lines by free-handing a curve through each point.

As I said above, an obvious way to create the drawings is to use a computer. Typically, a spreadsheet's graphing program can create an "x-y scatter" chart from two columns of data. The first column is generally the "x" or horizontal location, and the second column is the "y" or vertical location. You should arrange the data from the offset table with the locations of the buttocks in the first column and their heights in the second. The offsets of the waterlines will go in the first column, and their locations in the second column. You should type the sheerline in with the offset in the first column and the height in the second. If you're including diagonal data, you'll need to use some trigonometry functions. The first column ("x") will contain the diagonal value times the cosine of the angle, and the second column ("y") will be the diagonal value times the sine of the angle plus the starting height.

Now you have two columns of numbers that may be in a somewhat random order. If you tried to graph this with the spreadsheet, you'd get lines going every which way to points that lie on the desired curve. To bring these into shape, use the spreadsheet sorting function. Sort the two columns on the second column. If all works out right, you'll end up with the first column starting and ending at zero.

Graphing this data will produce a curve that resembles the form. Some spreadsheets even include a curve-smoothing function. Again, smooth lines are not required, but if the software will do it for you, why not use it? Unfortunately, spreadsheets are not designed to create scale drawings. Figure 4-3 shows something similar to Figure 4-2, but it's flattened and needs to be scaled to the right proportions. This may be possible with the spreadsheet, but it will be difficult. A drawing program or a computer-assisted design (CAD) package can do this better.

You need to get the curve produced by the spreadsheet into the drawing program. If the spreadsheet lets you save vector graphic files, give that a try. An easier method may be to "copy" the curve and "paste" it into the drawing program. To maintain the greatest accuracy, make the curve as large as possible before copying. After pasting it into the drawing program, draw a rectangle the size the form is supposed to be. The software may let you enter dimensions directly, or you can use the rulers. In Form 7, for example, the rectangle is 9.58×11.75. Now scale the form to fit the rectangle. Double-check a few of the points to make sure the transfer worked.

Most drawing and CAD packages will let you create a drawing that is bigger than one piece of paper. This drawing can be printed out on several pages and taped together. The software will also probably be able to give you a mirror image of the half-form, so you'll have both sides.

If you end up going to several sheets of paper, put some reference lines on the drawing so that you can get everything lined up right when you tape the pages together.

Of necessity, I'm being a little vague on the directions for computer drawings because there are too many platforms, with too many different software packages, to get very specific. What works on a Macintosh running Excel and MacDraw will not necessarily work on a PC running Windows with Lotus and Corel Draw. But at least the basic concepts I've mentioned should apply. I've described a simple method with basic software that should translate to other unsophisticated software but, of course, you may not need the spreadsheet or the drawing package to get good results. You may well

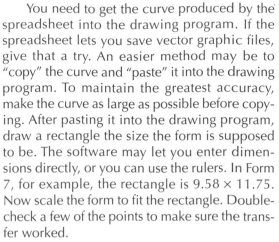

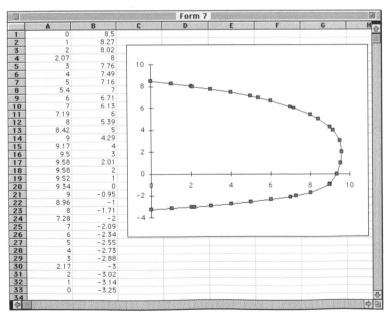

Figure 4-3. *You can also draw the forms with the aid of a computer spreadsheet and graphing program. The resulting graph will need to be scaled to achieve the right proportions. See text for details.*

have something that works better, but whatever you use, take a ruler to it and verify a few dimensions before you commit your results to wood. Computers will do exactly what you tell them; unfortunately, that may not be what you *thought* you were saying.

Offsets for the End Forms

The patterns for the end forms and cockpits are more straightforward. At least there are fewer numbers to deal with at once.

Unlike the cross-sectional forms, the end forms are oriented fore-and-aft, each one defining the shape of one end of the boat (see Figure 4-12). Each end form requires a set of lines defining its outline, and a guideline to limit the taper that we will grind into its outside edge where the wood strips meet along the stem or stern.

The cockpits are defined with just a single line, except in the case of the Guillemot—but we'll come to that later.

Drawing the Patterns

Whether you used a pencil and ruler, or a computer and printer, you will eventually have drawings of all the forms. Remember to include the CL, DWL, diagonal line, and sheerline on the final drawings because they serve as reference lines when you start building. If you have only one side of each form so far, flip this half-pattern over and copy it onto larger paper, so you'll have a mirror image and can then place the halves together to make the drawing of the whole form. Brown packing paper is a good source of large paper.

In Chapter 5 we're going to glue the drawings to plywood and slice them to pieces, so if you want to make a copy of your work, now's the time to do it. And while you're drawing the patterns you should also locate on them the cutouts for the strongback. When you set up the forms to build the boat, you'll need a beam on which to mount them in their proper positions

and attitudes. For this purpose we'll use a strongback (see Chapter 5), which, for our little boats, can be a simple 2 × 4.

The strongback will extend into the end forms, and I typically locate the bottom of the strongback hole at, or just above, the waterline (DWL). There's nothing magic about this location, but it usually lets the strongback run through most of the forms. The hole for the strongback measures 2 inches by 4 inches, even though a 2 × 4 these days measures 1½ inches by 3½ inches. The extra size will permit you to move the forms around to compensate for the inevitable irregularities of the 2 × 4.

Some of the forms near the end will not be big enough to accept the whole 2-inch by 4-inch hole but if there is room for some of its height, the strongback may be tapered by trimming off the bottom. Draw the rectangle of the strongback hole at the same location, relative to the DWL, on each drawing when you draw on the reference lines. As long as the rectangle is completely contained within the outline of the form, you can use the full-sized strongback. If the rectangle is only partially contained or it comes very close to the edge of the form, you'll

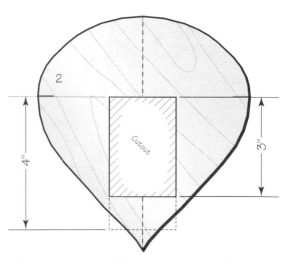

Figure 4-4. *Some of the cross-sectional forms near the end may not be big enough to accept the whole strongback. For example, Form 2 of the Guillemot, shown here, will need a smaller hole. You'll then have to taper the end of the strongback to fit the hole.*

want to taper the strongback in this area. And if the rectangle falls completely outside a form, you'll need to cut the strongback short before it gets that far. Try to locate the rectangle so as to reach the greatest number of forms.

The forms that the strongback cannot reach will be held in place by the end forms, and the strongback should extend almost 1 foot into each end form. Draw the strongback cutouts in the end forms as shown in Figures 4-8, 4-12, and 4-16.

Still confused? Get some graph paper and try it for yourself. You'll find it's easier to do than it is to read about it. But if you're really in trouble, full-sized drawings of all the forms and patterns are available from the author. See Appendix 3 for sources of plans for these boats and others.

Making Small Changes

Each of the boats included in this book has slightly different details that require a little explanation. You may want to take ideas from one boat and incorporate them in another. For example, you may like to adopt the Guillemot's cockpit recess on your Great Auk. Well, feel free to take the idea and modify it to your needs.

Great Auk Offsets

Deck Buttocks (Heights)

Long Position (ft)	1/2	1	2	3	4	5	6	7	8	9	10	11	12	13	14	15	16	16 1/2
11 in								4.73	4.93	4.55	4.12							
10 in							4.92	5.28	5.32	4.78	4.32	4.01						
9 in						4.90	5.38	-	-	-	-	-	4.17	3.89				
8 in					4.45	5.40	-	-	-	-	-	-	4.06	3.73				
7 in					5.39	-	-	-	-	-	-	-	-	3.98				
6 in			5.41	-	-	-	-	-	-	-	-	-	-	4.10	3.91			
5 in			5.89	-	-	-	-	-	-	-	-	-	-	-				
4 in			6.16	-	-	-	-	-	-	-	-	-	-	-	-	4.07		
3 in		-	-	-	-	-	-	-	-	-	-	-	-	-	-	-		
2 in		-	-	-	-	-	-	-	-	-	-	-	-	-	-	-	-	
1 in		-	-	-	-	-	-	-	-	-	-	-	-	-	-	-	-	-
Deck Peak	8.04	7.86	7.84	8.07	8.44	8.84	9.24	9.60	9.53	7.37	5.68	5.33	5.07	4.84	4.64	4.51	4.46	4.47

Hull Buttocks (Heights)

Long Position (ft)	1/2	1	2	3	4	5	6	7	8	9	10	11	12	13	14	15	16	16 1/2
Keel	-0.04	-0.80	-1.37	-1.89	-2.34	-2.70	-2.97	-3.16	-3.25	-3.23	-3.14	-2.98	-2.76	-2.49	-2.14	-1.70	-1.17	-0.77
1 in		1.96	-0.97	-1.66	-2.18	-2.58	-2.88	-3.09	-3.19	-3.16	-3.05	-2.87	-2.62	-2.29	-1.85	-1.29	-0.02	
2 in		6.83	0.28	-1.32	-1.98	-2.44	-2.78	-3.01	-3.11	-3.08	-2.96	-2.76	-2.47	-2.08	-1.55	-0.75	3.04	
3 in			2.54	-0.61	-1.73	-2.29	-2.67	-2.92	-3.03	-3.00	-2.86	-2.64	-2.31	-1.86	-1.20	0.30		
4 in			5.27	0.51	-1.31	-2.10	-2.41	-2.81	-2.94	-2.90	-2.75	-2.51	-2.15	-1.61	-0.68	2.16		
5 in				2.21	-0.64	-1.83	-2.38	-2.69	-2.83	-2.79	-2.63	-2.36	-1.96	-1.29	0.19			
6 in				4.38	0.40	-1.37	-2.16	-2.54	-2.70	-2.66	-2.49	-2.19	-1.70	-0.77	1.85			
7 in						2.06	-0.69	-1.79	-2.33	-2.53	-2.50	-2.30	-1.94	-1.30	0.18			
8 in						4.40	0.54	-1.24	-1.96	-2.27	-2.25	-2.00	-1.55	-0.60	2.42			
9 in							2.96	-0.25	-1.43	-1.86	-1.85	-1.56	-0.89	0.87				
10 in							1.81	-0.46	-1.22	-1.24	-0.75	0.50						
11 in								1.71	0.06	0.00	1.02							

Waterline (Offsets)

Long Position (ft)	1/2	1	2	3	4	5	6	7	8	9	10	11	12	13	14	15	16	16 1/2
9 in							-	-	-									
8 in		-					-	-	-									
7 in	0.76	2.07	-	-	-	-	-	-	-									
6 in	0.63	1.74	4.23	-	-	-	-	-	-									
5 in	0.53	1.54	3.87	6.37	7.70	8.87	9.88	-	-	-								
4 in	0.43	1.37	3.50	5.79	7.81	9.34	10.46	11.29	11.80	11.76	11.17	10.05	8.42	6.81	5.47	4.38	2.13	0.94
3 in	0.33	1.19	3.16	5.36	7.38	9.01	10.30	11.26	11.81	11.80	11.36	10.61	9.52	8.11	6.34	4.26	1.99	0.84
2 in	0.24	1.01	2.80	4.89	6.97	8.69	10.05	11.07	11.66	11.68	11.25	10.48	9.37	7.90	6.06	3.94	1.74	0.68
1 in	0.11	0.78	2.39	4.33	6.42	8.26	9.71	10.78	11.40	11.43	10.99	10.21	9.06	7.50	5.58	3.46	1.42	0.50
DWL		0.47	1.82	3.60	5.67	7.62	9.18	10.32	10.97	11.00	10.54	9.73	8.51	6.85	4.83	2.77	1.01	0.28
-1 in			0.95	2.55	4.51	6.61	8.32	9.53	10.22	10.25	9.76	8.88	7.52	5.62	3.46	1.60	0.26	
-2 in				1.91	4.43	6.50	7.91	8.69	8.66	8.01	6.82	4.78	2.36	0.50				
-3 in							2.10	3.35	2.99	1.58								

Long Position (ft)	1/2	1	2	3	4	5	6	7	8	9	10	11	12	13	14	15	16	16 1/2
Sheer Offset	0.94	2.11	4.34	6.33	8.00	9.37	10.48	11.32	11.84	11.81	11.35	10.59	9.51	8.12	6.39	4.38	2.12	0.94
Height	7.74	7.06	5.83	4.93	4.41	4.08	3.84	3.69	3.60	3.55	3.57	3.57	3.57	3.65	3.78	3.96	4.24	4.35

Figure 4-5. The Great Auk is easier to draw than the other boats because the deck has a lot of straight lines. You can draw a line straight between the sheer and the deck peak, or, if you want to round off the transition between the deck and the hull, you can follow the deck offsets and then draw a straight line to the deck peak. The difference is shown in Figure 2-17, Chapter 2.

Great Auk

The Great Auk has the simplest lines of the three boats, and part of that simplicity lies in the design of the V-shaped deck. To reduce some of its angularity, the transition from deck to hull is curved. In the center section, the deck smoothly curves away from the hull before straightening out to continue on to the peak at the center. You'll see that the offset table has gaps in it where the deck is straight; it's unnecessary to include all these points because they lie on a straight line.

The curved section makes the deck harder to build, so if you want to keep the boat as simple and easy to build as possible, you can just draw a straight line from the sheer up to the peak of the deck. This would change the look of the boat slightly and make the deck marginally lower at the sides, but the difference is small and the straighter version would be easier to build. This is a good modification if you want to use the sheerclamp method of attaching the deck that is described later.

Great Auk Cockpit

Long Position	Cockpit
0 "	0 "
2 "	7.65 "
4 "	8.70 "
6 "	9.11 "
8 "	9.30 "
10 "	9.34 "
12 "	9.30 "
14 "	9.20 "
16 "	9.03 "
18 "	8.78 "
20 "	8.45 "
22 "	8.04 "
24 "	7.52 "
26 "	6.88 "
28 "	6.10 "
30 "	5.03 "
32 "	3.36 "
33.5 "	0 "

Figure 4-6. In the Great Auk's cockpit offsets, the long position starts with 0 inches at the back of the cockpit and the offsets are measured from the centerline to the edge of one side. Use a flexible piece of wood or metal to draw a smooth curve through the points. Draw one side and flip over the pattern to make the other side. See Figure 2-17, Chapter 2, for the location of the cockpit.

Great Auk End Form Offsets

Length	Stern			Bow		
	Bottom	Top	Taper	Bottom	Top	Taper
0 "	-1.72	4.52		-1.38	7.87	
1 "	-1.68	-		-1.33	-	
2 "	-1.64	-		-1.28	-	
3 "	-1.59	4.51		-1.24	7.85	
4 "	-1.55	-		-1.19	-	
5 "	-1.50	-		-1.14	-	
6 "	-1.46	4.49		-1.09	7.84	
7 "	-1.42	-		-1.05	-	
8 "	-1.37	-		-1.00	-	
9 "	-1.33	4.47		-0.95	7.86	
10 "	-1.28	-	-1.26	-0.91	-	-0.84
11 "	-1.24	-	-1.19	-0.86	-	-0.73
12 "	-1.19	4.47	-1.13	-0.81	7.89	-0.62
13 "	-1.15	-	-1.05	-0.76	-	-0.44
14 "	-1.10	-	-0.97	-0.72	-	-0.20
15 "	-1.06	4.48	-0.86	-0.62	7.97	0.12
16 "	-1.02	-	-0.74	-0.48	-	0.55
17 "	-0.95	-	-0.54	-0.23	-	1.10
18 "	-0.85	4.49	-0.20	0.20	8.06	2.04
19 "	-0.68	-	0.33	0.81	-	3.52
20 "	-0.41	-	1.19	1.94	-	5.42
21 "	0.28	4.50	2.77	4.03	8.22	7.49
22 "	1.76	4.51		6.61	8.27	
22.73 "	4.51	4.51				
22.69 "				8.31	8.31	

Figure 4-7. With the numbers in this table you should be able to recreate the drawing in Figure 4-8. All measurements are relative to the DWL, and negative numbers are measured below the waterline. The "Bottom" column contains the numbers coming up from the keel, and the "Top" column contains the numbers for the deck. As the deck has very little curve, you could draw the forms with a straight line for the top and later plane away a little in the middle to give it a slight curve. The "Taper" measurements serve as a guideline for grinding the ends.

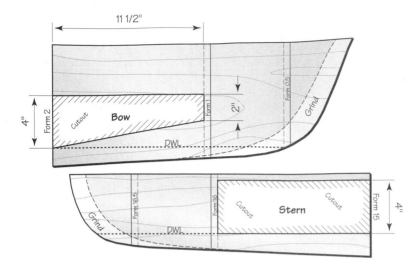

Figure 4-8. End forms for the Great Auk. The table in Figure 4-7 does not contain numbers for the taper guideline going all the way to the top, so just approximate the line to roughly match the bevel line shown in this drawing. The top of the end form also should be beveled slightly to accommodate the V of the deck. The cutouts indicate where the strongback enters the forms. Cut the bow end of the strongback to match the bow form.

Guillemot Offsets

Long Position (ft)	1/2	1	2	3	4	5	6	7	8	9	10	11	12	13	14	15	16	16 1/2
Deck (Heights) 10 in									2.80	3.40	3.01							
9 in								4.29	4.81	4.73	4.27	3.64	2.31					
8 in							4.75	5.39	5.73	5.22	4.46	4.28	3.62					
7 in						4.85	5.62	6.13	6.52			4.61	4.16	3.50				
Buttocks 6 in					4.65	5.61	6.19	6.71	7.22			4.84	4.49	4.01	3.01			
5 in				3.79	5.46	6.10	6.61	7.16				5.04	4.70	4.34	3.77			
Deck 4 in				5.23	5.93	6.42	6.91	7.49				5.23	4.87	4.55	4.13	3.29		
3 in			4.88	5.79	6.22	6.64	7.15	7.76				5.38	5.02	4.69	4.37	3.98		
(Heights) 2 in			5.86	6.11	6.39	6.81	7.37	8.02				5.51	5.14	4.81	4.52	4.31	4.13	
1 in		7.27	6.31	6.28	6.52	6.98	7.58	8.27				5.61	5.24	4.92	4.64	4.52	4.97	
Deck Peak	8.95	7.68	6.44	6.35	6.62	7.14	7.80	8.50				5.71	5.33	5.00	4.73	4.62	5.25	5.99
Keel	5.85	2.78	-0.41	-1.74	-2.42	-2.84	-3.08	-3.25	-3.37	-3.42	-3.39	-3.27	-3.11	-2.91	-2.48	-1.62	0.83	3.32
1 in		4.77	0.51	-1.08	-1.98	-2.56	-2.91	-3.14	-3.29	-3.34	-3.31	-3.18	-2.97	-2.64	-2.04	-0.85	2.11	
2 in			1.55	-0.49	-1.58	-2.29	-2.73	-3.02	-3.19	-3.25	-3.21	-3.07	-2.81	-2.41	-1.69	-0.31	3.65	
3 in			2.91	0.15	-1.16	-2.00	-2.54	-2.88	-3.08	-3.14	-3.11	-2.94	-2.65	-2.18	-1.37	0.26		
Buttocks 4 in				0.88	-0.71	-1.69	-2.32	-2.73	-2.95	-3.03	-2.99	-2.81	-2.49	-1.96	-1.05	1.66		
5 in				2.56	-0.18	-1.34	-2.08	-2.55	-2.81	-2.91	-2.87	-2.67	-2.32	-1.73	-0.65			
Hull 6 in					0.61	-0.92	-1.80	-2.34	-2.65	-2.77	-2.73	-2.52	-2.15	-1.49	0.85			
7 in						-0.29	-1.43	-2.09	-2.47	-2.62	-2.58	-2.36	-1.96	-1.09				
(Heights) 8 in							-0.82	-1.71	-2.21	-2.44	-2.42	-2.18	-1.70					
9 in								-0.95	-1.77	-2.13	-2.15	-1.83	1.05					
10 in									0.72	-0.78	-0.37							
Long Position (ft)	1/2	1	2	3	4	5	6	7	8	9	10	11	12	13	14	15	16	16 1/2
8 in	0.57							2.07										
7 in	0.37	1.26				0.85	3.65	5.40	6.33									
6 in	0.05	1.39	1.77	2.41	3.80	5.25	6.38	7.19	7.68									
5 in		1.10	2.92	4.26	5.66	6.84	7.75	8.42	8.82	8.65		5.21	3.13	0.06		0.93	0.90	
Water 4 in		0.63	3.22	4.94	6.40	7.61	8.52	9.17	9.59	9.70	9.38	8.52	7.34	6.02	4.42	2.96	2.05	0.44
Lines 3 in		0.17	3.04	5.06	6.63	7.87	8.81	9.50	9.96	10.13	10.00	9.50	8.68	7.55	6.00	4.18	1.70	
2 in			2.40	4.84	6.56	7.88	8.86	9.58	10.07	10.29	10.22	9.81	9.07	7.94	6.30	4.13	0.89	
1 in			1.49	4.13	6.24	7.70	8.76	9.52	10.03	10.25	10.18	9.76	8.99	7.80	6.05	3.66	0.08	
(Offsets) DWL			0.48	2.77	5.29	7.27	8.50	9.34	9.89	10.14	10.06	9.62	8.82	7.54	5.64	2.59		
-1 in				1.13	3.37	5.83	7.77	8.96	9.66	9.95	9.88	9.41	8.58	7.10	4.16	0.76		
-2 in					0.96	2.99	5.29	7.28	8.57	9.27	9.31	8.66	6.81	3.80	1.10			
-3 in							0.49	2.17	3.63	4.26	3.93	2.55	0.79					
Diagonal (1.44", 70°)			1.51	3.39	5.10	6.60	7.85	8.80	9.51	9.93	9.97	9.57	8.79	7.43	5.60	3.28	0.32	
Long Position (ft)	1/2	1	2	3	4	5	6	7	8	9	10	11	12	13	14	15	16	16 1/2
Sheer Offset	0.58	1.43	3.23	5.06	6.64	7.90	8.86	9.58	10.07	10.29	10.22	9.81	9.08	7.96	6.34	4.31	2.06	0.91
Height	8.13	6.43	4.03	3.20	2.75	2.41	2.17	2.01	1.89	1.83	1.83	1.86	1.92	2.04	2.24	2.67	3.92	5.08
Cockpit Recess Offset									5.31	8.32	8.45							
Height									7.62	5.22	4.46							

Figure 4-9. The Guillemot, because of its complicated shape, is the most demanding boat in this book to draw. Column 7 is highlighted with double lines to help you when referring back to Figure 4-2 to see where all the numbers come from. This table includes a row of "diagonal" measurements that help you draw the tight curve of the chine. The bottom two rows define the edge of the cockpit recess. Draw the deck around to this point and then horizontally across to the centerline.

Guillemot

The Guillemot has a small area around the cockpit where the deck flattens out. (See Figure 6-51, Chapter 6.) This recess in the deck is horizontal across the boat and serves two purposes: it permits the cockpit coaming to be lower, and it provides some contour underneath for your knees to grab. A lower coaming is good for performing Eskimo rolls and lets you hold the paddle a little lower, which is more comfortable. Your knees need to be able to grab the boat when you roll and for other paddling techniques. The cockpit cutout also reduces the amount of upward bending needed to install the lip of the coaming and that makes it easier to install. For this reason, you may want to create a similar cockpit cutout on the other two designs.

In order to make this cockpit cutout section, you will be laying strips horizontally across the boat. You don't want any of the forms in the way of the horizontal strips, so you'll want to end the forms below cockpit level. But it helps to keep the strips fair if you have some forms above the cockpit, and for this reason the offset table includes information for the forms above the cockpit, but it also includes a cockpit height.

Guillemot Cockpit Offsets

Long Position	Offset	
	Recess	Cockpit
-19.31 "	0.00 "	
-18 "	4.46 "	
-16.50 "		0.00 "
-16 "	7.29 "	3.61 "
-14 "	8.17 "	6.50 "
-12 "	8.49 "	7.68 "
-10 "	8.66 "	8.20 "
-8 "	8.75 "	8.39 "
-6 "	8.77 "	8.40 "
-4 "	8.72 "	8.27 "
-2 "	8.59 "	8.04 "
0 "	8.39 "	7.73 "
2 "	8.11 "	7.34 "
4 "	7.76 "	6.84 "
6 "	7.34 "	6.18 "
8 "	6.83 "	5.28 "
10 "	6.21 "	4.07 "
12 "	5.36 "	1.87 "
12.97 "		0.00 "
14 "	3.97 "	
16 "	1.82 "	
17.43 "	0.00 "	

Figure 4-10. *Because the Guillemot has a recessed cockpit, this table includes a column of figures giving the shape of the recess as well as that of the cockpit. The zero point for these offsets corresponds to Form 9. Place a mark on your drawings so you can align this point with the form when you draw the outline on your deck.*

Guillemot End Forms Offsets

	Stern			Bow		
Length	Bottom	Top	Taper	Bottom	Top	Taper
0 "	-1.78	4.63	-1.43	-0.68	6.45	-0.42
1 "	-1.66	4.65	-1.27	-0.54	6.49	-0.21
2 "	-1.55	4.66	-1.07	-0.38	6.54	0.03
3 "	-1.41	4.67	-0.86	-0.21	6.59	0.30
4 "	-1.26	4.71	-0.63	-0.01	6.66	0.58
5 "	-1.08	4.76	-0.40	0.20	6.74	0.87
6 "	-0.89	4.80	-0.16	0.44	6.83	1.17
7 "	-0.68	4.84	0.10	0.71	6.94	1.48
8 "	-0.42	4.92	0.37	1.03	7.05	1.80
9 "	-0.15	5.00	0.65	1.35	7.19	2.13
10 "	0.15	5.08	0.96	1.72	7.33	2.47
11 "	0.46	5.16	1.29	2.11	7.51	2.84
12 "	0.78	5.26	1.66	2.54	7.69	3.24
13 "	1.14	5.38	2.04	3.00	7.88	3.67
14 "	1.51	5.49	2.45	3.50	8.08	4.15
15 "	1.89	5.61	2.86	4.03	8.29	4.66
16 "	2.32	5.73	3.28	4.58	8.50	5.21
17 "	2.76	5.87	3.72	5.17	8.73	5.81
18 "	3.22	6.00	4.16	5.79	8.95	6.45
19 "	3.71	6.14	4.62	6.45	9.18	7.16
20 "	4.20	6.28	5.08	7.18	9.40	7.91
21 "	4.75	6.42	5.60	8.03	9.63	8.77
22 "	5.36	6.53		9.03	9.63	
22.71 "	6.21					
22.18 "				9.43		

Figure 4-11. *This table contains the information needed to create the Guillemot bow and stern forms shown in Figure 4-12.*

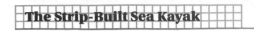
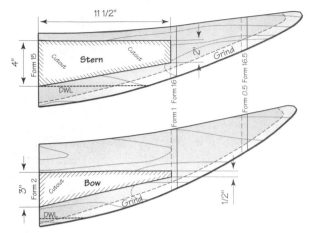

Figure 4-12. *The Guillemot's end forms. You'll need to taper the ends of the strongback to match the cutouts in the end forms.*

Figure 4-13. *The Guillemot Double is big and therefore has a lot of numbers in the offset table. The waterline numbers printed in boldface are below the sheerline.*

Guillemot Double Offsets

Long Position (ft)		1/2	1	2	3	4	5	6	7	8	9	10	11	12	13	14	15	16	17	18	19	19 1/2
	13 in										4.64	4.87	4.88	4.75	4.31							
	12 in							4.67	5.38	5.54	5.58	5.54	5.42	5.17	4.67							
	11 in						4.69	5.81	6.03	6.11	6.10	6.05	5.93	5.69	5.31	4.49						
	10 in						5.99	6.43	6.54	6.58	6.54	6.47	6.36	6.13	5.77	5.20						
	9 in					5.79	6.72	6.96	6.99	6.96	6.90	6.83	6.72	6.50	6.17	5.68	4.78					
	8 in				4.70	6.66	7.38	7.44	7.37	7.28	7.19	7.13	7.02	6.83	6.52	6.08	5.39					
Deck	7 in				6.32	7.39	7.96	7.88	7.70	7.54	7.44	7.38	7.29	7.10	6.83	6.43	5.85	4.76				
Buttocks	6 in			5.63	7.16	8.00	8.45	8.28	7.98	7.76	7.65	7.59	7.51	7.35	7.09	6.74	6.25	5.49				
	5 in			6.93	7.83	8.49	8.87	8.64	8.21	7.94	7.83	7.77	7.69	7.55	7.33	7.03	6.60	5.99	4.58			
(Heights)	4 in		6.90	7.73	8.35	8.86	9.20	8.92	8.38	8.08	7.96	7.90	7.83	7.72	7.54	7.28	6.90	6.40	5.74			
	3 in			8.03	8.33	8.72	9.15	9.46	9.13	8.50	8.18	8.07	8.01	7.94	7.84	7.71	7.49	7.13	6.71	6.24		
	2 in		8.77	8.72	8.76	9.00	9.36	9.65	9.27	8.58	8.25	8.14	8.08	8.02	7.93	7.83	7.62	7.28	6.89	6.55	6.45	
	1 in		9.96	9.17	9.05	9.20	9.52	9.77	9.35	8.62	8.29	8.18	8.12	8.06	7.99	7.89	7.68	7.33	6.96	6.69	6.79	6.86
	0 in	11.40	10.33	9.40	9.19	9.32	9.64	9.83	9.37	8.63	8.30	8.20	8.14	8.08	8.00	7.91	7.76	7.40	6.97	6.70	6.90	7.44
	0 in	6.53	3.70	-0.36	-2.30	-3.38	-3.87	-4.05	-4.11	-4.14	-4.16	-4.16	-4.15	-4.13	-4.09	-4.02	-3.90	-3.58	-2.73	-1.37	0.98	2.34
	1 in		5.51	1.49	-1.18	-2.72	-3.50	-3.86	-4.00	-4.06	-4.09	-4.10	-4.09	-4.07	-4.00	-3.88	-3.67	-3.17	-2.00	-0.10	2.92	5.87
	2 in		7.04	2.55	-0.32	-2.12	-3.14	-3.64	-3.86	-3.95	-4.01	-4.03	-4.03	-4.00	-3.91	-3.74	-3.44	-2.80	-1.41	0.88	4.51	
	3 in			3.43	0.49	-1.51	-2.74	-3.39	-3.69	-3.83	-3.92	-3.95	-3.96	-3.92	-3.81	-3.60	-3.22	-2.46	-0.87	1.76		
	4 in			4.38	1.27	-0.86	-2.31	-3.10	-3.49	-3.69	-3.81	-3.86	-3.87	-3.83	-3.70	-3.45	-3.00	-2.12	-0.30	2.63		
	5 in			2.06	-0.19	-1.81	-2.77	-3.26	-3.53	-3.68	-3.76	-3.77	-3.73	-3.59	-3.30	-2.78	-1.77	0.34	3.92			
Hull	6 in			3.16	0.51	-1.26	-2.38	-3.00	-3.34	-3.54	-3.63	-3.66	-3.61	-3.45	-3.14	-2.56	-1.34	1.08				
Buttocks	7 in				1.27	-0.68	-1.95	-2.70	-3.12	-3.37	-3.49	-3.52	-3.48	-3.31	-2.96	-2.29	-0.80	2.06				
	8 in				2.71	-0.03	-1.47	-2.34	-2.86	-3.17	-3.32	-3.37	-3.32	-3.14	-2.77	-1.94	-0.07					
(Heights)	9 in					0.85	-0.89	-1.93	-2.56	-2.93	-3.12	-3.19	-3.14	-2.94	-2.50	-1.44	1.05					
	10 in						-0.11	-1.41	-2.17	-2.62	-2.88	-2.97	-2.91	-2.68	-2.11	-0.63						
	11 in						1.62	-0.65	-1.63	-2.21	-2.54	-2.67	-2.60	-2.29	-1.48	1.02						
	12 in							1.27	-0.71	-1.56	-2.03	-2.21	-2.11	-1.63	0.08							
	13 in									0.21	-0.99	-1.36	-1.14	0.55								

Long Position (ft)		1/2	1	2	3	4	5	6	7	8	9	10	11	12	13	14	15	16	17	18	19	19 1/2
	11 in	0.60																				
	10 in	0.89	0.91																			
	9 in	0.95	1.94	1.44	1.23	1.98	3.55	4.63	3.66													
	8 in	0.69	2.11	3.04	3.59	4.71	6.00	6.92	6.70	5.92	4.58	3.68	3.08	2.25	0.35							
	7 in	0.25	1.98	3.95	4.92	6.20	7.55	8.59	8.92	8.96	8.67	8.44	8.08	7.39	6.36	5.10	3.61					0.94
	6 in		1.35	4.24	5.83	7.32	8.78	9.99	10.71	11.05	11.21	11.21	11.10	10.84	10.31	9.45	8.20	6.64	4.98	3.54	2.34	1.03
	5 in		0.68	4.26	6.17	7.91	9.53	10.89	11.86	12.41	12.71	12.85	12.85	12.68	12.27	11.55	10.36	8.69	6.74	4.80	2.26	0.74
Waterlines	4 in		0.18	3.68	6.24	8.14	9.82	11.16	12.16	12.82	13.24	13.49	13.59	13.50	13.15	12.46	11.30	9.62	7.50	5.03	1.67	0.41
	3 in			2.50	5.91	8.08	9.87	11.23	12.23	12.92	13.38	13.67	13.79	13.70	13.32	12.62	11.50	9.86	7.56	4.38	1.04	0.15
(Offsets)	2 in			1.44	4.93	7.66	9.65	11.10	12.15	12.85	13.34	13.64	13.75	13.65	13.25	12.52	11.34	9.56	6.95	3.28	0.54	
	1 in			0.64	3.65	6.66	9.12	10.76	11.92	12.69	13.19	13.51	13.64	13.52	13.10	12.30	10.99	8.96	5.90	2.14	0.11	
	DWL			0.12	2.39	5.27	8.04	10.10	11.48	12.36	12.94	13.31	13.47	13.34	12.86	11.97	10.46	8.07	4.48	1.10		
	-1 in				1.19	3.80	6.46	8.83	10.60	11.77	12.51	12.99	13.21	13.07	12.51	11.46	9.61	6.66	2.75	0.22		
	-2 in				0.25	2.20	4.63	6.88	8.85	10.36	11.38	12.04	12.34	12.17	11.51	10.22	7.84	4.36	1.00			
	-3 in					0.56	2.35	4.33	6.01	7.49	8.72	9.53	9.88	9.65	8.74	6.80	4.01	1.45				
	-4 in							0.27	0.98	1.58	2.13	2.43	2.44	2.00	1.01	0.17						

Long Position (ft)		1/2	1	2	3	4	5	6	7	8	9	10	11	12	13	14	15	16	17	18	19	19 1/2
Sheer	Offset	0.96	2.12	4.29	6.25	8.17	9.90	11.24	12.23	12.92	13.38	13.68	13.80	13.71	13.32	12.62	11.50	9.88	7.67	5.07	2.40	1.07
	Height	9.22	7.69	5.29	4.14	3.68	3.43	3.26	3.13	3.03	2.95	2.89	2.88	2.89	2.93	2.99	3.05	3.14	3.40	4.21	5.61	6.42

Thus, when you first make the forms, cut them whole, including the part above the cockpit. Then cut horizontally across at the cockpit height and tack-glue the top back on temporarily. You'll be able to break off the top of the form to strip across the cockpit unimpeded when you need to.

Guillemot Double

The double has two cockpits, but as they're the same shape I've included only one set of offsets.

By the way, note the position of the Guillemot Double's strongback. In order to make it as long as possible, I don't place it on the waterline, as before. In this design, the 2 × 4 can reach further if it's 2 inches higher.

Guillemot Double Cockpit

Long Position	Cockpit
0 "	0.00 "
2 "	8.07 "
4 "	9.22 "
6 "	9.62 "
8 "	9.84 "
10 "	9.93 "
12 "	9.92 "
14 "	9.78 "
16 "	9.53 "
18 "	9.19 "
20 "	8.77 "
22 "	8.26 "
24 "	7.68 "
26 "	7.00 "
28 "	6.19 "
30 "	5.22 "
32 "	3.05 "
32.95 "	0.00 "

Figure 4-14. These offsets for the Guillemot Double cockpit may be scrapped, and those of the Guillemot substituted, if you want a smaller cockpit. All the designs in this book have slightly different cockpits, but they are somewhat interchangeable.

Guillemot Double End Forms Offsets

Length	Bow Bottom	Bow Top	Bow Taper	Stern Bottom	Stern Top	Stern Taper
0 "	-2.38	7.37	-1.76	-3.42	4.70	-3.04
1 "	-2.13	7.42	-1.50	-3.27	4.69	-2.88
2 "	-1.89	7.47	-1.23	-3.12	4.68	-2.72
3 "	-1.61	7.52	-0.95	-2.96	4.68	-2.55
4 "	-1.32	7.57	-0.67	-2.80	4.68	-2.37
5 "	-1.04	7.63	-0.35	-2.63	4.67	-2.19
6 "	-0.72	7.70	-0.03	-2.46	4.69	-2.01
7 "	-0.38	7.78	0.28	-2.29	4.70	-1.82
8 "	-0.05	7.86	0.62	-2.11	4.72	-1.61
9 "	0.30	7.95	0.98	-1.92	4.75	-1.41
10 "	0.68	8.04	1.34	-1.73	4.79	-1.20
11 "	1.07	8.15	1.71	-1.53	4.83	-0.98
12 "	1.45	8.26	2.12	-1.32	4.89	-0.74
13 "	1.88	8.39	2.52	-1.11	4.94	-0.47
14 "	2.31	8.54	2.96	-0.87	5.02	-0.18
15 "	2.78	8.70	3.42	-0.63	5.10	0.16
16 "	3.26	8.89	3.90	-0.38	5.19	0.51
17 "	3.78	9.09	4.41	-0.09	5.29	0.92
18 "	4.32	9.34	4.95	0.25	5.42	1.39
19 "	4.90	9.60	5.54	0.72	5.55	1.94
20 "	5.52	9.88	6.20	1.29	5.67	2.61
21 "	6.21	9.89	7.08	2.01	5.74	3.54
22 "	7.07	9.58		3.09	5.83	
21.58 "			8.18			
21.62 "						4.78
22.70 "				5.05	5.05	
22.79 "	8.51	8.51				

Figure 4-15. This offset table for the end forms of the Guillemot Double does not include the backward-curving taper at the tops. That's because you don't need precision here—just do your best to approximate the broken line in Figure 4-16.

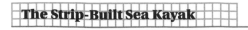

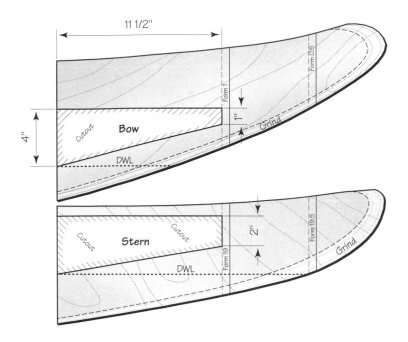

Figure 4-16. *End forms for the Guillemot Double. Note that the strongback will need to be tapered to match the cutouts in the end forms.*

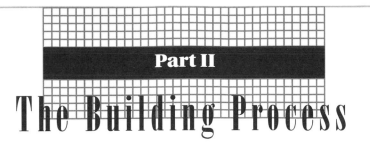

Part II

The Building Process

Setting up your shop correctly to begin with saves time and frustration in the end. When it's easy to put your tools down in places where you'll quickly find them when you need them, you won't waste time looking for them. When your materials are organized and close at hand, you'll choose the best piece for the job instead of the most convenient piece.

Where to Build

You don't need a large space in which to build a kayak. A garage, barn, breezeway, basement, or living room will all work. It should be a minimum of about 6 feet wide, and it should be a minimum of about 4 feet longer than the boat. That gives you just enough space to get all the way around the boat.

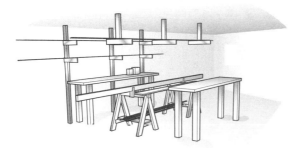

Figure 5-1. *My ideal kayak-building shop has tables providing work surfaces on either side of the sawhorses that hold the strongback. A rack along one wall holds strips and uncut wood. Some T-shaped racks hanging from the ceiling store strips close by for easy access. More strips can be stored on the sawhorses under the strongback. A plank laid across the sawhorses provides a convenient spot to put down tools. And there are some windows to provide natural light.*

Shelter

Unless you can guarantee that it won't rain for the duration of the project, you need to keep the boat under shelter. You can work outside, but you'll need shade from the sun to avoid problems with the epoxy. Until you start working with the resin, extremes in temperatures are not too much of a problem, but once you reach the epoxy stage, you run into snags. If the weather's too hot, your epoxy will cure too fast. If it's too cold, it'll seem like the stuff will never harden. Despite your doubts, the epoxy will eventually cure, even in cold weather, but it may not be as strong. Cold-weather epoxy is available, however, and specially formulated to work at lower temperatures.

Wide variations in temperature and humidity can cause problems with the unprotected wooden strips, too. Before you coat them inside and out with fiberglass, the strips will expand and contract with the weather, and these changes could cause the boat to warp. For this reason, it's important to keep the boat on the forms as much as possible until it's fully encapsulated.

As a matter of fact, both the resin and the wood will be happier with low humidity. Given a choice, most of the materials work better when it is cool and dry than when it is hot and humid. This is convenient for me, because I do, too.

Builders in northern climates looking for a winter project should have a heatable space. Conversely, if you'll be epoxying when it is 90°F outside, you may want to consider installing an air conditioner, or at least working at night when it's a little cooler. The ideal temperature is around 70°F.

Ventilation

Remember that you're going to make a mess, and that some of the materials you're using are hazardous. A basement usually is well climate-controlled, but the family may not appreciate the dust and resin smells in the rest of the house. I made my first strip-built boat in my parents' basement with polyester resin, and we had to throw out all the crackers in the house because they absorbed the taste of the resin. Epoxy doesn't smell as bad as polyester resin does, but it's a good idea to put up some temporary plastic walls around your work area to control the dust and fumes. The fumes produced by both epoxy and polyester are potentially hazardous to your health, so good ventilation is vital while you're using resin. Plenty of opening windows or a fan will make the task more pleasant if weather permits, and a fan blowing through a furnace filter will help clean the air while you're sanding. Please read the safety instructions in Appendix 6, as well as those that come with your materials, and follow them carefully.

Light Is Important

When it comes time to do the finish sanding and varnishing, it's important to have good light. Drips and ripples that are invisible in dim lighting will stand out plainly when exposed to the bright light of day. Don't wait until launching day to find out your that finish is wavy. Install some good bright lights for sanding and varnishing.

In passing, let me tell you the secret to a really fine varnish job: no dust. Dust landing in the wet varnish will make specks, and your finish will appear less glossy. It may be hard to find a dust-free varnishing space and you may need to vacuum up around your work space to eliminate most of the dust, and then let the remaining dust settle. Springtime, when the pollen is making everyone sneeze, is not a good time to varnish outdoors. There are days when the pollen will make your kayak yellow. Finally, try to pick a day without wind.

Removable Shelf

The stuff you need is *always* on the other side of the kayak, and it's a long walk around the end of the boat to get it. This is a constant source of frustration.

One solution is to have two of every tool. Some of the tools are so cheap that you may be able to afford this solution. Certainly, getting two dispensers of glue is a reasonable idea, because you'll go through two bottles of glue before the end anyway. But the chances are good that *both* bottles will end up on the wrong side. So what can you do? One solution is to nail a little shelf in the middle of the strongback where you can put stuff down and easily reach it from both sides. Of course, this won't be any good to you when the time comes to flip the boat over, because the shelf will be upside down. So here's a better solution: Make a little removable shelf that slips over the strongback. See Figure 5-2.

Figure 5-2. I made a little platform that fits over the strongback. This gives me a storage place for tools and glue that I can reach from both sides of the boat.

Figure 5-3. *Sort your strips out into bundles of different colors. A few nails pounded into the crosspiece of the sawhorses serve to keep the bundles separate.*

Storing Your Strips

The strips are so long that it's hard to store them out of the way, yet still have them accessible. There are several places where you can put them. Figure 5-1 shows several solutions. One is to make a rack above the kayak that is accessible from both sides. To this end, a set of T-shaped hangers suspended from the ceiling is a practical solution in some shops. The strips can be arranged on both sides of the T, and you just need to reach up to select the next strip.

If you're using several different varieties of wood, you'll want to be able to separate them. Another crosspiece or two is one solution, or some nails sticking up vertically can provide some bins to sort the strips into.

With a cross-piece on your sawhorses you can put shorter strips below the boat and off the floor. This keeps them off the moisture of a concrete floor and lets you clean underneath. But you need to be careful, when you're building the boat, that you don't spill too much glue on the strips below.

A wall-mounted wood rack is helpful to store wood that hasn't yet been cut into strips, or strips you won't be using immediately.

Another important requirement is some good work surfaces not too far away from the boat. They will tend to serve as level places where you can put down tools, but they'll also have an uncluttered edge where you can work on strips. Another convenient work surface is a plank placed on top of the sawhorses on either side of the strongback. It's useful when you're planing tapers into the strips.

As you can see, I'm full of good ideas about how to organize a shop to make work easier and more efficient, but I'm not very good at following my own advice. I'm sure you can come up with ideas of your own. Each space is going to have its own set of problems and advantages. The goal is to keep everything you need close at hand. You don't want to have to walk across the room each time you need a new strip. Keep your forms, work surfaces and storage areas close together.

Figure 5-4. *A neat shop would make life easier, but as you see, I'm not very good at keeping things clean. I do have room to move around the boat, however, and level places close at hand to work on.*

Cutting the Strips

When you're building a kayak, cutting strips is the only task that requires a big power tool. A table saw can pretty quickly turn a 12-inch board into strips, although even this is easier with some help. Set up the saw with long extensions and an extended fence. Use feather boards to hold down the board you're cutting. Some people use feather boards to hold the wood up against the fence, and while this will help assure more uniform strip thickness, you'll need to readjust the feather board after each cut. I don't feel it's worth it. Instead, build an extension to the table and fence.

Figure 5-5. Ten-foot-long boards serve as table extensions on my table saw. Vertical fences attached to the table extensions help keep the stock running straight. A notch cut into the extension on the infeed side gives me a place to grab the stock as I feed it into the saw. A hinged board supports the ends of the extensions.

I made two table extensions from 10-foot pine planks. To these I added a fence on one side. The fence extensions extend onto the saw table and are clamped parallel to the fence. With a 10-foot infeed table and a similar outfeed table I have a 20-foot fence, so there's not much chance of cutting the wood off-true. I cut a gap in the table extension so I could push the plank through the saw when it became narrower than the table extension, and in this way I'm able to cut strips without assistance.

If you have help, it's generally easiest to have one person at the saw feeding the wood through the blade, while the helper supports the end of the board. The helper should keep an eye on the edge of the board next to the fence. There should be no gap. The helper should not try to move the board, but just support the end and keep it feeding straight. The tendency is to try to speed up the cut by pushing on the board, and this will usually result in a crooked cut and possibly a stalled saw. The best way to hold the board is with your hands underneath, so there's no way to push.

Find as thin a saw blade as possible to minimize the waste. You may find that a thinner 7½-inch blade works well. If the table saw insert has a large gap, you'll want a "zero tolerance" insert to keep the strips from getting caught. This is just an insert with a narrow slot so there's little or no space around the blade. You can cut a piece of wood to replace the existing insert and, starting with the blade lowered all the way, slowly raise the blade so it cuts through the new insert.

Your strips will probably end up with some irregularities in thickness, but that won't really be a problem as long as they aren't too thin. If you have a thickness planer or sander you may consider running the strips through to make them uniform. I don't believe it's worth it, though, because you'll need to cut the strips oversized in order to have something to plane away. In any case, even the thickness planer will not do a perfect job—it will tend to have some tearout. A thickness sander will do a better job, but as I've said before, there's not much point in devoting great effort to achieve smooth and uniform strips.

You're going to be planing all the strips when you're done stripping the boat, anyway, and the original smooth surface will be removed.

If you want, you can use a bandsaw instead of the table saw, and a bandsaw has the advantage of having a thinner kerf, so you won't waste as much wood. The thinner kerf also offers less resistance to the wood and may be faster than a table saw. But bandsaws make a much rougher cut than table saws do, and in this case I have to admit that the rougher surface will make planing the finished boat a slightly longer job.

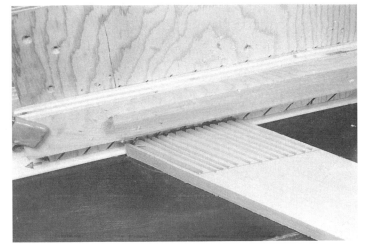

Figure 5-6. When you're milling the coves and beads you don't want your fingers to come anywhere near the cutter. Feather boards serve to keep your fingers away while holding the strips tight against the cutter. The upper feather board is cut from a piece of plywood and has a board in front of it to help hold it in place with some spring clamps.

Milling the Coves and Beads

You'll need a router or shaper to put coves and beads on the edges of your strips, and if you're using a router it will have to be mounted in a router table and not used freehand.

Your first job is to cut the bead, because cutting the cove produces delicate wings that can easily be broken off. To minimize waste, set up the fence so the deepest part of the cutter just misses the edge, and carefully center the cutter so it doesn't leave a ledge on either side of the strip.

You'll want to install one feather board to hold the strip down and another to keep the strip hard against the fence. Make certain that the bit cuts into the incoming strip instead of pulling the strip in. For a bit that turns counterclockwise, you will want to feed the strip in from right to left.

The bead is pretty easy to cut and you'll be able to feed the strip through pretty rapidly. Use the next strip to push the previous one

through the cutter, and inspect the strips as they come out, to make sure everything is working well. If you're getting splinters torn out of the bead, slow down your feed rate.

Figure 5-7. This shows what's happening behind the feather boards in Figure 5-6. The strip is being fed from right to left, with the cutter turning counterclockwise. You always want to push the stock against the direction of tool rotation. Here, I'm using a router bit mounted in a shaper to cut the bead.

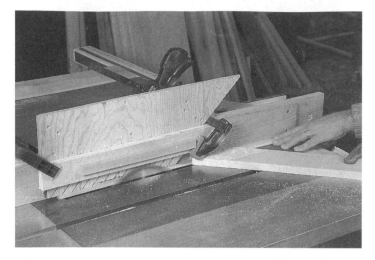

Figure 5-8. Here, I'm cutting the bead off a strip for use as the sheer strip. Had I planned ahead, I would have left the bead off a few strips. The plywood feather board holds the strip down against the saw, and the pine one coming in from the side holds the strip against the fence.

When you've cut all the beads, it's time to mill the coves. Adjust the elevation of the bit so it cuts into the center of the strip. The fence should be set so the cove fills almost the whole edge of the strip. You don't want to cut too deep because that will give you extremely fine-feathered edges. This feather edge is delicate and unnecessary. If possible, leave a small flat spot on the edge of, say, $1/100$ inch or so. You don't need to measure this. You'll know it when you see it. Cut some sample strips and check them. If the edges of the coves look very flimsy, move the fence out so the bit doesn't cut so deep.

Often, you'll need some strips with only either the bead or the cove, and the other edge left square. For example, the sheer strips may only need a cove. Now, instead of going through the work of milling both edges and then cutting one of them off, just mill one edge. I sometimes use a strip with two coves as the center strip on the keel. Now is your chance to make some.

To estimate the number of strips you'll need, see Figure A1-1 in Appendix 1.

Cutting Forms

The ultimate success of your project depends on preparing the forms correctly. They're arranged on a 2 × 4 and they must be aligned straight and true. Take some extra time early on, and you'll avoid problems later. Remember, too, that you have reference lines on the forms to make sure the kayak will not end up twisted and misshapen.

The easiest way to cut the forms is with a bandsaw or an upright jig-saw, although a power sabersaw or a handheld jigsaw will also work well. With the form patterns drawn out full-size, I rough-cut them outside the finished outline with scissors, then glue them with spray adhesive onto the form material, which can be cheap plywood, chipboard, particleboard, or whatever is available. If you need to buy some

Figure 5-9. With the paper form patterns cut out roughly, use spray contact adhesive to secure the patterns to the form material. Use a handheld jigsaw to rough-cut the form material into easy-to-handle pieces before doing the final cut with the jigsaw or bandsaw. At right are some finished forms with the reference lines still visible.

Figure 5-10. *When you're cutting out the hole for the strongback, it helps to have a working surface that lets the pieces fall through. Here, the author's brother, Eric Schade, uses the open frame of his old table saw. You could also use a garbage can. Drill holes in all four corners of the strongback holes and cut out the rectangle with a jigsaw.*

material for the forms, use ¹/₂-inch plywood. Remember to draw the reference lines on the patterns: the waterline, the sheerline, and the centerline, which will help you to align the forms on the strongback. Include the 2-inch by 4-inch rectangle for the strongback cutout, and make the rectangle that exact size, not the size of a 2 × 4, which is 1¹/₂ inches by 3¹/₂ inches. Sorry for the repetition, but it's important.

If you're cutting the forms from a large sheet of plywood, first cut the pieces out rough, leaving about 1 inch around the forms. There's no need to follow the exact shape of the forms, just cut each form free of the sheet. The smaller pieces will then be easier to work with. I usually cut the forms free with a sabersaw and then bring them to the bandsaw. Because the paper patterns were rough-cut outside the final outlines, your finish saw cut will be through paper as well as wood and if the paper is well stuck

down to the wood, this will cause no problems. You'll end up with building forms with all their reference lines in place on the paper that's stuck to the wood.

Cut out the strongback rectangle by drilling holes in the corners, then cut along the lines with a jigsaw. I usually use a trash barrel for my work surface, so the scrap from the holes falls directly into the trash.

You can save yourself the work of cutting the forms by buying precut forms from the sources in Appendix 2.

Breakaway Forms

When it comes time to build the cockpit, it helps if the forms are not in the way. The forms are designed to keep the deck fair around the cockpit, but they're not needed to make the cockpit. I cut the top off the forms under the cockpit and then use a couple

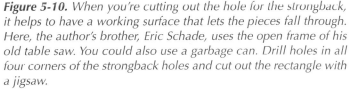

Figure 5-11. *Chris Hardy, of Marine CAM Services, has a computer-controlled router that he uses to cut forms for kits. If you're designing your own boat on a computer, this is a good way to get accurate forms.*

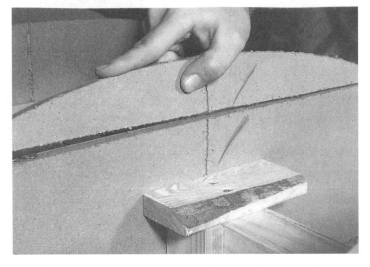

Figure 5-12. The breakaway section of a form that extends up into the cockpit will make the construction of the cockpit easier later on. See text.

If the forms do not have a mark to guide you, a bevel starting ³/₄ inch to 1 inch back from the edge is usually enough. Note that the plans in this book assume that the end forms are ¹/₂ inch thick. If you use thicker material you will need to bevel further back.

You can make this bevel with several different tools. A disk sander with a very coarse disk will work quite quickly, for example, and a coarse rasp is effective although it will take you longer. This is also a good task for a block plane. Whatever tool you use, you do not need to make a knife-edge. Leaving the edge about ¹/₃₂ inch wide will be enough.

of dots of hot-melt glue to tack them back together. This permits me to use them for stripping the deck, but I can break off the top when I need to build the cockpit.

Form Spacing

The plans in this book have a spacing of 1 foot between forms. This gives good support to the strips when you're sanding and provides many points to control the shape on kayaks with sharp curves. Other designs may have different spacing, and such close spacing may not be required if the design has more gradual curves, but every 18 inches is probably the furthest apart they should be. Any further can complicate sanding, especially if you use strips thinner than ¹/₄ inch.

End Forms

Cut out the bow and stern forms in a similar manner to the others. At the ends of the boat, the strips will be coming into the forms at an acute angle. Because you need a surface to staple to, you need to bevel the edges to bring the forms to a sharp point.

Figure 5-13. The author cuts out the end form of the Guillemot Double on a bandsaw. It's the easiest tool to use for this purpose, but a jigsaw does just as good a job.

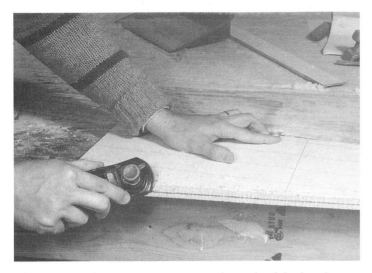

Figure 5-14. The strips coming up to the ends of the kayak meet the forms at an acute angle. Use a plane, rasp, or power sander to bevel the outer edge of the end forms. Be sure to bevel both sides of the form back to the taper guidelines so the end of the form comes to a ¹/₃₂-inch-wide edge in the middle of the plywood.

My brother actually makes the beveled section out of a separate piece of wood, then he cuts the form out along the back edge of the bevel line and tapes or tack-glues the beveled piece to the form instead of beveling the form. This

Figure 5-15. You can make an internal stem piece by cutting off the front of the bow form at the taper guideline and making a matching piece out of cedar. Bevel this piece on both sides so it is triangular in section.

lets him glue strips directly to the beveled section, which he leaves in the completed boat to create an interior stem piece. If you use good-quality wood for the end form, this piece can be made by beveling the end form normally then cutting off the bevel at the bevel guideline. Otherwise, cut the end form normally and then, without beveling, cut at the bevel guideline. The piece you removed may now be used as a pattern for cutting the stem piece out of a ¹/₂-inch-thick board.

You don't need to bevel the ordinary sectional forms because the strips lie almost flat across most of them. This is good enough to staple to, and the strips don't need to fit flush against the forms. Incidentally, some sectional forms are glued to the end forms to complete the end-form assembly.

The Strongback

The traditional strongback for strip-building is a ladder arrangement where the forms are secured to the rungs. Some kayak builders use this method. They first strip the hull and then they remove the forms from the strongback and flip the boat over. Some people precut the forms to include the deck, and these forms need to be held to the strongback with a separate piece of wood. The forms and the supporting wood are screwed together and the boat is removed from the strongback by removing the screws holding the forms to the support pieces.

Others integrate the support piece into the form. They don't completely cut out the deck, but instead leave enough wood to hold the form to the support. Then they cut the

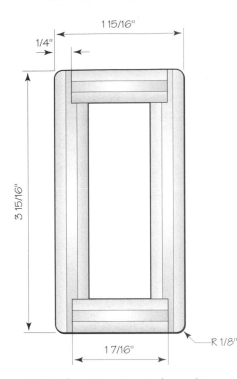

Figure 5-16. *If you're going to be making several boats, you may find it worthwhile to make a box-beam type of strongback to the dimensions shown here. Use high-quality plywood or particleboard, and rabbet the side pieces to accept the top and bottom. The resulting box should be just under 2 inches by 4 inches, so the forms slide on easily.*

across the sheerline. More importantly, it holds the forms together securely when you start work on the deck. If you remove the forms from the strongback, as the above methods require, you run the risk of the forms coming loose and upsetting their alignment. With the strongback strung through the forms, it will remain inside the boat while you are working on the deck and it will remain as a single unit that's easy to remove and replace when you start fiberglassing.

It's true that a 2 × 4 is not as stiff as a ladder strongback, and you certainly need to be careful that everything stays in line while you are setting up, but once you start stripping, the forms stiffen up considerably. With a ladder-type strongback there may be nothing holding the forms in place once you remove the hull from the strongback.

One problem with a 2 × 4 is you will rarely find a straight one. Since you want a straight kayak, you need to align the forms to each other, not to the strongback. That's why the holes in the forms are bigger than the 2 × 4: they permit you to move the forms around the strongback.

The 2 × 4 is a good solution for making one or two boats, but if you plan to make more, or just don't like the idea of using a 2 × 4, you can also make a 2-inch by 4-inch box-beam from

remaining bit to remove the boat, and strip the deck on the same forms as the hull—or they may use the supports remaining on the strongback as a female form.

If you found this difficult to follow, don't worry. The long and short of it is that I have found that the ladder-type strongback unnecessary. I find that a 2 × 4 strung through holes in the forms works just as well. What's more, there are several advantages to this technique. You save a bit of time and money making the strongback, for a start, and you save more time setting up the forms. It also lets you do interesting things like run strips

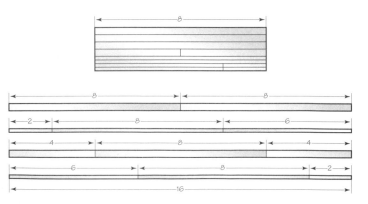

Figure 5-17. *You should stagger the joints of the box-beam, as shown here, to avoid weak spots. From one 8-foot sheet of plywood you can cut four wide side pieces and four narrow top and bottom pieces. Stagger the joints by cutting one of the wide pieces in half and cutting 2 feet off two of the narrow pieces.*

Figure 5-18. *It takes some time to get good square corners in the strongback holes through the forms, but if you leave the corners rounded you won't be able to slide the forms over a box-beam, if you're using one instead of a 2 × 4. Instead of taking all that time to get good corners in the holes, use a router to round the corners of the box beam.*

plywood or particleboard. Plywood is stronger and lighter, and particleboard is generally smoother and more dimensionally consistent. Use at least $1/2$-inch material. For a 16-foot strongback, cut four pieces of plywood $3^{15}/_{16}$

inches wide by 8 feet long on a table saw. Rabbet the edges with a router or a dado blade in your table saw to accept the thickness of your material, leaving $1/4$ inch of thickness beyond the rabbet. Cutting four pieces of plywood $1^{7}/_{16}$ inches wide by 8 feet long will provide enough material to make a $1^{15}/_{16}$-inch by $3^{15}/_{16}$-inch box beam. The slightly smaller size is to make it easier to slide the forms on. With smooth and dimensionally consistent material, and precise holes through the form, you can eliminate this fudge factor and make an honest-to-goodness 2-inch by 4-inch beam.

The forms that come with a kit may have a radius in the corner of the strongback holes. If so, use a router with a $1/8$-inch radius or a larger round-over bit to take the sharp corners off the strongback, so that it matches the holes.

Cut the forms to length as specified for the design. The length is usually 2 feet 1 inch shorter than the finished boat. (The odd inch comes about because the strongback stops short of the two half-inch-thick section forms at each end.) The ends of the strongback may need to be trimmed to fit into the small area in the ends of the kayak. Cut the required taper into each end as illustrated in Figures 4-12 and 4-16 in Chapter 4. The taper will always be on the bottom side of the strongback.

Aligning Forms

When you're ready to start setting up the forms on the strongback, the reference marks on each form will give you something to sight along. If your forms don't have any reference marks, you should add some. See Chapter 4.

Figure 5-19. *You can also use pipe for a strongback. Here, I'm using a piece of PVC pipe for a Little Auk kayak. But, because PVC pipe is flexible, I wouldn't use it for a boat longer than about 10 feet.*

Figure 5-20. Section forms and end forms cut out and ready for use. Reference lines that will help align the forms on the strongback are visible on the paper patterns glued to the wood.

To set the strongback up on the sawhorses, start by cutting 2-inch-wide, 3-inch-deep, slots in the ends of two 1-foot-long 2 × 4s. These are the cradles for your 2 × 4 strongback. Screw the cradles upright to the sawhorses, with the slots upward, and nestle the strongback into these with the narrow edge up. You can now mark the form positions. These will usually be 1 foot apart but because the coordinate system is based on the completed boat, the 1-foot form may not fit on the strongback. Remember, it's 1 foot from the bow of the finished boat, and the finished strips protrude past the end forms. The first

Boat Stands

Instead of building the kayak on a set of sawhorses, you can build a boat stand that you can use both for building the boat and storing it when you're done. The stand comprises four inverted Ts held together in pairs with cross-pieces.

A strap of webbing or old carpet makes a sling between the ends of the Ts to hold the boat. The two slings are fastened in slots cut into the uprights to accept a 2 × 4 on edge. You can either fasten the sling permanently in the slot or you can make some toggles out of dowels as follows:

Make a sawcut most of the way down the middle of a 4-inch-long dowel. Slide some webbing into this slot and run a screw through it to secure it in place.

Now you have removable slings, and you can use your stands to build the boat, with a 2 × 4 strongback running lengthwise through them, and to store the boat afterward.

I actually make my stands so they can be easily disassembled. To this end, I cut two mortises in the uprights and tenons on the ends of the cross-pieces. Holes through the tenons accept pegs that lock the stand together. The result is a handy stand that fits in the back of my car.

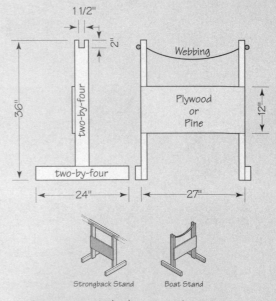

Figure 5-21. A dual-purpose boat stand is an alternative to a sawhorse. This stand will support the strongback while you're building, and the finished boat afterward.

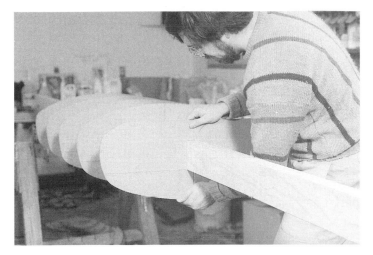

Figure 5-22. *Sliding the forms roughly into position on the strong-back.*

form that is actually on the strongback is usually the 2-foot form. Because you have to fit the strongback into the narrowing bow, the beginning of the strongback will usually lie somewhere between the 1-foot and 2-foot forms. The location of the first form on the strongback, relative to the forward end of the strongback, is 11½ inches for all the designs in this book. Mark 1-foot increments starting from this first form and label the locations accordingly.

Tap a nail into the middle of one end of the top side of the strongback. Stretch a string tightly between this nail and another at the far end. Use a pen to carefully mark where the string crosses each form location mark. These marks will form

the centerline of your kayak. You could snap a chalkline to create this reference line, but it is likely to be less precise.

Next, put a nail 2 inches down from the top on one side of the strongback, at either end, and tie a string between them. If the 2 × 4 curves upward in middle, place the nails higher: The object is to create a line that's no more than 2 inches from the top anywhere along the length of the strongback. Mark this line in the same way you did the centerline. This will be an elevation reference and it corresponds to the middle of the 2-inch by 4-inch hole in the forms.

In sequential order, slide all the forms, except the end forms, onto the strongback, lifting it out of the cradles to get the forms into the middle section. Roughly align them to their locations, and be aware that it will be easier to see the reference lines if they are facing the nearer end of the boat.

Now, remember that the forms represent the shape of the cross section of your kayak at the exact location of the mark you've made on the strongback. So which side of the mark do you place the form on?

Well, since your kayak tapers toward the ends, and since the forms don't have beveled edges, you should place the forms on the side

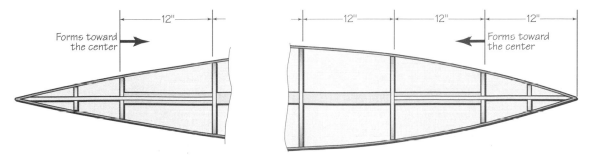

Figure 5-23. *Because the strips taper inward toward the ends, they touch the edge of the form that is closer to the end. In order to have the strip touch exactly at the mark, the forms should be placed on the side of the form mark that's toward the center of the boat.*

of the mark that's closer to the middle of the boat. It will mean changing over in the center, of course, but this method will ensure that the strips will touch the forms at the correct location. See Figure 5-23.

You now need to screw to the strongback some cleats that will eventually hold the forms securely in place. You can make cleats from any scrap wood cut into pieces about 2 inches wide and 6 inches long. To make sure the forms end up in the right place, you need to put each cleat on the side of the form mark that's *away* from the center of the boat. In other words, the cleats on the forward half of the boat should be in front of the form location marks and the cleats on the after half should be behind the marks.

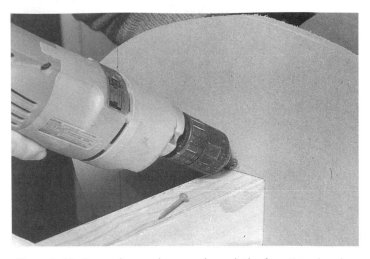

Figure 5-25. *Run a sheetrock screw through the form into the cleat to secure it in place.*

Align one face of the cleat with the form location mark. Use a square to make sure the cleat is at a right angle to the strongback and secure the cleat on top of the strongback with two sheetrock screws.

Use the square to line up another cleat vertically on the side of the strongback. Again you will need at least two screws to secure it in place. See Figure 5-24. Double-check that your

forms are on the correct side of the cleats as you screw the cleats down.

Go back and make sure your centerline and elevation marks are going to be visible when you put the forms in place, and extend them as required. I usually start by aligning each form to the centerline, raising it to the proper elevation, and putting one sheetrock screw through the centerline of the form into the cleat to hold the form in place (Figure 5-25).

Now sight down the middle. The reference lines will probably not line up exactly. Try rotating each form around its single screw to bring the reference lines into alignment. Hopefully, they will come close. If not, back off the screw for the uncooperative form and move it as required. Now sight down the reference lines on the side (Figure 5-26). These should be almost in line. Some forms may need to be rotated slightly, or moved.

It can help to clamp a strip parallel to the reference line on the middle form to extend it out where you can see it more easily. When the forms look good, run a couple of sheetrock screws into each cleat, locking the forms in place, and when you've done that, go back and recheck all the reference lines.

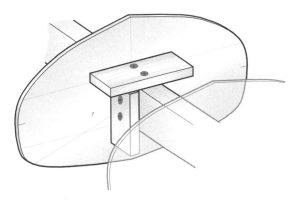

Figure 5-24. *Wood cleats secure the forms in place. Use a square to make sure the cleats are at right angles to the strongback.*

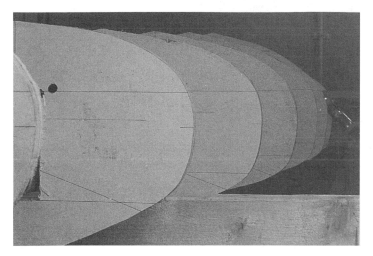

Figure 5-26. Forms lined up and ready to be secured. This is how the reference lines should appear.

Installing End Forms

To complete the assembly of the end forms, you need to glue on some section forms. But first you need to make those section forms narrower, by the width of your end form. If you are using $^1/_2$-inch wood for your end forms, this means you need to cut away $^1/_4$ inch of wood on either

Figure 5-27. Completing the end form assembly by gluing cross-sectional forms to either side of the end form. Before this job, however, you must remove the center of the sectional form, to account for the thickness of the end form. See Figure 5-28.

side of the section form's centerline. The two halves can then be glued on either side of the end form.

The plans in this book have sectional forms 6 inches from the end, as well as 12 inches. These 6-inch forms may be quite small and seem pretty useless, but they can help hold the strips at the end where there tends to be quite a bit of curvature. Remember that the form locations correspond to distances from the bow of the finished boat (that is the outside of the strips) which are not the same as the distances from the end of the form. So be sure to make your measurements from the flat inboard end of the end form, not the pointed outward edge.

Now you can install the end forms. A reference line at the waterline can be used to ensure the end form is on straight. You don't want it sagging or pointing up in the air. The waterline should be parallel to the strongback. Align the form to the centerline of the other forms. Sight down the form to make sure it is not pointing off to one side. Some pieces of scrap wood glued or screwed on either side of the end form will hold it in proper alignment.

When all the forms look right, make sure they're secure. You don't want them shifting as you work. Double-check that all the reference lines are lined up as they should be and, finally, run a strip of tape around the edge of the forms to keep glue from adhering to them. Masking tape, duct tape, fiber tape, Scotch tape, any tape will work. Use whatever's cheapest or whatever you have on hand. Some people rub a candle around the edge instead of using tape, and there's nothing wrong with that, either.

Now stand back and look at what you have accomplished. The shape of the kayak is there before you, like a skeleton, but you can already picture how beautiful the boat will look. It's kind of a shame that the building form is not something you keep, but the boat itself will look better yet.

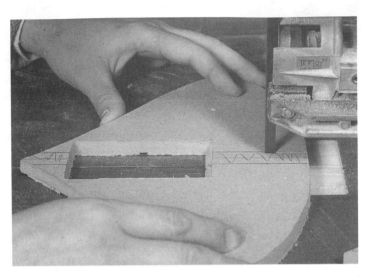

Figure 5-28. The author uses a bandsaw to cut away ¼ inch of wood on either side of the centerline of a sectional form that will be glued onto the end form. This accounts for the ½-inch thickness of the end form. See Figure 5-27.

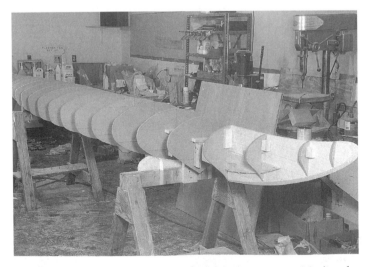

Figure 5-29. The fully assembled form gives you a good feeling for how the finished boat will look. This is the form for the Guillemot Double.

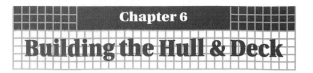

hile the skeletal form is beautiful in itself, it is by enclosing it in strips that you flesh out the kayak. Stripping is the fun part. The strip method of boatbuilding is very tolerant in that it doesn't demand the skills of an experienced boatwright to achieve beautiful results. The tasks involved are small and undemanding, and mistakes do not cost a lot. You're working with small pieces of wood, so if you mess up one piece you can put it aside and use it elsewhere later. Small gaps between strips, while frustrating to the perfectionist in all of us, are not major disasters. They will not significantly weaken the boat, nor will they cause leaks.

There are as many different ways of stripping a boat as there are builders. I will cover the way I do it, and try to touch on some of the techniques other people use. I can guarantee that you'll have an idea or two of your own, too, and just because I don't mention it, that doesn't mean it isn't better than anything I suggest.

Actually, I never build a boat the same way twice. A lot of the fun in building, for me, is experimenting with new ideas. So you should feel free to experiment, also. If an idea doesn't work as expected, you'll learn more from making a mistake than you would from doing it perfectly the first time.

Stripping the Hull

I usually start on the hull first, rather than the deck, because it's not as visible. If I'm going to make mistakes, I would prefer they not be too visible. Working on the hull gives me the opportunity to experiment and perfect my technique before I get to the more visible deck. The hull is probably a little more difficult than the deck, but this gives you a good chance to hone your skills.

It's easiest if the first strip on each side is a full-length strip. This will help to give fair curves to the following strips. If you don't have any full-length strips, scarf and glue two strips together to make one long enough. The strongest scarf for this purpose is cut diagonally to the thickness. (See the sidebar on scarfing later in this chapter.) This strip needs to be strong because it will start out unsupported by neighboring strips. Later strips don't require this strength.

The Sheer Strip

The most important strip is the first one you fit, because it

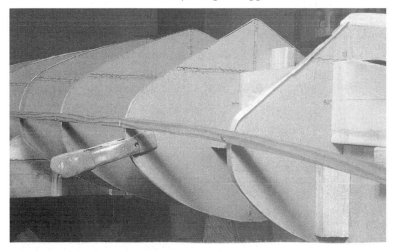

Figure 6-1. *The first strip to go on the boat is the sheer strip for the hull. Carefully sight down the strip to make sure it bends fairly and has no sudden, uneven-looking humps.*

defines the sheerline and the curve of all the other strips. If it isn't fair, none of the other strips will be, either. This probably won't affect the boat's performance, but it may look funny. The sheer strip also defines the transition from deck to hull.

If you're using cove-and-bead strips, you'll need to cut the edge off either the cove or the bead for this strip. Either use a table saw to square up the edge, or plane it down by hand. I usually place my strip with the cove (hollow) side up—that is, pointing away from the sheer and toward the keel. (See the sidebar that follows.) In this case, I have to remove the bead.

If you plan ahead, however, you can simply not bother milling the bead on a few strips. This non-beaded edge will need to be beveled slightly so when you install the deck sheer strip there will not be a big gap. It doesn't need to be perfect yet, but it helps to get the bevel close to correct. I'll tell you how.

Starting at the bow, hold the strip on the forms next to the sheerline marks with the square edge lowermost, next to the mark. Estimate by eye the angle needed to make this bottom edge level with the floor, and then use a block plane to try to match that angle (Figure 6-3). Look at the angle on a couple of forms at

Which Side Up?

When you're using cove-and-bead strips you have to decide whether you will strip with the cove (hollow) or the bead (rounded) side out (that is, toward the next strip to be laid). The cove side is delicate; the edges of the cove are easy to break or mash. Because of this, you may want to strip with the bead side out, so that you can push down on the cove to force the strips together. In this way you are less likely to mash and wreck the cove.

Unfortunately, you will eventually come to a point where two strips come together (see Figure 6-20) and you'll need to fit another strip between the two. If both the existing strips are showing a bead, you'll need to create a cove in the end of the third strip. If they're both showing a cove, you'll need to create a bead. Now here's the point I'm coming to: it's more difficult to make a cove than a bead, although it's possible to make a cove with a round file.

The easiest solution of all may be to remove the bead from the strip that will mate with the end of the third strip. You can do this if you're careful with a jackknife or a chisel.

On the other hand, it's not at all difficult to add a bead to a strip with a few strokes of a block plane (see Figure 6-21). With this in mind, if you strip with the cove side out, when you reach that point where you fit a strip between two others, you just need to add a bead to the end of the third strip.

To make the bead, you first knock the corners off the edge of the strip so the edge of the strip resembles part of a stop sign. You then knock the corners off this octagon. You don't need to make a perfect half-round—it just has to fit quite snugly into the cove.

While it's easier make a bead to fit into a cove than the other way around, the fact remains that in order to get a tight joint between adjoining strips, you'll still need to push on the delicate cove edges. In reality, though, those edges aren't so delicate that they can't withstand a little pushing. To be safe, however, you can use as a pusher a short piece of strip with the cove removed. If you insert the bead of the pusher into the cove of the strip you are laying, you can safely apply pressure without risking damage to the strip.

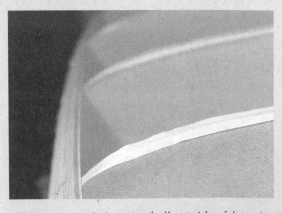

Figure 6-2. *With the cove (hollow) side of the strips facing up, you'll find it easier to finish the bottom.*

Figure 6-3. *If you're not using cove-and-bead strips, you'll have to bevel the edges of many strips to achieve a tight fit. Lean the plane slightly, so you start by removing one corner of the strip. Test the fit as you go. You'll also need to bevel the edge of the sheer strip, where the deck and hull meet, even if you're using cove-and-bead strips.*

If the first strip looks good, however, secure it in place by stapling it to the forms. If it's hard to keep in place, run a small finish nail through it into the form.

Next, trim the ends off with a razor saw. Hold the saw against the opposite side of the end form and follow the angle the opposite strip will take as it meets the first strip. (See Figure 6-5).

Apply a little glue to the newly cut face and install the first strip on the opposite side. Eyeball it again to make sure it looks fair and symmetrical to the other side. Trim the excess using a razor saw. Congratulations: your two sheer strips are installed. Take the opportunity to look down their length to make sure they are fair.

a time and notice how the bevel angle changes between forms. Try to roll the bevel so it changes smoothly from one angle to the next, and work on a few feet at a time. Don't concentrate your effort exclusively on one section. Hold the strip back in place now and then, examine your work, and move down the length of the boat as you get it about right. Once again, perfection is not required yet.

By the way, as you work on this bevel you may have time to wonder whether a cove-and-bead joint between the hull and deck would have been easier. Well, yes, except that the need to separate the hull from the deck at various stages of construction would expose the cove or bead to a lot of abuse.

Once you're satisfied with your rolling bevel, lay the strip with its lower edge along the sheerline. Use some of the U-shaped clamping fixtures mentioned on page 80 in the sidebar on Dealing with Staple Holes to hold the strip in place temporarily. Eyeball this strip to make sure it follows a fair curve without any sudden angular changes. If it doesn't, now's the time to adjust it and, if necessary, the forms.

Stripping the Topsides

Quite a bit of care is required to make a perfect joint where the strips coming from either side meet at the bow and stern. Using the taper in the end forms as a guide will usually produce a close fit but sometimes you just miss, and it comes out wrong. Consequently, you may end up with some gaps.

Don't feel bad. A perfect joint is not necessary. Minor gaps and misalignments will be covered before the boat is finished. If you really screw up, you can either put that strip aside and use it later, or cut a small wedge to fill the gap.

The next strip goes right on top of the previous strip, that is, on the same side as the second sheer strip. I balance my strips as I build the boat. If I put the first sheer strip on the left, I then put the other sheer on the right, followed by another strip on the right. Then I go to the left side and install two strips before going back to the right. This will form a bow and stern that look like interlocking fingers.

The third strip can extend out beyond the ends of the boat when you glue it on. Put a small

Dealing with Staple Holes

Stapling or nailing the strips to the forms makes holes that will show in the finished boat. While these holes are hardly noticeable, some people find them offensive. There is no structural problem with the holes; they just don't conform to some people's aesthetic standards. If you can't bear the thought of staple holes, there are several ways to eliminate them.

The first suggestion is to fill the holes afterward. Some people will insert toothpicks into each hole with a little glue, but that's a time-consuming task. You need to be sure you don't insert the toothpicks so far that they go into the form as well, as this will attach the boat to the form and make it difficult to remove. Of course, a toothpick may show as a light spot in the hull strip, instead of a dark spot

as a hole would appear. You need to decide if this is an improvement.

You could also fill the hole with a little putty made from sanding dust and epoxy. This is relatively painless, but does take some extra time. Note that sanding dust taken from the same wood you intend to fill will end up darker than the wood. You will need to mix in some lighter-colored material to make a filler that matches.

But the best way of all to eliminate the holes is not to put them there in the first place. After all, the staples are only used to hold the strip in place

Figure 6-4. To avoid staple and nail holes, you can fit U-shaped pieces of plywood over the strips and hold them in place with spring clamps until the glue dries. This technique also works well for holding particularly stubborn strips, but you need to wait for the glue to dry before you can install the next strip.

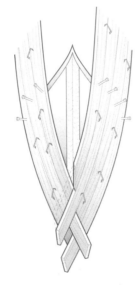

Figure 6-5. The simplest way to deal with ends is to create a "finger joint." Let your first strip overhang the end then cut it at approximately the angle at which the strip on the other side will hit it. Install this next strip and leave it overhanging. Repeat this for each new level of strips, alternating sides as you go. Use staples to hold the strips together and if they are really uncooperative use a small finish nail driven into the form.

bead of glue along the upper edge of the previous strip. (A reminder: All the strips are edge-glued together. They are not glued to the forms.) Press the new strip in place and staple it to the forms. You then cut the third strip as you did the first strip, using the end forms as a guide.

Incidentally, if the strips pull away from each other between the forms you may need to add a couple of staples bridging the two strips to hold them tight. If you're using cove-and-bead strips, the bridging staples are probably not required. What you will find, however, is that when you try to put the next strip on the other side you won't be able to make a snug fit at the ends because the cove or bead of the sheer strip on the other side won't let the strip nestle properly.

while the glue dries, so most of the stapleless methods involve installing one strip and holding it in place until the glue dries before installing the next strip.

Holes drilled in the form can be used as clamping points for spring clamps or C-clamps but it's hard to get a hole everywhere that you need one. Instead, you can use a U-shaped piece of plywood as a clamping fixture. The strip is put in place and the U-piece is slid over the strip next to the form, the fixture is then clamped to the form to hold the strip in place. Even if you are not trying to eliminate staples, this is a good way to secure recalcitrant strips.

Each strip is clamped in place and the glue is permitted to dry, and then the next strip is installed and clamped. Depending on how fast the glue dries and how much time you have free to work on the boat each day, this may result in only one or two strips being installed daily.

A faster method is to use hot-melt glue to secure the strip to the form. Hot-melt glue sets up quickly and you can continue to strip quickly. Normal yellow glue is used between the strips. The trick here is to make sure the hot-melt doesn't stick to the forms too permanently, as you need to get the boat off the forms eventually. Actually, hot-melt doesn't stick that well, so if you have tape around the edge of the form, this shouldn't be a problem. But, remember, you do want the

glue to hold long enough to keep the strip in place while the yellow glue dries. On a simple shape, similar to the Great Auk, this should not be a problem, but the hot-melt may not be strong enough for more complex shapes that tend to spring away from the form with more force.

After you've finished stripping, you'll have to remove all the hot-melt from the inside of the boat. This is when you hope it didn't stick too well. You may be able to peel it off by hand or with the help of a paint scraper but if the glue gets a good bond to the strips it can be hard to remove. Some concerted scraping should eliminate most of it but as you work the glue it will tend to heat up and soften, making it harder to deal with. Eventually, you'll get it to the stage where it can be removed by planing, although it may gum up your plane a little. You cannot sand hot-melt glue because it gets hot, melts, and clogs up the sandpaper quickly.

For my part, I don't bother with toothpicks or hot-melt glue. I just want to get the boat done. Staples are quick and easy, and the holes they produce are small. From 10 feet away you can't even see them. The boat will look good even with these small holes so I don't think any of the methods to eliminate the holes is worth the effort. I just use a stapler and get on with it. Maybe I should have higher standards.

Figure 6-6. *When you're making the finger joint in Figure 6-5 with cove-and-bead strips, you'll need to make a cove in the top of the previous course of strips. A small round file such as a chainsaw file works well for this.*

No matter. If you're stripping cove-side-up, you can cut a cove into the sheer strip with a 1/4-inch round file. If you're going bead-side-up, you may need to make some saw cuts and whittle a bead with your jackknife.

If you're not using cove-and-bead strips, you'll need to make a rolling bevel on the edge of the strip, as you did for the sheer strip. Here, it's easier to see if you are getting it right because you have the previous strip that you must match. It will be easier if you plan ahead and bevel the top edge of the strip while you are at it. Approximating the bevel you think you will need will make

Figure 6-7. The strips are edge-glued together. They are not glued to the forms. The duct tape in this picture ensures that the strips will not stick to the forms. With the cove side up, you can dispense a bead of glue right into the cove.

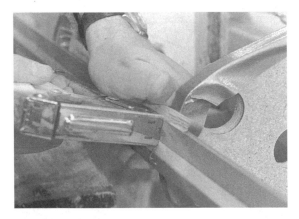

Figure 6-8. A simple hand-stapler with ceiling-tile staples is usually enough to hold the strips in place while the glue dries. Note the strip of wood under the author's hand. It protects the edges of the cove while he applies pressure for a good tight joint between strips.

the bevel on the next strip less severe. You won't need to bevel the strips where the section shape has a gradual curve.

If the sheerline has a strong curve, you can make your life easier by adding "cheater" strips. To do this, lay down a full-length strip as usual, but where the sheer curves away don't pull the next strip all the way down to the curve. Leave a gap narrower than the width of your strips, tapering away gradually to nothing. When this strip is secured in place, fill in the gap by planing a strip to fit. You get a fairer (smoother) curve by fixing the long strip before shaping the cheater. To mark the shape of the cheater strip (#3 in Figure 6-9), hold the strip up against the gap with one edge following the edge of strip 2. With one end of the strip at the narrow end of the gap between strips #1 and 2, mark the width of the strip at the wide end. Draw a line on the strip between that mark and the end. Use a jackknife to rough out the shape of the strip. Then use a sharp plane to close in on the line. The narrow end of the strip will become very flexible and hard to plane but a really sharp plane doesn't need to be pressed as hard to make a cut, so it won't bend the strip so much. You can clamp the strip to another strip that will give support as you plane, or you can put the strip down on your workbench and plane it there.

Try the fit of the cheater strip. Note where it stops when you try to insert it into the gap. Look to see what part of the strip hit, and stopped you pushing it in all the way. This will usually be somewhere in the middle, so plane away at the middle of the strip a little and give the edge of the strip a slight concave curve. The curve should be smooth and fair, with the nar-

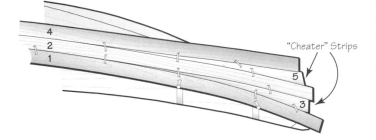

Figure 6-9. If the design has a lot of upward sweep, or your strips are particularly stiff, you may need to install "cheater" strips such as those marked 3 and 5 here. Fix the strips in the order numbered here. By installing the longer strips first you'll get a tighter joint.

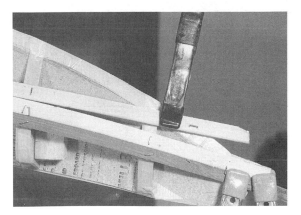

Figure 6-10. You can either make the space for the cheater strip one strip wide, as shown here, or you can make it wider and use several cheaters to fill the gap.

Figure 6-11. When planing a cheater strip to a thin taper, you will need to support the back of the strip so it does not bend away from the plane.

Figure 6-12. Guiding the cheater strip carefully into place. You can push it fairly hard to get a tight fit.

Figure 6-13. If you choose to use an internal stem piece, glue the strips directly to it. In the finger joint, you only glue the strips to each other.

row point coming in sharp and even. Try the strip again, looking for the binding point, and planing away at that area first. When it fits, mark the end of the cheater strip for the miter angle so the strip on the other side will fit in over it. You'll need to cut this miter first in order to fit in the other strip.

You'll make things easier for yourself later if you balance the strips at the front and back. Because the bow of a kayak generally sweeps up higher than the stern, you should put a couple more cheater strips in the front than the back so that you'll reach the keel at about the same time in the bow as the stern. Measure down from the keel at each end to get an approximation of how balanced the ends are. If the distance from the centerline down to the strips is more at the bow than the stern, add another cheater strip.

If you're using cove-and-bead strips, you'll need to put a bead on the side you're tapering so that it will mesh into place. You can plane this in with your block plane—see the sidebar below entitled Fitting Ends of Strips. After each adjustment of the taper, you'll need to recarve the bead.

Continue stripping until you have covered the sides of the kayak. Alternate sides as you go, to keep from putting too much pressure on one side of the boat and distorting the forms.

Scarfing

Most people consider the "ideal" strip to be as long as the boat or the part of the boat it's covering, but it's getting harder to find these long pieces of wood, and if the boat is really long it's just plain impossible. It's also unnecessary. Shorter strips are actually easier to use. When you're working on the bottom of the boat, you often must fit the strips in at both ends and this requires some very precise fitting. It's easier if you can fit one end without worrying about the other end, then join them together somewhere in the middle where it's easier.

The traditional boatbuilder's way to join lengths of wood is to "scarf" them together. A scarf is a long-angled joint that maximizes the glue area between the two pieces while making the transition from one piece to the next as gradual as possible. You can cut a scarf in a strip by cutting diagonally across the width of the strip, or you can cut diagonally across the thickness.

The cut you choose depends on what you want to achieve. Cutting across the thickness will probably be stronger and less noticeable, but sometimes you want the joint to be noticed, in which case a scarf cut across the width can be a nice-looking detail. See Figure 6-14.

The longer the scarf, the stronger it will be, but this doesn't really affect us much because you don't generally need a strong scarf for strip-built kayaks.

I use a belt sander to cut my across-the-thickness scarfs. Here's how:

- Clamp the sander upside down to the workbench.
- Put a small block of wood at the back, behind the belt.
- Place a mark beside the belt, near the front of the flat part. Turn on the sander and place a strip on the block at the back, with the front lined up with the mark.
- Slowly tilt the front of the strip down onto the moving belt.
- Sand the end down to a sharp point.

Repeat this for the end of the strip you want to scarf on. By placing the strip on the block and sanding to the mark each time, you'll be sure to repeat the correct angle.

Now apply a little glue to both scarf faces and press them together with some clamps. Make sure that the thicknesses match up correctly and

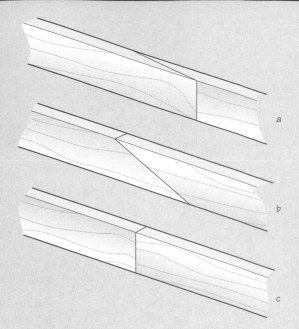

Figure 6-14. Strips can be connected in a various ways to make a longer strip: (a) is a through-the-thickness scarf; (b) is an across-the-width scarf; and (c) is a butt joint. Of the three, (a) is probably the strongest and (c) is the easiest.

that the strip is straight. After the glue dries, the strip is ready to use.

The across-the-width scarf and the butt joint are both variations of a single idea. The difference is just the angle you cut. A butt joint is a 90-

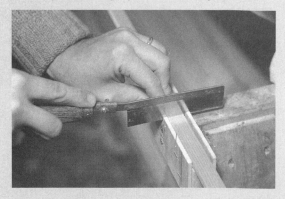

Figure 6-15. A little homemade miter box attached to the end of the sawhorse provides a convenient place to cut the ends of strips for a butt joint.

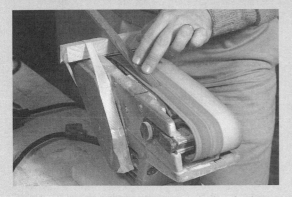

Figure 6-16. *For consistent through-the-thickness scarfs, align the end of the strip with a mark placed at the side of the belt sander while you support the back of the strip with a small block of wood and press down slowly. Be careful; you can easily give yourself an unwanted manicure while doing this.*

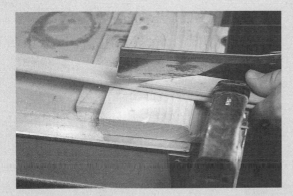

Figure 6-17. *You can match an across-the-width scarf by using the previously cut strip as a saw guide for your next one.*

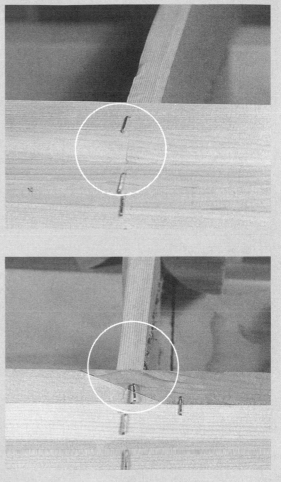

Figure 6-18. *A finished butt joint, or through-the-thickness scarf (top), and an across-the-width scarf (bottom).*

degree cut, while a scarf is cut at an acute angle. You can, of course, cut at any angle in between, and for this reason I sometimes make a miter box. I put a fence on either side of a ¾-inch piece of wood and cut some guide slots in it at the angle for my scarf. Or, I just freehand the first scarf and use the end of that strip as a guide to cut the next strips. After cutting the first piece, I clamp it, or the scrap that came off, to the next strip. I use this to guide my sawing. To tell the truth, the angle at which you choose to cut is not critical. I generally make my across-the-width

scarf about 2 inches long, but since the scarf doesn't serve much structural purpose, the angle you choose depends more on aesthetics than anything else.

I don't preassemble strips when I use an across-the-width scarf or butt joint. I glue in the first strips, and just snug up the second strip. You don't need to put any glue in the joint.

And when you're fitting both ends of a strip, but have a gap in the middle, it's easiest to get an accurate fit if you just use butt joints between the two fitted pieces.

If you're using strips that are shorter than the length of the boat, you can join them together in place. The easiest joint is just a straight butt joint where you cut the ends of the strips square, put some glue between them and press them together. A scarf joint may be used if you don't like the looks of the butt joint—see the sidebar entitled Scarfing.

As I told you when I was discussing making the end forms, you can make the bevel of the end forms into a separate stem piece. If you do this, don't extend the strips much beyond the end of this piece. You also won't need to make the interlocking finger pattern I described above. Instead, you cut the strips very slightly beyond the stem piece, to be trimmed later. Glue the strips directly to the stem and staple them in place while the glue sets.

Where the forms have a tight curve, there may be gaps between adjacent strips even if you're using cove-and-bead strips. In these situations, the narrower the strip, the more easily it will conform to the curve of the hull. I saw a half-dozen strips in half to make thinner strips for tight curves such as chines and areas where the strips twist a lot. Narrower strips are also easier to sweep upward to follow the sheerline. If you are using cove-and-bead strips, plan ahead and mill a dozen narrow strips as you mill the normal-width strips.

Details of the Bottom

As you strip from the sheer toward the bottom, you'll eventually come to a point where the strips on either side joining at the stem and stern meet more horizontally than vertically, and a strip running down the centerline would touch them—try to plan your cheater strips so this happens simultaneously at the bow and stern.

At this point, I run two strips together down the centerline from bow to stern. These two "keel strips" will result in two half-moon shapes that we'll fill in later with strips.

Figure 6-19. *At this point, the strips coming up the side are starting to wrap around to the bottom at the bow. It's now time to think about how you are going to finish the bottom.*

At this point I run strips on either side of the keel. When I use cove-and-bead strips I put the cove on the outside, away from the centerline. Before installing these keel strips, cut off the bead, and bevel the edges as you did the sheer strips.

We'll do the two keel strips one at a time. You need to join the ends of the first keel strip to the strips coming up from the sheerline. Do this in the manner described in the sidebar entitled Fitting Ends of Strips. The only difference is that you don't have a strip to fit against. Fit the first keel strip with its beveled edge aligned with the boat's centerline.

Once you have one end of the keel strip fitted, you need to fit the other end. Secure the strip in place using clamps, with the first end fitted correctly. Mark the length needed and cut the strip a little bit long. Mark the taper similarly to the first end. When you are planing the taper, don't cut quite to the line—make sure you don't cut the strip too short. Try the fit. Concentrate on getting the fit of the taper right first. Worry about the length later. When you get the taper right, check the length. With any luck, it will be too long. In fact, it will probably seem way too long.

With nice even pressure, take one plane cut off the taper. Notice that because of the acute angle of the taper, a little bit of material off the

Fitting Ends of Strips

There is really only one skill that you must learn to make a strip canoe or kayak and that's the ability to fit the end of one strip up against the side of another. Everything else is just placing strips side-by-side.

But you'll need to put a taper on the end of one strip to get it to fit against the side of another—see Figure 6-20. Once you can do this, you'll be able to assemble any pattern of strips. This isn't a hard skill to learn and it's tolerant of mistakes.

The basic process is to mark the required taper, rough it out, clean it up, try the fit, and adjust it until it fits. With a little bit of patience while you're learning, you'll soon become so proficient that it will take less than a minute for each end of the strip.

The first step is to mark the angle of the taper. You'll be laying your new strip parallel to what I call a "side strip," and marking the angle made by

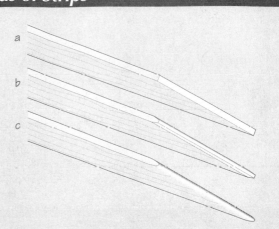

Figure 6-21. *You can quickly put a respectable bead on the end of a strip (a) by first knocking off the corners (b), then removing the corners again (c).*

an "end strip." With plain-edged strips this is easy because what you see is what you get. With cove-and-bead strips, however, you need to account for the invisible hollow of the cove.

Use a straightedge to mark the depth of the cove on the side and end strips. Draw a line ⅛ inch in from the edge of the gap. You can now lay your new strip up against these lines to determine the angle. Lay the new strip parallel to the side strip, with the end aligned with the point

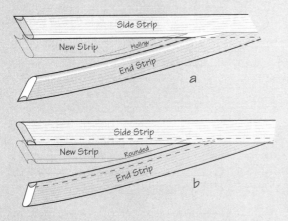

Figure 6-20. *A new strip is placed parallel to the "side" strip, and its end is fitted into the "end" strip. To slide the new strip all the way into the space you'll need to shape the ends to join the edge of the end strip. In case (a) the new strip will need a hollow carved in the end and in case (b) you just need to round the end. It is much easier to round the end than it is to carve a hollow. You will naturally reach case (b) if you start stripping at the sheer with the cove side up. Notice that, because of the cove, the space to be filled in (b) extends into the strips farther than you can see. It helps you draw the extent of this hollow on the strips (see dotted lines) before trying to fit the new strip. Use the drawn on lines as your guides.*

Figure 6-22. *Start fitting a strip by placing it beside your "side" strip with the end aligned with the point of the gap, hidden behind the new strip. Mark where the "end" strip intersects the new strip. If you are using cove-and-bead strips, mark the depth of the cove on the existing strips and align to these marks.*

(Continued)

Fitting Ends of Strips (continued)

Figure 6-23. Draw a line between the end of the strips and the mark made in Figure 6-22.

Figure 6-25. You can get a pretty close fit with a knife.

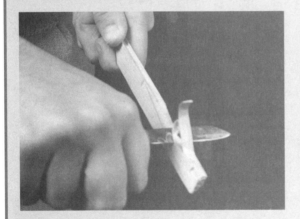

Figure 6-24. Whittle down close to the line made in Figure 6-23.

Figure 6-26. Even out the taper with a block plane. You can either push the plane or pull it. I hold it whichever way makes it easier to see my mark.

where the end strips and the side strips meet. Make a mark on the new strip where the edge of the new strip crosses the side edge of the end strip.

Draw a straight line from the end to this mark. This line defines the taper the strip needs to fit in place. Use your jackknife to trim off most of the excess material, leaving a little wood proud of the line. Clean up to the edge with your block plane. Your plane stroke should run the full length of the taper. This will produce the best, straightest cuts. Avoid short choppy strokes with the plane because they'll produce an uneven

edge. Put a bead on the newly planed edge if you're using cove-and-bead strips.

Now try the fit. If it doesn't go in all the way, and there is a gap at the point or "toe," remove material from the "heel." If the strip goes all the way in place, but there is a gap toward the back, you need to remove material from the toe. Remove the strip and take a couple swipes off the point.

When you try the fit, the strip may touch somewhere in the middle, with gaps at the toe and the heel. In this case the taper may need to be somewhat concave. Remove material in the

Figure 6-27. *At first try, the "heel" is a little tight. Remove some material from the heel and try again.*

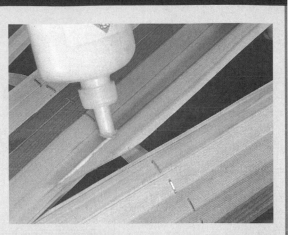

Figure 6-29. *Once you are happy with the fit, apply glue to the end and the side and install the strip.*

Figure 6-28. *You will quickly get a very tight fit like this one.*

middle, using plane strokes that do not run the full length of the taper. When you get it close, use one long stroke with good pressure against the strip to clean up any roughness produced with the short strokes.

By this time you may have figured out that if the strip goes all the way in, touching at the toe and heel, the taper needs to be convex. Remove a little material from the toe and the heel and use one long stroke with just a little pressure to clean up the edge.

Depending on what side of the strip your line is on, you might find it easier to pull the block plane instead of pushing it. You always need to

cut down the line from the thick part of the strip to the narrow point (heel to toe). In order to see the guideline you marked, you may need to hold the strip with the long part going away from you and hold the plane with the front towards you. A block plane is small enough to fit well in your hand whichever way you use it.

All of this fitting will soon take less time than it took me to explain it. You'll soon be able to create a tight joint, ready for gluing, with very little fuss. Once you know how to do this, there's nothing involved in stripping a boat that you can't do, because everything else is just a variation on this theme.

Figure 6-30. *Fitting a keel strip. The procedure is the same as that shown in Figures 6-22 to 6-29, except that you use the centerline on the forms as a guide instead of a "side" strip.*

Figure 6-32. *Beveling a keel strip. Each one will need one side beveled, so you get a tight fit along the centerline.*

taper will make a more significant change in the length of the strip. Make sure that the angle of the taper stays correct as you cut it back. Each time you try the fit for length, double-check that the taper still fits correctly.

When you get the first keel strip fitted, repeat the process for the other keel strip. Check the bevel down the centerline to make sure it's a tight joint. Apply glue to the joint.

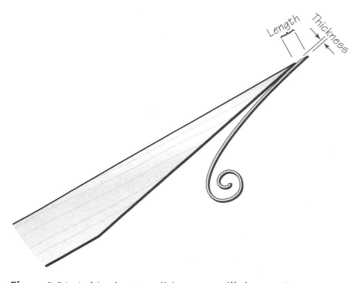

Figure 6-31. *A thin shaving off the taper will shorten the strip more than you might expect, so use very fine cuts when you're shaping a strip for an exact fit.*

You'll need to put some staples across the joint between the forms because the strips will tend to pull away from each other.

You're now left with two bell-shaped areas on the bottom, one on either side of the keel strips. These also need to be filled, of course, and I do it by running strips alternately parallel to the sides and parallel to the keel. I like this pattern because it looks good and because it doesn't create a crease in the skin. If you run your strips all the same way, you'll tend to create a sharp angle in the surface where one strip joins another strip going in a different direction. Careful work can eliminate this crease, but any way you do it will involve about the same amount of fitting, so why not do it in a way that's easy and looks good?

The fitting of the strips proceeds in the same way as the keel strips. Fit one end, then measure the length and fit the other end. This is easier if you're using shorter strips, so fit in one strip that is shorter than the space to fill. Cut the end of this strip with a right angle so that the cut falls on one of the forms. Then fit another strip at the other end. Mark the length where this strip overlaps the

Filling the Bottom and Deck

There are many ways to arrange the strips for the bottom and the deck, and Figure 6-33 shows four of them.

Style (a) is the pattern I typically use. I think it looks nice because the curved strips on the side accent the curves of the bilge or sheer, while the straight strips in the center accent the keel or top of the deck. More importantly, the strips conform well to the shape of the boat. Admittedly, this method requires a lot of joints where the end of one strip hits the side of another but the joints in this style are generally easier to make than the other types. And you'll need two final strips—the hardest kind to fit—whereas some of the other styles require only one. You don't need to worry about these final strips in the deck, though, because the presence of the cockpit means you only have to fit one end of the strip. I feel the nice looks of this layout are worth any slight additional effort.

Style (b) has all the strips parallel to the centerline. This system works well for a V-shaped hull or deck, as long as there is not a lot of curve near the edges. The strips may not be able to conform to a curved chine or the edge of the deck, however. Try laying a strip in a few places to see how well it can conform. In my opinion, this pattern looks best on a kayak with simple lines and not much curvature. It gives a nice straight-ahead and fast look to a deck.

Style (c) is the typical "football" fill pattern used in strip-building many canoes. In this method, one side of the bottom is stripped first, and the strips are permitted to go well beyond the centerline. When the first side is done, the centerline is drawn using a string in the way we marked the center of the strongback. Then, using a framing square as a guide, the excess length of the strips is carved back with a chisel and a block plane. The strips on the unstripped side are put in place using the same method I describe for fitting ends. The advantage of this method is that you need only fit ends for one side of the boat. The disadvantage is that cutting a straight centerline can be difficult, and any mistake will be highlighted since the curve of the strips tends to point your eyes toward the centerline. I feel it's easier to fit each strip individually than it is to cut the long centerline of style (c).

Style (d) avoids the long cut in style (c) by making each end fit in much the same way as style (a) does for each half of the boat. This is a good solution for a flat-bottomed or flat-decked boat, but even shallow V-shapes can make the fitting together difficult.

Any combination of these four styles can be adapted to give any look you want. The choice of pattern will affect the look of the boat. The strips can be used to highlight or camouflage a feature of the shape. I prefer style (a) because it seems to enhance the natural shape of the kayak without drawing attention to the ends of the strips. In the end, all that matters is that you cover the forms with strips.

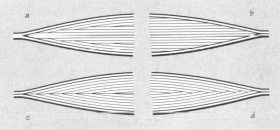

Figure 6-33. *Possible variations for stripping the bottom or deck. What you choose depends on the shape of the boat, the look you want, and how much trouble you are willing to go to. Examples (a) and (c) are good for boats with a V-shaped keel line and an otherwise rounded bottom. Style (b) is good for a V-shaped keel line and otherwise fairly flat bottom. Style (d) is only good when the boat is fairly flat at the keel.*

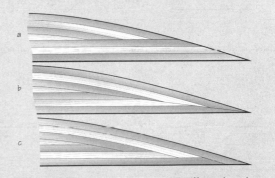

Figure 6-34. *Lining up your joints will tend to draw attention to them and may cause a kink in the surface that's hard to fair out. Example (a) will show up as a fairly abrupt transition. Style (b) will draw your eye to the intersection of the strips. It is also the most difficult to make. Example (c) is easy to make and does not draw your eye.*

Figure 6-35. Making reference marks. When you need to fit both ends of a strip into a space, first get one end to fit well then make a mark on the new strip and the existing adjacent strip, so you can fit the other end without constantly inserting and removing the first end. See also Figure 6-37.

square end of the previous one. When you cut this strip off at a right angle at the mark it should drop into place, making a tight butt joint. If you're using cove-and-bead strips, they will be nestled down into a cove. You will need to flex

Figure 6-36. Plane the taper of the second end of a two-ended strip until it is about right, then try the fit. If it looks good, check the reference marks shown in Figure 6-35 to see if the length is right. Shave down the end until the marks line up.

the strips a little to line up their ends and snap them into place.

If you're using long strips, you need to get the fit of the ends right simultaneously with the length. This can be a little tricky and you'll get tired of installing the strips at both ends and trying the fit. With cove-and-bead strips it can, in any case, take a little bit of wrestling to get the strip in place.

To avoid this wrestling match where you are apt to break something, use a register mark. Fit one end of the strip as usual. Hold the strip in place and, as close to the other end as possible, make a pencil mark across the strip onto the neighboring strip (Figure 6-35). You can now remove the strip and use the register mark to align the strip as you fit the new end. Again, start by making the strip too long and whittle back until the register marks line up.

As the strips get shorter, it gets harder to install them, especially if you're using cove-and-bead strips. The space you need to fit the strip into is smaller than the strip, because the cove extends deep inside the strips already installed. You will need to bend the strip into a bell-shaped curve, with each end lying flat against the forms and the middle bulged up. Sometimes it feels like you need three hands to guide the strip into place. Luckily, the strips are flexible and can withstand some abusive handling.

Watch the shrinking space between the strips. When it gets to be less than three strips wide you need to start planning for the last strip. Lay some scrap strips in the gap to measure. You want the gap smaller than three strips wide but bigger than two strips. If you are using cove-and-bead strips you will need to cut the cove off the second-

Figure 6-37. *Flexing a strip into place. Constantly inserting and removing a strip while you're trying for an accurate fit is difficult and tedious. With cove-and-bead strips, you won't be able to just drop your strip in place. Because of the hidden depth of cove you are fitting the new strip into, the strip will have to be longer than the space you can see. Here, I have inserted one end in place, and by bending the strip I can slide in the other end. If my length is right, it will snap into place.*

strip, make a register mark and start working from the other end. When you get it close, sometimes you can lightly tap it into place with a hammer. It helps to plane it slightly wedge-shaped (narrower on the inside) so that it tightens up when pushed in.

Stripping the Deck

You are now ready to strip the deck, which you do without removing the hull from the forms. If you originally built a pair of boat stands, rotate the stands now, install the webbing and place the kayak right-side-up in the stands. If you've just been using sawhorses, cut some curved cradles from foam, and tape them in place on top of the sawhorses. If you don't have any foam yet, install some vertical posts on either end of the sawhorses. Suspend some carpet, webbing, or rope between the posts, and rest the kayak in the resulting cradle. I have to tell you, though, that this doesn't work as

to-last strip and the bead off the final strip, so you don't need to fit the final strip inside a space bigger than the available gap. When you cut the coves off, make sure the gap for the final strip will be narrower than a strip with both the cove and the bead cut off. If it isn't, you'll just need to fit two more strips instead of one.

The last strip is the hardest. Here's what you do:

Cut a strip a bit longer than the gap and mark the shape of the strip by eye. Mark the length and then measure the width of the gap in several places. Transfer this width to the strip and then connect the marked widths with straight lines. Rough out the shape of the strip a little oversized with a jackknife or saw. Starting at one end, carefully plane the strip to fit, a little bit at a time. Try to push it into place. Plane off the high spots. When you can fit it in all the way to the middle of the

Figure 6-38. *Testing the width of the gap with scraps of strips. When the hole is less than three strips wide, it's time to cut the cove off. See text.*

Figure 6-39. *Laying the final strip over the hole before marking the shape from below.*

even before them, for that matter. Don't do anything special in the area of the hatches when you're stripping. Just ignore the fact that there's to be a hatch when you're done. You don't need to strip all the way over the cockpit, though—just far enough over to ensure that you have enough wood around the edge, and enough to keep the deck fair.

When you're done, take another opportunity to step back and admire what you've achieved. From a pile of thin strips of flexible wood you've created a beautiful boat shape. When you tap on the skin, you're greeted with a solid knock.

The Cockpit Recess

The cockpit recess is an optional detail. It's a small inset area around the cockpit perimeter that creates a transition from the deck to the coaming (Figure 6-50). I include it only in the design for the Guillemot, but you can incorporate it into any design. It's an extra step, but it does make attaching the lip to coaming easier because it reduces the amount of curvature at the front and back of the cockpit. It also looks cool.

Nothing special needs to be done while you're stripping the deck to prepare for making the recess. If the design includes a pattern for a recess, you can transfer the outline after you finish the main stripping of the deck. You don't need both halves of the pattern to mark the outline. Align the centerline of the pattern with the centerline of the deck. Because the deck may have more contour than the pattern can conform to, the pattern will probably not lie flat. Mark it out as best you can (Figure 6-45). It does not need to be too precise. Fair out the curve with a thin strip of wood.

well as foam because the boat tends to swing as you plane and sand during the fairing stage.

Start stripping the deck just as you did the hull, beginning with the strip at the sheer. But here's an important reminder: Do not put glue between this strip and the sheer because this is where the deck and hull will separate when you're done stripping. You can often put in the centerline strips right after the sheer strips, or

Figure 6-40. *Fitting the final closing strip. Start at one end and gradually taper it to fit. Press it in place and mark where it gets too tight. Plane at this point and try again. See text.*

Dealing with Tough Curves

There may be places where the curves of the hull become too severe to force the strips around. Cheater strips help when the curvature is lengthwise, such as where the bow sweeps up, and beveling helps with around-the-hull curvatures like those at the bilges. But if these solutions are not enough, cut the strip in half down its length. This makes a more flexible strip, and one that conforms better around the hull. I often use half-width strips for the sheer and around the bilge (Figure 6-42).

Try to limit the degree of twist in the strips by running them parallel to feature lines. For example if the chine is "hard," that is, sharply curved, don't try to wrap strips across the chine line. It may help to run a strip along the chine before you reach it with the strips coming up from the sheer. Fill the space between the sheer and the chine afterwards.

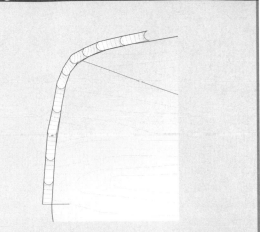

Figure 6-42. *Stripping around the chine is easier with narrow strips. They will conform to the shape better and are easier to bend.*

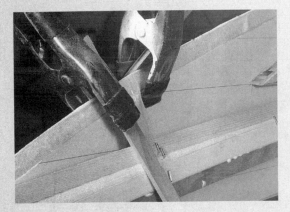

Figure 6-41. *Some strips just don't want to stay where you put them. Here, I'm using a strip and a clamp to apply pressure to a recalcitrant strip.*

Figure 6-43. *With a short, wide boat there can be a lot of bend along the length of the strip. Sometimes it is easier to start a new course of strips with less bend, then go back and fill in the gap.*

Measure the width to make sure it's wide enough for you. If you want a wider or longer cockpit, now is your chance to modify it to your needs.

You are the person handling the saw, so you can choose to make the cockpit any size you want. One person making one of my designs decided he wanted to paddle with his small son, so he cut a 5-foot-long cockpit. If you want

to use a spray skirt, make sure you can find one to fit.

You can use your razor saw to cut the outline. I have found it helps to bend the saw into a curve. This lets you make a nice clean cut with a little care. You can also use a power jigsaw, which is quicker, but it can be difficult cutting through the forms, and you may need to lift it to keep from cutting your strongback in half.

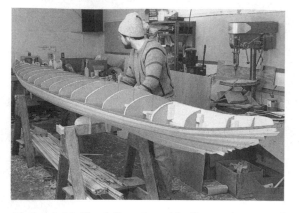

Figure 6-44. *The fully stripped hull turned over and in position for work to start on the deck.*

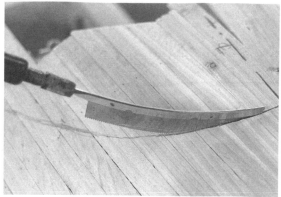

Figure 6-46. *Cutting out the cockpit with a bent razor saw. You can also use a flexible Japanese saw, a coping saw, or a jigsaw.*

Figure 6-45. *Marking out the cockpit (or recess) hole using a pattern of one side of the hole. Flip the pattern over to get the other side symmetrical. Note that I didn't bother to strip all the way across the cockpit.*

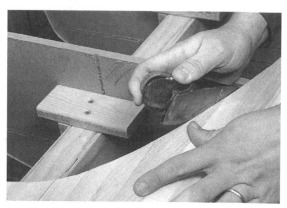

Figure 6-47. *Cleaning up the edge of the cockpit hole with a plane and sandpaper.*

Clean up the edge with a block plane or file when you are done.

You can now break off the top of the forms that you precut and reglued. This will make it easier to work on the cockpit.

Now you need to fill the recess back in, if you're making one. Not all the way, just enough to make the cockpit the size you want. Start at the front of the cutout and cut a triangular piece to fit into the front of the hole. You'll need to bevel the ends to make a tight fit, then apply some glue and insert it in place. Hold it there with some masking tape.

Fit four or five strips, going all the way across the front of the cutout. Tape them in place as required.

Work down each side of the cockpit with pieces that don't go all the way across (Figure 6-49). They just need to reach the edge of the final cockpit outline. Strips 2 inches to 3 inches long will suffice. As you get near the middle of the cockpit, you can use shorter ones. Every four or five strips, put in a strip that spans all the way across. This will help keep the shorter strips from drooping and falling off. Continue down each side until you

Figure 6-48. Starting the cockpit recess with strips that will later be cut back to the finished shape of the cockpit. Staples and tape help hold the pieces in place while the glue dries.

are near the middle. Then repeat the process, starting at the back and working toward the middle.

Where you meet in the middle, you'll need to make a filler strip, possibly a wedge-shaped one. When you're done, find something else to do while the glue dries for about 12 hours.

While these end-glued strips may seem fragile, remember that the strips will be covered

Figure 6-49. Strips for the recess run horizontally across the cockpit. You don't need the strips to go all the way across, although a few strips spanning the gap now and then will help keep the shorter strips from drooping.

in fiberglass and that the final result will be very strong.

You can avoid all the stripping in the recess cutout if you use a piece of 3-mm (⅛-inch) marine plywood. Rough out the shape of the plywood to match the hole, leaving it a little oversized. Make a 6-inch hole in the middle, big enough to fit your hand in. Bend the plywood into place, reach through the hole and mark the inside edge of the cutout. Use a block plane to trim back toward this line. Try the fit occasionally so you get a snug fit in the middle. Plane around toward the ends gradually. Work for a snug fit all the way around. Before you glue it in place take the opportunity to cut out the shape of the cockpit. Apply glue around the edge and secure it in place with masking tape or strapping tape.

The Cockpit Coaming

Draw the outline of the cockpit using the design template. Cut the recess out in the same way as you did the cockpit cutout (Figure 6-50). Now it's time to make the vertical part of the coaming.

Cut a basketful of 2-inch-long strips. You'll need about 125 cove-and-bead strips per cockpit, so use all the short strips left over from stripping the boat. Cut them on a bandsaw or table saw or in a miter box with a hand saw. If you use two different colors you can alternate strips for a nice pattern (Figure 6-51).

Start at the forward end of the cockpit. Plane the bead off two strips and bevel them so they fit together on either side of the centerline. Put a little bit of yellow glue on the vertical joint and a bead of hot-melt glue near the bottom of the outside face. Press the strips into the

Figure 6-50. The final recess—just a small perimeter around the actual cockpit hole. In this case, I fiberglassed before cutting out the hole, but you don't need to do this.

inner edge of the cockpit hole. The hot-melt glue will grab quickly, so you can let go and install the next strips with yellow glue between the strips, and hot-melt holding them in place, too. You can use hot-melt between the strips as well, but it tends to set quickly so you need to line them up carefully. Try to keep the strips vertical as you proceed towards the middle of the cockpit. The strips should protrude downwards past the deck slightly at their bottom ends.

Figure 6-51. Short strips glued in vertically form the cockpit coaming.

Don't go all the way around. Stop in the middle, and then start again from the back. Now work toward the middle again. You will need to fit a wedge-shaped strip into the final gap.

After the glue dries, go back and clean it up. You won't be able to sand the hot-melt glue, so cut it out with a knife. Leave the top edge rough until the coaming lip has been installed.

For kayaks without a lot of contour around the cockpit, such as the Great Auk and the Guillemot Double, you can make the vertical part of the coaming with laminated hardwood. Cut out a plywood form, using the cockpit pattern. Half-inch or thicker plywood will work well. Drill a series of large clamping holes around the edge. Cut some 1/8-inch-thick by 2-inch-wide veneer of ash or some other flexible hardwood. You will need four pieces each about 6 inches longer than half the circumference of the cockpit. Mix up a small amount of epoxy. Paint a thin coat on two pieces of veneer. Mix some silica into the epoxy to create a mayonnaise-consistency glue. By this time the thin coat on the wood should have soaked in somewhat.

Apply an even coat of the thickened glue and stick the two veneers together. Starting at one end of the form, clamp the veneer in place. Leave a couple inches hanging out beyond the end. Carefully bend the veneer around the form, clamping as you go. After the glue cures, remove the result from the forms. Repeat this process for the other side.

You now have two pieces that must be fitted into the cockpit hole. The pieces won't fit perfectly at first because they need to be trimmed to length and twisted some to match the contours of the deck. Glue them in place with yellow glue, using tape and strips sprung across the

Figure 6-52. The last strip in the coaming is tapered, so it wedges into place.

opening to hold them while the glue dries. Don't worry about the veneer hanging down below the deck, because you'll trim it later. Just make sure you leave at least 1 inch above the deck all the way around.

There is yet another way to make the coaming, but it's best done after you've fiberglassed the outside of the deck. I describe it here just to keep it near the other cockpit methods. Using ¼-inch plywood, you can cut a series of rings the shape of the cockpit—enough for four or

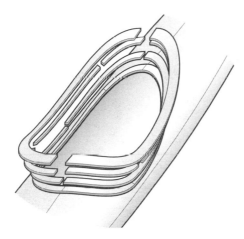

Figure 6-53. Plywood laminations make an alternative cockpit coaming. Don't cut complete rings because this will waste material. Use a series of ring segments with staggered joints. The top ring, which forms the lip, will be wider than the others, and should be made of one or two pieces, no more.

five layers, each about ½ inch wide, plus one or two more layers about 1 inch to 1½ inches wide for the top lip. This is installed after the deck has been glassed. The layers are glued, stacked, and clamped together around the cockpit hole. Be sure to give the underside of the cockpit lip a good coat of epoxy to protect it from water. Clean up any glue that oozes out.

After the glue dries, clean up any remaining drips and file and sand the surfaces smooth. I have a philosophical problem with this method because it's very wasteful of wood, but it's used to good effect on many plywood-built kayaks and there is no reason why it can't be used as a somewhat easier solution on a strip-built kayak.

Finishing the Ends

You can leave the ends of the hull just as they are. When you start fairing out the hull, plane off the ends of the strips so they're flush on both sides. If there are any gaps where you didn't fit the strips quite right, fill them with resin thickened with wood flour. If you want a neater look, install a stem piece.

The Stem Piece

You can get rid of any sloppiness at the ends by planing it off, then laminating on some hardwood. This makes an attractive detail. Plane off

Figure 6-54. The finger joint used at the ends may look a little messy. Plane around it to clean it up a little bit before installing a stem piece.

Figure 6-55. *Plane the rough ends of the strips on the bow and stern to a smooth, fair surface.*

Figure 6-56. *Packing tape holds the laminated hardwood strips in place while the glue dries. The strips will form a stem piece. As you can see, ash will bend around a very tight curve.*

the sharp edge of the bow and stern to give a flat edge that is perpendicular to the centerline of the boat (Figure 6-55). Set the blade of your block plane fairly deep so it cuts quickly, but back it off as you finish up. Plane until the edge is about ³/₈ inch to ¹/₂ inch wide. Make a nice fair curve coming from the keel all the way to the tip. On the double kayak you may want to go around up onto the deck.

Some layers of hardwood such as ash will be laminated onto this edge. Cut some hardwood ¹/₁₆ inch to ¹/₈ inch thick, and ¹/₂ inch wide, long enough to cover the edge. Use carpenter's glue to attach the laminations. Apply some glue to the edge and glue together the layers of hardwood strips (The exact number of layers is your call, but two or three is usually enough.) While the glue is still wet, tape the stack of strips to the end, starting at the keel. Use packing tape to hold the hardwood in place as you gradually bend it down around the end. Keep the strips centered on the edge as you go. Gradual, even pressure can bend ash around an amazingly tight radius. If you're having trouble coaxing the bend, and you fear you'll break the strips, use a heat gun or a hot hair drier to heat the wood. The hot wood will be more flexible.

If you want, you can use a solid piece of wood instead of a lamination. Cut and plane a piece of wood to match the planed curve of the stem. Glue it in place, using tape to hold it. This system works just as well as the lamination method above but requires more care to get the fit tight.

Almost all the wood is now in place for the finished boat. Standing back, you can now fully see its shape. Now I have to tell you that I'm

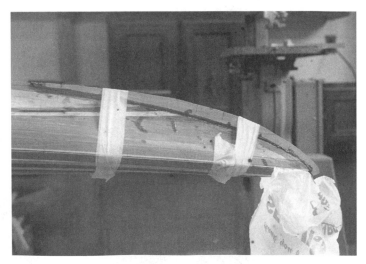

Figure 6-57. *Instead of laminating on multiple thin layers, as depicted in Figure 6-56, you can glue on a solid piece of wood cut to fit.*

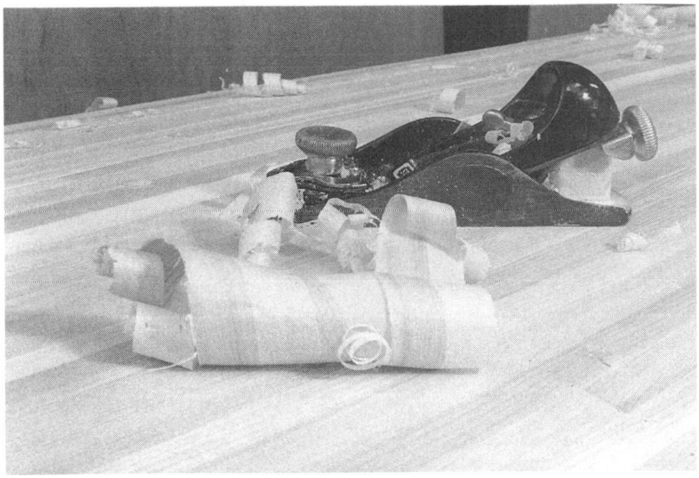

Figure 6-58. *A good sharp plane makes quick work of fairing the boat. If it's properly set up and sharpened, you can pull off paper-thin strips of wood.*

the transformation even more. Don't worry, the feeling will pass.

Fairing

There are few things more satisfying than pushing a sharp plane across a section of cedar. A parchment-like curl of wood coils out of the plane, leaving a smooth surface where there was once rough wood. The sweet scent of cedar is released with each stroke. Some consider fairing the hull an onerous task, but if you're properly equipped with the right hand tools, it can be downright exhilarating.

never completely satisfied at this point. The boat looks rough. There are sharp angles between some of the strips. The boat is full of staples. The wood is dull. There may be drips of glue. When it comes right down to it, the boat doesn't look very beautiful. Ugly may be too strong a word, but it may occur to you. This is a good mood for starting the next task because it will highlight

Removing Staples

First you need to remove the staples. This is a somewhat tedious job, but with the right tools it can go quickly. A staple remover will make quick work of the average staple and you can probably remove all the staples in an hour or two. You can use a screwdriver by inserting it under one side of the staple and prying it up, but use a scrap of wood to protect the boat from dents. Often a screwdriver will leave one leg of the staple stuck in the form. A pair of pliers will remove the remaining leg. Keep a cup handy to collect all the staples your remove.

If you used some nails, a standard claw hammer will pull them. Again protect the wood. Try to pull the nail out straight, so you don't get an elongated hole.

Don't remove all the staples right away, though. Leave a row of staples along the sheerline to hold everything in place while you're doing the initial planing. Pull them out later when you need to fair the sheer region. If you're going to leave the boat for a while without work-

Figure 6-59. *Before you can plane, you must get rid of the staples. Here, Cathy uses a heavy-duty office staple remover. It is quick and easy. (However, there are a lot of staples.) You can also use a screwdriver, pliers, or the blade of a scraper.*

ing on it, run a few staples back in, to keep the boat from deforming. If it does deform, bend it back in shape and staple it there for a while.

Just removing the staples will improve the looks of your boat. It's not a waste of time to take a seat now and admire your work for a while. Call it "bonding time." You're building a relationship with your creation. Get a feeling for the inherent strength of what you're building so you won't be afraid to put it in the water. Don't lose sight of the fact that it's a boat and it will not be completely happy until it is out on the water.

Planing

If you didn't overdo the glue, you won't need to scrape much. Use a paint scraper to remove the gross drips (Figure 6-60). This will make the planing easier.

I'm never completely satisfied with the shape of the boat until I start planing it. You'll find that you can remove a lot of the most blatant mistakes in stripping by planing off the high spots, and the rough surface of the strips quickly disappears in thin curls of wood. The sharp lines between the strips soon blend into a pleasingly smooth surface.

Figure 6-60. *A paint scraper removes hardened drips of glue.*

Planing the outside. A block plane is the best tool for most of this job. Adjust the blade to be quite shallow and adjust the gap in front of the blade to be quite small. With nice long strokes, push the plane in the same direction as the strips. Hold the plane at an angle to the direction of motion, with one hand guiding on the front knob and the other pushing from behind. If the blade grabs wood and tears it, plane the other way. You may need to retract the blade and/or close up the gap in front. If you still have problems, sharpen the blade.

The uneven surface of strips that are not lined up perfectly can be cleaned up quickly by cutting diagonally across the strips. Hold the plane parallel to the strips and push it at about a 45-degree angle.

A large jack plane can help fair large, basically flat areas. The intent is to remove the high spots. Plane only enough to touch everywhere once. Plane until the rough-sawed surface of the wood is removed. Don't get stuck in one place. Move around and work gradually on the whole boat.

Planing concave regions. The flat bottom of a standard block plane can only smooth flat or convex surfaces. Concave regions can be hard to smooth. The modified plane I described in Chapter 3, Tools and Materials, does a good job of cleaning up sections that the block plane can't reach. It's especially good for the hollow sections near the bow of the hull. Plane in the direction of least curvature, which is not necessarily parallel with the strips. Any remaining unevenness will be removed by sanding.

A spokeshave is particularly good for smoothing the upsweep on the bow and stern of the deck. The short foot of the spokeshave permits smoothing of quite tight curves, and the handles on the sides of the tool also give good control on sharp convex surfaces such as the chine. You can either push it or pull it, depending on the grain and how

Figure 6-61. Holding the plane somewhat diagonally for an easier cut. Two hands on the tool will help keep it from "chattering."

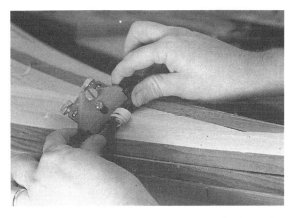

Figure 6-62. A spokeshave works well where the boat is highly rounded or where there are concave curves. The bow and stern of the Guillemot are both rounded and concave.

you can most easily reach the part you want to smooth. Like the plane, it's easier to cut with the shave held at an angle to the direction of motion. If the tool chatters and skips, hold it at a sharper angle, push down more, or retract the blade.

The planing is your first chance to fair out the boat. It does much quicker work than sanding. Don't overdo it, but careful work now will save time later. If you are worried about the plane being too aggressive, adjust it to a shallower cut. It will do a better job, with more control, than trying to do the fairing with a power sander.

Filling

After planing, but before sanding, it's time to go back and fill any gaps between strips. I know, if you did a perfect job this wouldn't be necessary, but get real. Everyone is entitled to mistakes and it really isn't a big deal.

Mix up some dookie schmutz of epoxy and sanding dust. If you don't have good clean sanding dust you can buy wood flour. If you have a sander with a dust collector, do some initial sanding on the boat to get some matching dust. The dust darkens in the epoxy, so you might want to mix in some lighter-colored material for a better match. Make a putty of peanut-butter consistency. Force the mixture into any cracks

Figure 6-63. If you do a good job with your plane, you won't have much sanding left to do.

Figure 6-64. Before you finish fairing, you can mix up some resin with sanding dust to fill any large gaps between strips.

with a putty knife. Press the putty into the cracks by pulling the knife flat across the seam. Clean up the excess by drawing the knife vertically down the length of the seam.

Let the putty cure. Clean up the excess with a plane. The putty is harder than the surrounding wood and if you were to try to sand it, you'd find that the sandpaper would remove the wood faster than it would the cured putty, leaving a high spot.

Big gaps can be better hidden with slivers of wood. Whittle down a wood scrap so it can be jammed into the hole. You can make a plug that will expand to fill a gap by first squeezing it flat with pliers or rolling it with a screwdriver handle. When you wet the compressed wood with glue it will expand back to its original thickness. Don't try to make the filler piece flush with the surface. Leave it standing a little proud and sand it smooth when the glue dries. Pick wood that nearly matches the color of the surrounding strips.

Sanding

After planing and filling comes sanding. For most people, this is the least enjoyable part of the project, but I kind of enjoy it. If you did a good job with the planes, sanding will go quickly. The planing will leave a smooth surface with some slight sharp corners between plane strokes. Sanding will easily knock the tops off these corners. The boat transforms from a rough form to a sleek kayak. Be sure to wear a dust mask while sanding, especially when you're using power tools.

Sanding the outside. The first sanding device I use is a hand tool. The fairing board is a long flexible sanding block that bridges high spots, removing the tops first. Use long sweeping strokes. Rock the sander over the chine, applying even pressure as you move from the bottom to the side. Run your hand over the surface to feel for irregularities and carefully work on those areas that need it. Feel free to sand in any direction initially. A coarse sandpaper, such as 60 grit, will cut easily for the initial sanding.

Eventually you must remove the cross-grain scratches by sanding only parallel to the grain with a small hand block. The fairing sander does not get into hollows but you can cut a curved bottom on a sanding block to finish concave sections. A random orbital sander will perform most of the work of a small hand-sanding block, and more quickly.

Don't use a disk sander in a drill unless it's all you have. A disk sander can be hard to control, and it will cut quickly. If you catch an edge, it will make a divot that can only be eliminated by removing a lot of surrounding wood. I only use a disk sander for the most stubborn hollows, and then only with great care, leaving the finishing for another tool.

A random orbital sander is much easier to control than a disk sander. Hold the face of the sander flat on the wood and keep it moving around. Stroking lengthwise will fair better than moving the sander across the boat. This will keep you from creating an unwanted hollow

Figure 6-65. One of my strips ended up too low. I could plane down all the surrounding wood to the same level, but it's better and easier to fit a piece into the hollow. It will be sanded flush, and no one will ever know I screwed up.

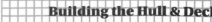

Figure 6-66. The long board, or fairing sander, is the most effective sanding tool. After planing, it will make quick work of any remaining high spots.

and let the dust get out from under the tool. Change the paper often, otherwise it will get dull and become less effective. Dull sandpaper will raise the grain by working faster on the softer parts of the wood.

Start out with a stiff backing pad and 80-grit sandpaper. For hollows, you can concentrate the pressure slightly on one side of the sander. Again feel the boat as you go, sensing irregularities. Don't be afraid of using your block plane to eliminate the worst.

Make sure you hit the whole surface with the sandpaper. Planed surfaces will show up as a slightly different color on the finished boat.

Figure 6-67. When sanding around a corner with the fairing sander, rock the board so you don't get a flat spot.

When you have done the whole boat with 80-grit, use 100-grit to reduce the scratches. Finish up with 120-grit sandpaper on a flexible pad. You don't need to go beyond 120-grit. This slightly rough surface will be good for the epoxy to bond to.

Incidentally, be careful not to sand all the way through the boat. It can happen, and if it does, swear and jump up and down, then sit down and sulk for a while. I don't suggest moaning, as it may attract the unwanted attention of the neighborhood tomcat. After you've gotten your frustration out of your system, carve a piece of matching wood to fit tightly on the back side of the hole. Glue the piece in place, and when it dries sand it smooth. Nobody will ever know. The mistake is no reason to have kittens.

Rounding the ends. Don't leave the bow and stern too sharp. The fiberglass will have a hard time wrapping around anything less than a 1/4-inch-diameter corner. Plane and sand the bow and stern to a nice round section.

Wetting down. Before you do the final sanding job, use a slightly damp rag to wet down the wood strips. This will swell and raise dimples created during building. Don't leave any water standing on the wood because you don't want to loosen up the glue holding the boat together.

Wetting the boat down is very satisfying because it brings out the true color of the boat. It is also a good way to highlight places you missed while fairing.

Sanding the coaming. This can be a little tricky because it's hard to get a good stroke on the vertical part. You can rip some thin strips of sandpaper, stick them to a length of fiber tape and pull them back and forth around the coaming. A power detail sander with an oscillating triangular sanding pad can also get into the hard-to-reach corner.

Smoothing the inside. Don't sand the inside until you have glassed the outside. This will make the skin strong enough to handle rough

Figure 6-68. Plane the inside so there are no steps between strips. *You don't need to be as neat here as on the outside, but a fair surface will end up stronger.*

treatment. One advantage of strip-building a kayak, compared with building a canoe, is that you don't have to do as fine a finish job on the inside of a kayak.

Plane down the high spots and sand vigorously with coarse paper. You don't want to sand right through, but you also don't want to leave big steps between strips because they tend to trap air under the fiberglass, which is hard to get rid of. You might want to do a finer job in the cockpit area for cosmetic purposes, but epoxy bonds better to a coarsely sanded surface. You won't need a better excuse to stop sanding at this point.

Around the underside of the cockpit, you'll need to trim off the excess strips or veneer hanging below the deck. This can be accomplished with a coping saw, rasp, or disk sander. Sand the coaming even with the underside of the deck and put a nice radius on the corner. Use a plane and sandpaper to clean up the inside of the coaming.

If you need to, you can make up some dookie schmutz to fill gaps on the inside. If you are filling gaps where they will be seen, do it before you finish sanding. If you are filling in mistakes up in the ends where they will not be visible, do it just before glassing. Clean up the excess putty so you can apply the glass right over the still-wet dookie schmutz.

All the planing and sanding required to fair out the boat is tedious to some people. This is understandable. It can be tedious. But with a good sharp plane and plenty of sharp sandpaper, it does not need to take very long. The transformation from the rough staple-ridden strips to the smooth fine shape after fairing is well worth the effort. Take all the time you need to make the boat look good, but don't become obsessed.

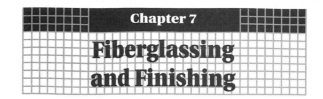
Many builders are daunted by the idea of epoxy and fiberglass. Most of the fears are a result of horror stories passed down by people who used polyester resin. In one way, polyester is easier to deal with because you don't need to worry about mixing ratios. But the stuff smells terrible and the imprecise measurement of catalyst means you are never sure when the mix is going to kick off and start hardening. Modern epoxy systems come with good measuring tools and you know one batch is going to react pretty much like the previous batch.

Fiberglassing

If you start out with a slow-curing resin and mix small batches, you won't have to feel rushed when you're using epoxy, and you'll be able to do a methodical and controlled job. When mixed epoxy (or polyester) is concentrated in a container, the heat of the chemical reaction accelerates the curing process. But if you use a shallow pan that lets the heat escape, and if you quickly spread most of the mix in a thin coat on the boat, you'll be left with plenty of time to get the details right.

Epoxy Sealer Coat

Before removing the deck from the forms, put a sealer coat of resin over it. If you're using a viscous epoxy, thin it down with 10 percent of epoxy thinner (use what is recommended by the manufacturer) or use a less viscous epoxy like some of the newer systems that are becoming available. If you're using polyester, thin it with acetone or toluol.

This sealer coat is not strictly necessary but it will make the deck stronger if you want to take it off while you're working on the hull. You could just carefully lift the deck off and put it aside, or you could leave the deck on while you work on the hull and put some wax paper through the sheer strips to keep drips off the outside of the deck. The sealer coat will also limit the amount of resin the wood absorbs when you apply the glass. Using a sealer coat is the safer way to go, although it involves more steps.

Prepare for epoxying by putting on protective clothing. See the appendix on safety before getting up to your elbows in epoxy. With proper handling, epoxy is safe, but it's by no means benign, so be careful working with it. Wear protective clothing and gloves. Under no circumstances should you allow uncured epoxy to contact your skin. Work in a well-ventilated space and wear an organic respirator.

Figure 7-1. *Protecting the deck while the hull is glassed. You can carefully remove the deck from the forms while you glass the hull, or you can tuck wax paper between the sheer strips to protect the deck from drips, as shown here.*

Mix up about one cup of resin to begin with. Spread the sealer coat with a roller, or a squeegee, or a cheap bristle brush. Some rollers lose their fuzz while rolling, and if the fuzz is pink it can be annoying. If it's white you probably won't see it when the boat is done. Cheap bristle brushes or "chip" brushes also lose their bristles but you probably won't see them either. I like using squeegees because they're quick and produce a thin even coat. Spread the resin over the whole hull, mixing more as required.

If you use the pumps that come with most epoxy systems, you'll find that one cup will be 3 or 4 pumps each of resin and hardener. Although these pumps are usually pretty accurate, you should pump into a calibrated cup, just in case the pump "burps." It's important that you get the mix ratio correct for the brand of epoxy you are using, and a burp or mispump may result in an inaccurate measurement that can throw off the ratio. If that happens, you should discard the mixed batch. By pumping into a calibrated cup, you'll be able to determine how much more you need without wasting any.

After the sealer coat has cured, pop the deck off the forms and put it aside. You may need to pull a razor saw along the seam at the sheerline to cut through any resin and glue that found its way there. Flip the boat over and put a sealer coat on the hull.

Let's pause here to note that most epoxies suffer from "amine blush." This is a result of the chemical reaction that hardens the epoxy. Epoxy will not stick to a previous layer of epoxy affected by blush, but luckily the blush is water-soluble. Wipe down the hardened sealer coat with a wet towel and scrub it with a green kitchen pot scrubber. Even epoxy without blush should be roughed up before you apply new layers of epoxy—it's best to sand cured epoxy to provide a scratched surface the next coat can bond to mechanically. The best bond is a chemical bond, which can be made if the epoxy has not yet cured completely. If you work fast and can apply the next layer of epoxy or fiberglass within 24 to 72 hours, you can usually avoid amine blush and the need to sand. Read the instructions on your epoxy for guidance. If you're in doubt, give

the boat a quick sanding to remove the surface gloss.

Preparing the Cloth

Set aside at least half a day to do the fiberglassing. Get all your materials and tools ready. Have mixing pots and stirring sticks, scissors, and squeegees close at hand. Although you don't need to rush the job, you don't want to stop midway.

Roll the glass out over the hull. Drape it diagonally so the length of the boat spans the width of the cloth. Let it hang over the edge and trim off the excess a little beyond the sheerline. I usually use a couple of layers of glass on the bottom, typically one layer over the whole bottom and another layer between the chines. You

Figure 7-2. *Fiberglass starts out white, but the resin will make it become clear. The result will be strong and beautiful.*

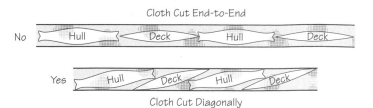

Figure 7-3. *The cloth roll is usually more than wide enough to cover the hull or deck in one piece. Avoid rolling the fiberglass out straight on the boat, as shown in the top illustration. Instead lay it diagonally—starting with the bow near one edge and finishing at the stern near the other edge—so you can nestle the pieces next to each other. This will save a lot of material and, because the cloth will be aligned on the bias, it will wrap around sharp corners more easily.*

may be able to use the scrap cut off the side of the first layer. Lay the second layer of glass on the bottom and neatly trim the edges to follow the chines. Use a pair of old scissors to cut the fiberglass. Several strips of bias-cut (diagonally-cut) cloth laid up on the bow and stern will provide for abrasion protection when beaching.

I usually stack the smaller pieces of fiberglass on the outside. Sanding would be easier with the smaller layer under the bigger layer, but the layup will be stronger with the smaller layer on top. A sharp transition in the thickness of the fiberglass can cause it to crack with hard use. By putting the smallest piece on the outside, you're able to feather the edge to create a gradual transition (Figure 7-5). With the larger piece on the outside, you would need to sand through the outer layer of glass to create the smooth transition, and then you'd be left without a continuous piece of glass covering the bottom.

If the boat has hard chines and you do a neat job of trimming the smaller piece, the edge will disappear in the chine. In this case, little sanding will be needed to smooth the transition, so the smaller layer can probably be laid under the larger layer without causing problems. But if a layer ends in a rather flat section there will be a noticeable step in thickness. In this case it's probably better that the smaller layer be laid on top of the bigger one. You could let the epoxy cure between layers and put on the smallest piece first and feather the edges when

the epoxy cures, and while this would save sanding later, it's difficult to keep from sanding too much into the raw wood. I don't recommend this method.

Wetting Out the Cloth

I used to wet out the glass one layer at a time. This reduced the amount of air trapped in the layup. However, if you let the epoxy cure fully you have to sand between the layers and clean off any amine blush, so I now wet out all the layers at once with a low-viscosity epoxy.

However you choose to lay out the glass, the wetting-out is accomplished in the same way. Lay out the glass and smooth it with a brush. If you have a drafting brush, it will work well, otherwise a clean paintbrush will do. Don't use your hand, because you may catch a wrinkle and mess up the weave, causing a blemish.

Pour a puddle of resin in the middle of the boat. Move the puddle with a squeegee, working from the middle toward the ends and sides. Hold the squeegee at about a 45-degree angle to move the resin quickly. Don't try to wet it out completely yet, just keep moving. The fiberglass will soak up the resin and become clear over about a minute or so. Hold the squeegee nearly vertical to move resin from wet to dry areas. Apply the resin to a large area and come back later to the areas that weren't wet out completely.

If you're using a fast-curing resin such as polyester, you have to move quickly. You don't want incompletely wet-out regions to start setting up. Use a bristle brush or roller to apply more resin as required. Don't apply so much resin that you can't see the weave. The cloth should appear wet but not glossy. You don't want the glass floating in resin, you want it tight to the wood. If you're doing one layer at a time you can apply the next precut layer now, or wait for the epoxy to harden.

On the sides, where the glass is vertical, it can be hard to get resin on without spilling a lot. Start out with a line of resin on the flat part

Glassing Schedule

Much of the durability of the finished kayak is a function of how much glass you lay on it. The trade-off for an indestructible boat is weight. More glass will make a more rugged boat, but additional glass means additional weight. Weight can be saved by careful planning of where you lay the fiberglass.

Obviously the deck is not going to see as much abuse as the hull, so you may want to use lighter glass on the deck. The keel at the bow and stern are going to take the most punishment, and you'll want some extra protection here. You may feel that the keel near the bow needs more protection than the stern because that is what will hit things first, but I've found the stern gets more wear because when I pull the boat up on a beach I usually drag the stern.

As we've already seen, the glass will provide the most strength from impact on the inside, where it's in tension. Glass on the outside provides abrasion resistance and protection from sharp objects. A simple lightweight layup consists of one layer of 4-ounce fiberglass everywhere.

This can be beefed up by substituting a layer of 6-ounce fiberglass on the inside of the hull. Extra glass around the cockpit strengthens this area for lifting the boat, and side-to-side ribs of glass behind the cockpit strengthen the deck to take your weight while you get in the boat.

One layer of 6-ounce everywhere, with some added abrasion

resistance on the bottom, is a good standard layup. Pads of glass inside, under your feet, protect the hull from wear, and a patch under the seat provides extra strength where your weight is concentrated. This standard layup will withstand a lot of abuse.

An expedition layup will have further protection on the bottom and extra reinforcement around the cockpit. For a super-heavy-duty layup, use 10-ounce fiberglass where the most strength is needed. You won't end up with a boat that's too heavy.

The glassing plan should be varied to fit your needs. If you tend to climb up the back deck as a self-rescue technique, you may want to reinforce that area. If you're trying to save every ounce you can, use lighter glass at the ends of the deck where less strength is needed. Exotic materials can be used where extra strength or less weight is required, and you know exactly what you want, but if you're not sure what you need, start with the standard layup, and you won't be too far off.

Figure 7-4. The fiberglass reinforcement you choose depends on the boat's intended use. Heavier-weight fiberglass, or more layers, means a heavier boat, and there is not much way around it. Try putting the fiberglass where it will do the most good, as shown here. Strategic points are the keel at the bow and stern, under the seat, and the deck behind the seat.

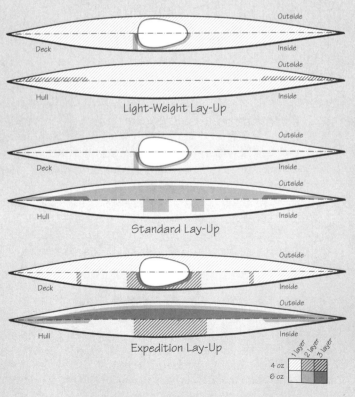

Light-Weight Lay-Up

Standard Lay-Up

Expedition Lay-Up

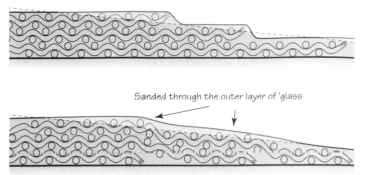

Sanded through the outer layer of 'glass

Figure 7-5. The strength of fiberglass lies in the long fibers. If these fibers are broken, much of the strength is lost. By laying smaller layers of glass on the outside you are less likely to sand into the fibers and reduce the strength.

above the chine. With an even pressure on the squeegee, pull the resin down over the chine and onto the sides. On a boat with hard chines you will have a tendency to apply more pressure at the chine and less below. Avoid this by keeping the squeegee at a constant angle relative to the surface. A steeper angle will move (and remove) more resin. Do not force resin into the glass, let it soak in naturally so as to reduce the amount of air trapped in the glass.

Figure 7-6. Use a clean dry paintbrush or a draftsman's brush to smooth out any wrinkles in the dry fiberglass. Do not use your hand because you could catch a wrinkle and make a permanent crease.

Figure 7-7. Mix up a small amount of resin and pour it out onto the fiberglass. An old bleach bottle with the side cut out makes a good mixing container. Incidentally, I should be wearing a respirator. Just because I'm stupid doesn't mean you should be.

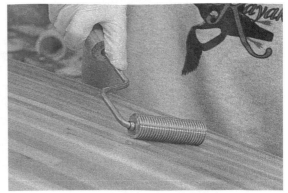

Figure 7-9. Using a grooved bubble roller to force bubbles to the surface and push the cloth down tight against the wood. Don't push too hard, as the roller can damage the fibers of the cloth.

Figure 7-8. Use a squeegee to move around the puddle made in Figure 7-7. Work quickly, but don't press very hard. Just try to move any wet spots to the nearest dry spot. See that container sitting there? It's a mistake. I'd be really annoyed if it had some wood chips stuck to the bottom. Keep the fiberglass clean. Don't put anything on top of it that might be dirty.

Getting the glass to lie flat at the bow and stern can be a pain. The cloth may need to be cut back along the centerline. The two halves may then be folded over the edge. Lay some bias-cut strips over the ends and part-way up the keel. The bias-cut fiberglass will lie more easily over the sharp angle and hold everything in place.

Getting Rid of Bubbles

Sometimes it just isn't possible to get rid of all the air bubbles, especially at the bow and stern, but bubbles with several layers of glass over them are not really a problem. If you find them offensive, sand down into them and feather the edges. Cut a piece of glass the size of the sanded area, and several smaller pieces, to bring the sanded area up to the same number of thicknesses of glass as the surrounding area. Lay these pieces down in order, largest to smallest.

Small bubbles in the glass can often be removed with a bubble roller. This is a specialized fiberglassing tool that looks like a small paint roller with grooves on it. Rolling the wet glass pushes it tight against the wood and forces resin and air to the surface. Using the bubble roller before squeegeeing off the excess resin will help produce a slightly lighter boat, but the kayak will be fine if you don't have a roller.

After you have wet out the whole surface, go back and even out the resin. Check for places you missed. Use a brush to dab on a little extra resin. After you made certain everything has been wet out you need to remove the excess resin.

Removing Excess Resin

With the squeegee held at a relatively high angle, pull the resin from the middle to the sides. Any excess resin should be scraped off and put in a waste cup. Don't press too hard. You don't want to starve the glass. The weave should look wet but not shiny, and it shouldn't appear

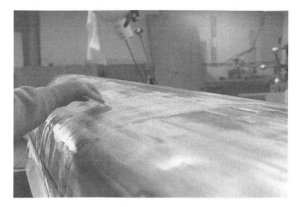

Figure 7-10. *Removing excess resin after the fiberglass has been completely wet out. You want the cloth to have an even, "dry" look, like the part I'm working on in the middle, with no shiny wet spots like those in the foreground. Scrape with an even gentle pressure, pulling from the center to the sides. Deposit the resin you remove into a cup and throw it away.*

whitish, which indicates resin starvation. If you are pressing too hard, white spots will appear on top of the weave. To fix this, move resin back in from an area that has excess.

Wait about an hour. If you didn't apply a sealer coat, some places in the glass will be starved of resin because the wood has soaked it up. Apply more resin to fill the dry spots. Squeegee off the excess.

The Next Coat

Let the epoxy cure until it is no longer sticky, but still a little soft. You want to fill the weave with more epoxy before the first coat of resin has completely cured. On a hot day, this may only be a couple hours after you applied it, but overnight is a typical period. Apply an even coat of resin with a paint roller. To remove any surface bubbles on the resin, "tip off" this fill coat by wiping the surface with a dry foam brush, or a section of paint roller stapled to a stick.

Leave the hull on the forms for several days while the resin is curing. Trim the excess glass that hangs off the edge with a sharp jackknife while the resin is still a little soft.

You can now get a good idea what the finished boat is going to look like. The resin brings out the color of the wood and the boat really glows. It has not yet achieved its final luster, though. It will look even better after varnishing.

Remove the hull from the forms by lifting at one end. You might need to break it free by pulling the sides away from the forms before starting the lift. Carefully place the hull aside.

Glassing the Deck

The rest of the deck goes the same way as the hull, except for the cockpit area. Lay the glass over the deck and trim it a little oversized. Cut a slit into the middle of the cockpit area, approximately down the centerline so it extends slightly beyond the outside of the coaming. Make a couple of diagonal cuts wherever the coaming has tight curves. Also extend these cuts slightly beyond the coaming.

Start wetting out the fiberglass around the cockpit and move toward the ends. If you have trouble making the fiberglass lie flat around the cockpit, make a cut through the fiberglass at the side of the cockpit all the way from the sheer to the cockpit hole. Overlap the two ends to remove any slack. When you are done, make sure there is glass all the way up the outside of the cockpit coaming.

Glassing the Coaming

The coaming can take a lot of strain when you enter or lift the boat. To ensure a strong joint between the coaming and deck I create a "fillet" to make the angle between the two less abrupt. I make the fillet by laying several strands of glass yarn or roving into the joint. This creates a nearly clear fillet. An easier method is to mix up some dookie schmutz and use a Popsicle stick, gloved thumb, or a rounded stick to make a $1/2$-inch-wide, rounded fill in the corner. The dookie schmutz should be mixed to a natural color, using wood flour so that it matches the surrounding wood as closely as possible. Carefully clean up any excess.

Temperature and Epoxy

Most epoxies are formulated to be used at a "room" temperature about 70°F (20°C). At this temperature, the resin will typically have a pot life of about 15 minutes and it will take a couple of hours to harden.

But for many people, building a kayak is a winter project, and they're working in an unheated space. This can have the advantage of lengthening the pot life, but the cure time can seem like forever. Rest assured that it will eventually cure, even if it takes a week. To speed up the cure you can do two things. You can heat up the workshop or you can use a faster-curing epoxy.

A warm shop is more pleasant to work in, but heating an uninsulated garage or outbuilding can get expensive, although a kerosene heater can provide relatively inexpensive heat near the boat. I have successfully built several boats with the help of a kerosene heater. One potential problem with them is the safety concern about an open flame. Luckily, epoxy is not that much of a fire hazard. The other problem is that kerosene produces water as it burns, and this humidity in the air can react with some epoxies to promote amine blush. The blush can be cleaned off with soap and water, but it's an added step.

If you cannot practically heat the whole work space, try heating just the boat. A few drop-lights hung under the boat can provide quite a bit of heat. You can also put a tent of plastic or blankets over the boat to contain the heat after you have spread the epoxy.

Take note, however, that with freshly spread epoxy in a warming shop, any air in the layup will expand, causing bubbles and pinholes that are hard to get rid of. You can avoid this problem by heating the shop before you start working and then turning off the heat when you have finished spreading the epoxy. Trapped air will cool and shrink, thus eliminating many of the bubbles.

By the way, storing epoxy in the cold can make the unmixed resin crystallize, turning it cloudy and stiff. All is not lost. Place the jug of resin in a tub of hot water. This will melt the crystals and make the resin completely usable again.

There are fast-curing epoxies specially formulated for working in cold weather, and for this reason most brands of epoxy will have several hardeners available. You can often mix the different hardeners to control the curing time. By mixing a little fast-cure in with the slow-curing resin, you can speed up the curing time for cool days, and by using pure fast-cure you can work on the cold days. I like having some fast-cure hardener around for small jobs that I want to cure quickly.

Hot days are another problem. Epoxy in the mixing pot may remain usable for only 5 minutes until it kicks off, after which the heat of the reaction can melt the mixing cup, leaving a smoking puddle. Don't use any epoxy that has started to "kick," or gel. You can tell it has kicked by the heat it suddenly starts to produce. To deal with this, try to spread your epoxy in a thin layer quickly. Pour the newly mixed resin in a flat pan to disperse it while you work, and pour it on the fiberglass quickly so you can spread it out. This will dissipate the heat of the reaction and keep it from accelerating. If you need to, you can place the pot in ice water, but be careful that you don't drip water into the epoxy or onto the fiberglass.

Use a slow-curing epoxy on hot days, and don't work outside in the sun. The heat of the sun will accelerate the reaction even further. Try to work in the evening, as the day cools, to limit bubbles. If you can work in an air-conditioned space you will have more control.

To get roving yarns, you can pull strands from woven roving (24-ounce fiberglass cloth), you can buy a spool of roving, or you can pull a bunch of strands off the edge of regular fiberglass cloth. The roving is then wrapped around the coaming and pressed down into the corner where the coaming joins the deck (Figure 7-11). Paint some resin into the corner to hold the strands in place.

Cut several narrow (1-inch) strips of fiberglass and cover the wet dookie schmutz or rov-ing. Bias-cut strips will be easier to lay in place. Then cover the outside of the coaming with wider strips of glass that extend down onto the deck. The inside of the coaming will be glassed as you glass the inside of the deck.

Glassing the Inside

After you have glassed the outside you can safely work on smoothing and glassing the inside. Then you can go to work on the deck.

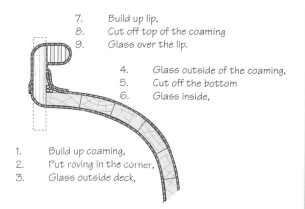

7. Build up lip,
8. Cut off top of the coaming
9. Glass over the lip.

4. Glass outside of the coaming,
5. Cut off the bottom
6. Glass inside,

1. Build up coaming,
2. Put roving in the corner,
3. Glass outside deck,

Figure 7-11. The cross-section of the finished coaming should look somewhat like this. The order in which you perform the steps to make the coaming can be varied, but this works. In step 2, the goal is to make a fillet. You can use roving, a bundle of small yarns pulled from cloth, or dookie schmutz.

The procedure for glassing the inside is the same as the outside. Cut the glass to size. Sometimes this is easiest to do by spreading the glass on the outside, cutting it, then rolling it up and laying it on the inside.

When it comes to epoxying inside, you don't need to fill the weave; you can save weight by leaving the weave showing. You will probably end up putting too much resin up in the ends, where it's hard to reach. This will end up as a puddle along the keel. There's no good rea-

Leaving the Project

When you leave the project for a couple of days, try to put the deck and hull back onto the form. Slight shrinkage of the resin or wood can distort the shape. If you can't put it back on the form, put some sticks between the gunwales (hull sheer strips) to hold the shape.

Don't seal only one side of the strips with epoxy and leave the project for extended periods, and by that I mean weeks or more. The wood on the inside may continue to shrink while the outside is constrained. If the boat is not on the forms, it can curl up like a rhododendron leaf on a cold day.

But even if this disaster does happen, you still needn't despair. Try to spread the piece out slowly by inserting progressively longer sticks between the sheer strips until you can get it on the form. With slow, even pressure you can probably get the boat back in shape.

son to leave it there, because it's heavy and it doesn't supply any needed strength, so scrape up the excess resin with a squeegee and put it into a waste cup. Don't be tempted to reuse this epoxy if it is full of air, though.

You might find runs appearing along the chines as well, so clean them up before the resin cures. Leave the cloth with an even, matte finish with no shiny spots.

Figure 7-12. Lay the fiberglass on the inside of the deck and remove any wrinkles. You will need to make some cuts in the cockpit area so the glass can lie up against the coaming.

Figure 7-13. On the inside, use a squeegee to pull resin up the sides from a puddle in the middle. In this case, my brother is putting on a sealer coat before applying the fiberglass. This is not a bad practice, but it does add an extra step.

115

The Coaming Lip

The cockpit coaming needs a small lip on top to hold a spray skirt in place. The lip should be at least $3/8$ inch wide, but wider is better. I'd say that $1/2$ inch is good and $3/4$ inch is not outrageous. The reason for having a wide lip is that if you're going to be paddling in rough seas or heavy surf, your spray skirt may be pulled off a narrow lip.

There are several methods of creating a lip on the coaming. The best-looking method is to laminate thin strips of wood together to build up a lip. Cut $1/8$-inch strips of wood or veneer about $3/8$ inch wide. Ash is one of the easiest woods for this because it bends easily. Use the cockpit coaming as a mold, apply glue or epoxy to the strips and the coaming, and assemble the strips in place on the coaming. You can put glue in between all the layers and wrap them all at once, but this can get unwieldy.

Instead, lay up one strip at a time, clamping it all the way around and keeping the height off the deck constant. I then put glue on the next strip, remove a clamp or two from the first strip, and place in the next one. Then I work around, removing and reclamping until the next strip is all the way around. If my strips are not long enough to go all the way, I just butt-join the next one in place and put a clamp over the joint after I get the next layer on. Run the strips parallel to

Figure 7-15. The wood strips are wrapped around the coaming, clamping while you go. Doing all the layers in one fell swoop like this can get tricky. The other choice is to clamp and glue one layer at a time.

the deck all the way around, as in Figure 7-11. This method looks especially good if you use woods of alternating color, such as ash and cherry. For cockpits with a small radius at the front, you may not be able to bend the laminations all the way around without breaking the strips. But there is an answer.

Instead of going all the way around, end the strips just shy of the front, leaving them rough. When the glue cures, cut the ends off at a diagonal that is tangent to the vertical part of the

Figure 7-14. Applying glue to thin wood strips that will be laminated together for the coaming lip. For a thicker glue, mix some silica into the resin.

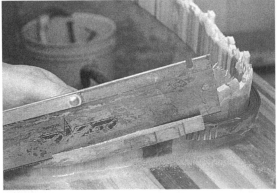

Figure 7-16. Because it can be difficult to bend the lip around the front of the cockpit and finish it off, it's easier just to let the strips run off straight. When the glue cures, cut off the excess wood flush with the coaming. Finish off the front as shown in Figures 7-17 and 7-20.

Figure 7-17. Finishing off the front of the coaming lip with shorter strips.

Figure 7-19. Cleaning up the top of the coaming. Here, a Japanese saw rasp makes quick work of the job without getting gummed up. You should round the edges of the coaming and cover it with fiberglass.

coaming, and then, to complete the lip, laminate on a few short layers to the front.

On boats with a V-shaped deck, such as the Great Auk, the coaming will meet at a sharp angle at the centerline. You won't be able to bend the lip around this corner. Instead have the veneer end at the centerline. Lay one strip in on one side and cut it to length in place. Then lay in the strip for the opposite side again cutting it in place. If you end up with gaps in the joint fill them in with dookie schmutz later. Alternatively, you may choose to do a recess around the cockpit. This will let you make a smooth curve around the front and back of the cockpit.

The easiest method of making a coaming lip may be to use hot-melt glue to tack a piece of rope all the way around the coaming, and then saturate it with resin. This actually looks pretty good and has a nice nautical flair to it, but it's hard to make a waterproof seal with a spray skirt. If you don't intend to use a spray skirt, the rope lip may be the way to go.

Another method I've used sometimes is to use a strong, yet flexible, foam. I used some fancy stuff I found in a dumpster somewhere, but even the blue insulation foam will work, as long as you're not using polyester resin, which will

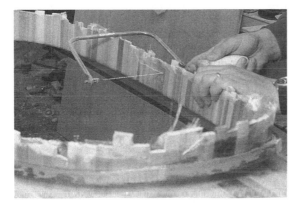

Figure 7-18. After the lip has completely cured, use a coping saw to cut off the excess coaming above it.

Figure 7-20. The finished coaming. The lump under the coaming is a knee brace—see Chapter 9.

dissolve styrene-based foams. Cut a strip about ½ inch square. Sand about a ¼ inch radius on two corners and then glue it in place. You'll need to glass over the foam to make it strong, of course, and if you used some ugly color, paint over it.

After the glue has cured on the lip, trim the excess coaming off the top. Use a coping saw to cut close to the lip and then plane and sand the rest of the way down. Round over the edges of the lip so that it does not cut into you or your spray skirt.

Making the Hatches

If you're building a kayak that will only be used for day trips or short local paddles, hatches are not required. You can always stuff gear into the ends from the cockpit, and airbags can be used for safety flotation instead of bulkheads.

But I like one hatch behind the seat, for easier access to storage space for lunch and dry clothes. For camping and extended expeditions, it's worthwhile having hatches in the bow and stern.

Figure 7-22. Marking out the shape of the hatch on masking tape. I like to make the sides parallel to the strips. Rounded corners will make it easier to cut with a jigsaw.

The shape of the hatch is up to you. I like a basically hexagonal shape. You can cut a pattern from a piece of paper folded in half, so when you unfold it the two sides are symmetrical. There is no particular reason for this, except that straight edges are easier to cut, and easier to fit a wood coaming to. Rounded shapes work just as well, however.

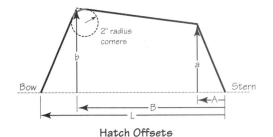

Hatch Offsets

	Great Auk		Guillemot		Guillemot Double	
	Bow	Stern	Bow	Stern	Bow	Stern
a	6	7	5 1/4	7	6 1/4	6 1/4
b	5 1/4	9	4 1/2	8	4 3/4	8 3/4
A	3 1/2	3 3/4	3	4 1/2	3 1/2	3 1/2
B	11 1/2	18	11	14 1/2	10 1/4	14 1/2
L	15	21	14	18	13 1/4	19

Figure 7-21. You can make your hatches almost any shape you want. Here are some sample offsets for hatches you can use as guides. Use the bottom of a coffee can as a template to mark rounded corners if you want them.

Figure 7-23. Starting the cut for the hatches with a jigsaw. This can be nerve-racking. Start the saw with the blade running parallel to the deck and the line you will be cutting. Slowly tilt the saw down as the blade cuts into the surface. When the blade makes it through, turn off the saw. Put a piece of cardboard under the front of the saw to protect the boat from scratches. Don't worry—this step is actually easier than it looks.

Figure 7-24. Insert the blade into the newly cut slot and start cutting the hatch. Always push away from you with slow, even pressure. If pushing feels awkward to you, stop the saw and move to a new position. Make sure the power cord is not hooked on anything. You get only one chance, so you want to do it right. Don't rush.

I like to make my hatch covers out of the same piece I cut from the hole, but again this is not required. A sharply contrasting wood would look just as good. Some people like the rubber hatches made by Valley Canoe Products (VCP) that are available on commercial kayaks. These are also a good solution because they are extremely watertight.

Lay out the position and shape of the hatch by drawing on masking tape placed in approximately the right place. Measure carefully to make sure the shape is symmetrical. You can cut to this line using a razor saw, a power saber-saw, or a fine knife blade. The hard part is starting the cut. With a razor saw, start by carefully scratching through the glass and wood along the marked line, until you've cut through. It's hard to cut curves with a razor saw but it can be done. With a sabersaw, align the saw over the mark with the blade running parallel to the surface. With the saw running, slowly tilt the blade down onto the mark. Put something in front of the saw to protect the deck while you are tilting the blade down. Keep tilting down until the blade pierces through. Stop the saw and lower the blade into the slot and cut normally. I do this with the deck on the forms and often cut right through the forms. The change in resistance

can make the saw hard to control, so be careful. You will be using the piece you cut out as the hatch cover, so take care as you cut.

If you messed up cutting out the hatch and ruined the cover piece, you can make a new one by stripping that part of the deck, fiberglassing it up and cutting it to size.

I like a flush hatch because it looks sleek, and reduces the amount of spray you get in your face when you're breaking through waves. A flush hatch is also easy to make.

Paint the edges of the hatch cover and the hole with some silica-thickened epoxy resin to seal the endgrain. Lay a 1-inch-wide extra layer of glass around the edge on the underside of the cover. When the resin cures, sand this smooth. This will be the seat for the gasket. Smooth out the edges.

Wax the inside and edges of the hatch cover heavily so that the epoxy will not stick to it. Put on several coats of carnauba-based wax and buff it smooth. Use "butcher's" wax (available at hardware stores) or, if you can find it, a mold-release wax. In most cases this will be enough. To be extra sure the epoxy won't stick, use a PVA (polyvinyl alcohol) mold release. This creates a thin, water-soluble plastic film when it's painted on and allowed to dry. Don't touch the PVA after it has dried, as the moisture of your hands may damage its mold-releasing properties.

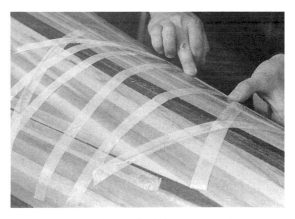

Figure 7-25. Making a flush hatch. Start by waxing the inside of the piece you just cut out, then tape it back in place. Seal up the cracks so resin will not leak out.

Sand the inside of the deck around the hatches to rough them up for glassing. Lay the hatch back in its hole and tape it in place from the outside (Figure 7-25). Seal up the seam between the deck and the hatch with tape on the outside.

Start by painting on a gel coat of resin all the way around the seam. Now, lay 3-inch-wide strips of glass on the inside of the deck, straddling the seam. Resin it down. Use about six layers of 6-ounce cloth all around. Let the resin cure but don't wait too long, because you don't yet want the epoxy to be super hard, which it will be after 6 to 24 hours. Remove the tape sealing the outside seam.

If you waxed it well, you will now be able to remove the hatch, but it may take some persuasion. Whittle a wedge-shaped strip of wood. A tapered piece of the wood you used for the coaming lip works well. Work the wedge under the glass (Figure 7-27). You will see a color change as the glass pulls away from the hatch cover. Work the glass free all the way around. Try not to over-stress the glass. You will see white spots appear in the weave if it is over-stressed.

When the fiberglass is free all the way around, try pushing on the middle of the hatch. If this does not free the cover, insert the wedge under the glass and twist it. Work all the way around to loosen the cover. This may be quite dif-

Figure 7-27. Forcing a thin wedge under the cured fiberglass. Work the wedge around until the fiberglass is released from the hatch all the way around.

ficult if you've let the resin cure completely, so try to do it within 24 hours. If you are still having problems, turn the boat over and scrape any resin out of the seam. When you get the cover off, you are left with a close-fitting lip around the inside of the hatch hole in the deck. Trim the rough edges to make the lip 1 inch wide.

A Plywood Hatch Lip

On fairly flat decks, or V-shaped decks, such as the Great Auk's, you can build the lip with marine plywood instead of fiberglass.

Figure 7-26. Lay fiberglass across the seam between the hatch and the deck, and soak it with epoxy resin. Here, I mixed some graphite powder in the resin to make it black.

Figure 7-28. A drum sander chucked into a drill makes a combined drain and finger hole at the lowest part of the hatch. Hold the tool firmly so it doesn't run away from you. If you want to be more careful, use a file.

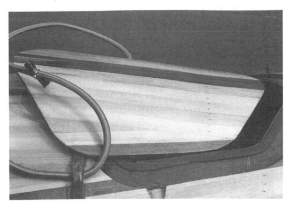

Figure 7-29. *The finished flush hatch. The fiberglass lip provides a good surface for a gasket.*

Figure 7-30. *If you are intimidated by the idea of using a jigsaw to cut the hatch, you can use a razor saw.*

Cut out a plywood shape with outer dimensions 1 inch larger than the hatch, and an opening in the middle 1 inch smaller than the hatch. Apply glue around the outer edge of this piece and the underside of the deck. Clamp this in place and clean up any glue that is squeezed out. After the glue dries, seal any exposed wood with several coats of epoxy.

Use a rasp or a 1-inch drum sander chucked into a drill to create a finger-hole/scupper on the bottom edge of the hatch—but use that sander very carefully. This hole allows water to drain out and provides a finger grip to lift the hatch off. Seal the grain of the scupper with several coats of epoxy.

achieve this, cut the miters at a slight inward angle, so that the upper edge of the strip is slightly shorter than the lower. Then build a rim downward around the hatch cover, similar to the one around the hatch hole. After the glue has dried, plane the top and bottom edges to match the contour of the deck.

Weather-stripping (Figure 7-33) makes a very waterproof seal when there is a good fit between the hatch cover and the lip. But whereas the fiberglass lip assures a good fit, with the wood lip you have to check carefully for a tight fit. Even then, some people don't trust these hatches to be waterproof enough,

An All-Wood Hatch

Purists will want an all-wood hatch. If you'd like to make a an all-wood hatch with a rounded outline, the rim may be created in the same way as the coaming. But it's a lot easier to use straight-sided hatches because you can use straight wood strips (1 inch to 1 1/2 inches wide) glued vertically along the edge (Figure 7-32).

The outer edge of these strips should tilt inward so that the hatch cover will fit over (Figure 7-33). To

Figure 7-31. *Straight sides cut with a razor saw can be fitted with straight wood sides to complete a raised hatch.*

Figure 7-32. The sides of the raised hatch must be sloped away from each other so that the top and bottom will fit together.

Rubber Hatches

Rubber hatches come with a round or oval plastic lip that must be attached to the deck. For the standard round hatch, cut a wooden ring about 11 inches in diameter. In the center of this, cut a 9¾-inch-diameter hole. Fair the cut edges. Sand a slight taper into the outer diameter for a snug fit into the deck. Cut a hole in the deck of your kayak to match the outer diameter of the ring. Start by cutting it a little undersized and file and sand it to fit.

Glue the ring in place with thickened epoxy. Run a nice fillet around the inside of the seam. Plane off the excess ring sticking above the deck, but don't cut into the glass. Finish up the top flush with the deck, using sandpaper. Round over the interior top edge with sandpaper or a router with a round-over bit. Seal the wood with several coats of epoxy.

Cut another ring from plywood with the same 11-inch outer diameter and an 8⅛-inch

and prefer the commercial rubber hatches like those made by VCP, which are definitely waterproof. The contrast of the black rubber against the wood looks good to some people.

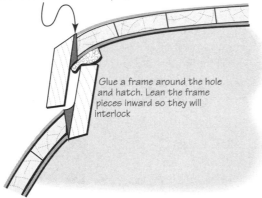

Fill the gap between the frame and hatch with thickened epoxy

Glue a frame around the hole and hatch. Lean the frame pieces inward so they will interlock

Figure 7-33. Weather-stripping on the inside of the hatch makes a watertight seal. The initially straight top of the raised hatch lip will need to be curved to match the contour of the deck. The bottom of the hatch cover lip will also need to be curved.

Figure 7-34. Rubber hatches like this one from Valley Canoe Products (VCP) are very watertight. The cover of this one is not shown. Jay Babina installed this hatch by making several rings of wood so he would have a flat surface on which to mount the ring.

inner diameter. Rough up the bottom of the plastic hatch lip with sandpaper in preparation for gluing. Mix up some more thickened epoxy and glue the plastic lip to the plywood ring. Clamp it centered on the plywood and wipe off any excess glue. When the glue cures, clean up any drips and sand the top surface of the plywood.

Glue and clamp the lip assembly into the bottom of the ring in the deck. Make sure the plastic lip is centered in the hole. After the glue cures, clean up any drips and seal all exposed wood with several coats of epoxy.

Installing Cheek Plates

I install a board on either side of the cockpit, hanging down from the coaming. For want of a better name I'll call these boards "cheek plates." They serve two purposes in the kayak. First, they keep your butt centered in the boat, which is required for rolling, and which also generally provides a more secure-feeling boat. They're also handy places to secure the backrest strap to.

I make them from a flat panel consisting of strips covered with glass on both sides, but 1/4-inch marine plywood, sealed with epoxy, would

Figure 7-35. *The cheek plates are attached to the deck only. They will be strong enough if you put a good fillet of fiberglass behind them.*

also work. The cheeks are mounted just slightly aft of center. Sand and plane the top edge to conform to the inside of the deck about 1/4 inch from the edge of the cockpit. Make some measurements to be sure it's not too tight a squeeze. Tack each cheek plate in place with a couple of dots of hot-melt glue, or quick-set epoxy, and secure it with tape until the resin has cured. These plates need to be able to take a lot of strain, so they must be securely joined to the deck. Create a good fillet of glass on the back side and apply several layers to the outside. Sand off any sharp edges and seal any exposed wood with several coats of resin.

While you are installing the cheek plates, it's also a good time to install some of the hardware needed for the seat (see the chapter on Outfitting). You will need a loop (or padeye) to tie part of the backrest to. This loop should be fixed to the underside of the deck, centered behind the back of the cockpit, and as close to the edge of the cockpit coaming as possible. I usually drill a 1/2-inch hole in the edge of a small piece of 3/4-inch-thick hardwood. Contour one side of this to conform to the underside of the deck directly behind the cockpit. Glue this down with thickened epoxy and lay some fiberglass over the top, so you end up with a small loop to tie to.

You can also make this loop by gluing down a piece of PVC or other pipe. Use some dookie schmutz to create a fillet, and then fiberglass over the top.

Joining Hull and Deck

The major pieces of the kayak are now complete. The remaining task is to join the deck and hull back together again. While this may not be the most enjoyable task, at least it's over quickly.

Before we start, let me urge you to wear a respirator while working inside the boat. As a minimum, have very good ventilation. In fact, don't listen to what I have to say on the subject, listen to the manufacturer. This joining process is the same for fiberglass sea kayaks and whitewater kayaks.

Aligning the Seams

Prepare the seams for gluing by sanding the interior edge. Clean up the rough edges of the glass with a plane. Try the fit to see if the joint will be tight. If there are gaps in the seam, adjust the bevel with your plane. If you plane the top edge of the hull level, or angled slightly inward, and do the same for the deck, chances are they will fit well.

Then start by laying the deck on top of the hull and aligning both ends. (By the way you are done with the forms now, so put them away; you won't be needing them again.) With the ends carefully aligned, wrap some tape around each end. Use fiber-reinforced packing tape for

this job because it's stronger and easier to remove than masking tape or duct tape. Next, go to the middle in the cockpit area and force the two halves together so the seams meet. You'll find that the hull and deck probably don't match perfectly any longer but if you've kept the hull and deck on the forms while you weren't working on them, the pieces should match up reasonably easily. They may have deformed a little and the edges might not meet right away, but there should be enough flex to make everything meet.

Run a strip of tape across the seam (Figure 7-37). Repeat this on the other side. You may want to wrap some tape all the way around to make sure it's secure. Move about halfway between this tape and the end tape and perform the same procedure. You may need to pry with

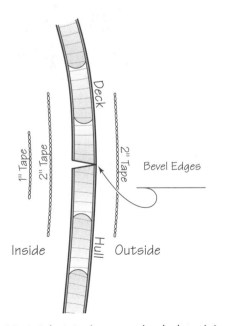

Figure 7-36. A tight joint between the deck and the hull is made by beveling the edges slightly inward (this illustration is exaggerated). Two layers of tape on the inside and one on the outside make this joint as strong as the rest of the boat.

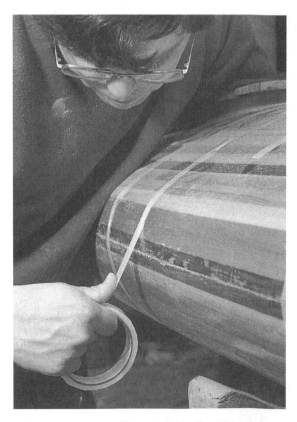

Figure 7-37. Using fiber-reinforced packing tape to hold the deck to the hull before fiberglassing the inside seam. Reach inside to push the joint into alignment.

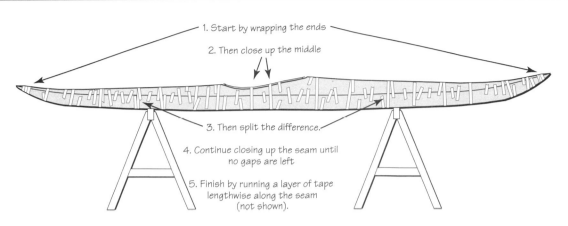

1. Start by wrapping the ends

2. Then close up the middle

3. Then split the difference.

4. Continue closing up the seam until no gaps are left

5. Finish by running a layer of tape lengthwise along the seam (not shown).

Figure 7-38. The joint between the deck and the hull must be aligned as well as possible. It cannot be moved after you fiberglass the inside.

a putty knife to force the seam to line up. Keep on aligning and taping until the whole sheerline is done. You will want to use long strips of tape across the seam because the tape does not always adhere too well to the resin. It helps to have the tape stuck to another piece. Tape sticks better to itself than to anything else.

Be aware that you may need to apply a fair amount of force to get the seams lined up. Where you can reach inside, you can apply pressure near the seam, and where you can't reach, use the putty knife or some other thin blade to lever the seams into alignment. Don't be timid about applying force, the boat can handle a lot. When you're done, the seam should feel smooth and flush. Finally, run tape along the length of the outside hull-deck seam so the resin won't drip out when you fiberglass the inside seam.

Taping the Interior Seam

Now cut some glass cloth tape for the interior seam. I use two layers, one 1-inch-wide layer, and one 2-inch layer. Tip the boat on one side and measure the tape by rolling it along the seam from the center of the cockpit to about a foot from the end. You will not be able to reach the tape all the way to the ends so don't cut it too long. Cut enough lengths to do both sides

Figure 7-39. Applying the tape to the interior seam. This is not much fun but it's over quickly. Fumes build up inside the boat, so make sure you wear a respirator.

and roll them into fairly tight rolls. It is easier to run two lengths from the center to each end than it is to run one long length the whole way.

The trick is to lay this tape along the joint between the hull and deck as far into the ends as possible. To do this, you must saturate the tape in resin then unroll it onto the seam, pushing it as far into the ends as you can reach with a stick. You will need a stick measuring 1 inch by 1 inch and long enough to reach into the ends from the cockpit. Sand or plane it smooth so there is nothing to snag the glass tape. Cut one end at a 45-degree angle and nail or tape a bristle brush to it, so the end of the brush reaches out beyond the end of the stick. Saw off the handle of the brush so it can fit further into the ends of the boat.

Mix up enough resin to saturate one roll of tape (about 2 ounces). Dunk one of the 2-inch-wide rolls in the resin. Let it soak. Work it with your fingers (always wear gloves) to help the resin soak in. While the tape is soaking, use the brush on the end of your stick to paint some resin down the inside seam.

The fiberglass is completely saturated when it no longer has any light-colored spots. Now squeeze it in your hand to wring out the excess resin (you are wearing gloves, aren't you?) and then, starting at the center of the cockpit lay the tape down on the seam (Figure 7-40). Roll it out as far as you can by hand. If you have hatches, reach in and keep unrolling. When you can push it no further, get out your stick. Use the end of the stick without the brush. Poke and prod, trying

to keep the tape centered on the seam. If you mess up, pull the tape back, re-roll it, add more resin, and try again. With the brush end of the stick, paint on more resin and smooth out the tape. Put one layer going into one end, then the other end, then back to the first with the 1-inch tape on top of the 2-inch. This keeps you from getting bubbles under the tape. Do one side and let it cure before flipping the boat over and doing the other side because it's no fun to have your just-completed seam come falling on your head.

If you survived doing the interior seam, you are over the hump; the remaining tasks are much easier. With both interior seams taped, pull off the strapping tape and stand back. You have a kayak.

Taping the Exterior Seam

The application of fiberglass tape on the outside of the hull-deck seam is the last job required to make your kayak seaworthy. First sand the joint smooth because there may be some residual adhesive and tape left from strapping the boat together. This can be cleaned off with paint thinner containing mineral spirits. Cut a length of 2-inch-wide fiberglass tape long enough to do the whole seam, then re-roll the tape. Paint some epoxy onto the joint. Roll the tape in place while keeping it tight. Wet it out, starting in the middle and working towards the end. Let the resin cure, then do the other side.

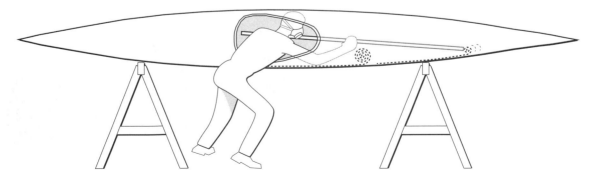

Figure 7-40. Run pre-saturated fiberglass tape as far up the seam as you can reach with your hands. Poke and prod the remaining tape the rest of the way with a stick.

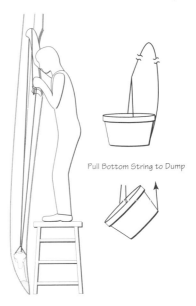

Pull Bottom String to Dump

Figure 7-42. *Using a dumper to keep from spilling goo all over the inside of the boat as you make the end-pour. Lower the dumper down into the end and pull on the bottom string to up-end the contents.*

Figure 7-41. *Running a strip of fiberglass along the outside hull-deck seam. Watch carefully for air bubbles.*

Making an End-Pour

Because you couldn't run fiberglass tape all the way into the inside ends of the boat, the bow and stern could use a little more reinforcement. I accomplish this with an end-pour. I mix up some resin with microballoons, sawdust, little scraps of foam, and so forth, to make a light-weight filler that I pour into the ends. Here's how:

Put a little masking tape along the hull-deck seam to seal it at the ends if needed. Stand the boat on end by leaning it against a house or tree.

Make a resin dumper from a disposable cup or other small container. Tie a string to the top to hang the cup from, and one to the bottom so the cup may be dumped. Make sure the string is long enough to reach the ends. Lower the dumper full of resin into the end and dump (you

Figure 7-43. *Finding a suitable place for your boat while you make the end-pour can be difficult. Make sure the boat will stay put.*

may have to stand on a stool or stepladder—Figure 7-43).

I make the end-pour large enough to accept a hole drilled through the bow and stern for a rope grab-loop. In actual fact, the end-pour is not completely necessary because sufficient strength is probably provided by taping the exterior seam, but I think it's justified for installing the grab-loop. This method of attaching a grab-loop is easy, strong, and neat looking.

Using a Sheerclamp

Although fiberglass taping inside and out is the best way to attach the deck to the hull in my opinion, because it's lightweight and strong, it is admittedly a bit of a pain to accomplish.

An easier way is to glue a strip of wood along the upper edge, or gunwale, of the hull. With a little fitting, the deck can be glued or screwed to this sheerclamp. This method works best with decks that join the hull at close to 90 degrees.

Cut two ³/₄-inch by ³/₄-inch strips of pine or spruce the length of the boat. Sand the inside

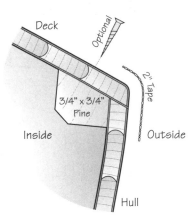

Figure 7-44. *The sheerclamp is an alternative to taping the interior hull-deck seam. Glue a piece of wood to the upper edge of the hull, and plane it to match the angle of the deck. Then glue the deck down onto this sheerclamp. You can hold the deck down with screws or temporarily tape it in place until the glue cures. Sand the edge smooth and apply a layer of fiberglass tape over the outside.*

upper edge of the hull to prepare it for glue. Try the fit with the 1-inch-wide side against the inside of the boat. If you're going to do an end-pour, don't bother making the sheerclamp fit all the way into the ends. If you're not planning an end-pour, you'll need to miter the two sides so they fit together all the way into the end.

Apply glue to both the sheerclamp and the boat, and clamp the sheerclamp in place with about ¼ inch sticking up above the edge of the hull. Incidentally, the pressure of the sheerclamp may change the width of the hull so measure the width of the deck and either pull the deck together with rope or tape, or spread it apart with sticks as required, until the sheerclamp glue cures.

Estimate the angle at which the deck meets the hull, and plane that angle into the top of the sheerclamp. Try the fit as you go and when you get a decent fit all the way around, seal all the exposed wood on the hull and deck with several coats of epoxy.

You can glue, screw, or nail the deck to the sheerclamp. Before gluing, rough up both surfaces with sandpaper. You may need to wrestle with the hull a little to make the width match the deck so try the fit before applying any glue. If you need to spread the hull, you can put the sticks back in, but remember to tie a string to them and lead it back to the cockpit so you'll be able to pop them out after the deck is attached.

If you have a good fit that won't have to be moved much once it's put together, you can apply a glue made of epoxy resin filled with wood flour. Spread the glue on the deck and the sheerclamp. Place the two pieces together and hold them in position with copious amounts of tape.

If the joint is going to take a lot of work to force together, you will probably end up pushing glue out of the seam and making a mess, in which case you may be better off using screws or tacks. Even if you plan to screw or nail the deck to the hull, you may want to hold the deck in place with packing tape while you secure it. Use corrosion-resistant bronze fasteners. Drive them as close to the edge as you can get while still hitting the sheerclamp (about ¹/₂ inch from the edge).

Whether you use glue or fasteners, you should put a layer of fiberglass over the seam after it's secured in place. Follow the directions given above. Cover the fasteners with the tape to keep them from pulling loose.

Now is your chance to pick up the finished kayak. It can be paddled now if you are impatient to get out on the water. Otherwise just go ahead and sit down in it. Lift it up and enjoy the feel of it.

Finishing Off

The finish of the kayak makes or breaks its final appearance. In fact, many first-time mistakes can be hidden behind the high gloss of a fine varnish. It takes some practice to get a good finish, but since a good finish requires multiple coats, you can practice while you are applying it. I will detail methods of creating a beautiful finish with inexpensive brushes.

Final Sanding

Sand with the fairing sander to remove high spots and to feather in the transitions between layers of glass. Try to remove a minimum of glass while still producing a smooth surface. Except for the edges of the layers of glass, you don't need to do more than touch the tops of the glass weave. Avoid sanding deeply into the weave as this will weaken the material. Light spots will appear as you touch the fiberglass. If you have sanded down to the weave and the surface is still not smooth, paint on another coat of resin. Start sanding with 80-grit sandpaper and finish with 120-grit.

Skim Coats

Some hollows are simply too deep to sand away. For example, if your original fill-coat of epoxy did not fill the weave completely, you won't be able to sand the surface smooth without sand-

ing into the fiberglass, and you don't want to do this. Instead, sand off the surface, do your major feathering, then go back and apply skim coats of resin.

Mix up a small amount of resin (2 ounces) and spread it on the boat, using a squeegee or roller. The squeegee applies a smoother and thinner coat than the roller does. Because it's thin, you may need more coats to do all the filling, but the sanding between coats will be easier because it's smoother. Keep applying and sanding the coats until you are satisfied with the smoothness of the surface. You could do the fill-and-sand routine with the varnish when the time comes, but the resin is stronger and more durable, so it's better to do the filling now.

Varnishing

I use a good oil-based, marine-grade spar varnish because I've found that even the best single-part polyurethane varnish seems to evaporate away within one season. The varnish should contain ultra-violet ray (UV) inhibitors because its purpose in life is more to protect the resin from the sun than to look good. The more coats you apply, the better it will look, and more importantly, the more UV protection you'll add with each coat.

You'll get a better-looking finish if you varnish in a dust-free work space. This isn't usually possible, but do the best you can. Wipe the boat down with a rag dampened with paint thinner, then wipe it again with a tack cloth immediately before varnishing.

A good varnish brush can be extremely expensive and it will probably shed bristles. Luckily, I find disposable foam brushes work very well. Pour some varnish into a cup through a paint filter, to remove any impurities. Don't ever dip directly into the full varnish can, as this will introduce crud. Dip the whole brush in the varnish and then wipe off the excess. Flow the varnish on in even strokes. Starting at one end, work down one side, painting from the center-line to the sheer. Maintain a wet edge as you go, that is, don't go so slowly that the finish starts to dry along a border. Brush only in one direction, along the length of the boat, not up and down, to minimize brush marks and don't try to go back and touch up a spot that has started to dry. You can sand out your mistakes later. Then do the other side. When the coat dries, flip the boat over and coat the other side.

Wet-sand with 220-grit and 400-grit paper between coats. I usually apply four to six coats, although sometimes I get impatient and put the boat in the water after two or three. It's okay if you do that. Just wash it off afterward, and continue with the remaining coats.

The Almost-Complete Kayak

Finally, stand back and look. What you see before you started out as a pile of raw pieces of wood, a roll of fabric, and a jug of goo. It is now a beautiful and functional boat that bears little relation to those initial raw materials. Already, the transformation is amazing, but you cannot truly appreciate what you've accomplished until you put your kayak in the water.

As good as the boat may look glistening in the sun in your back yard, it looks even better with beads of water running off the deck as you paddle away from shore. The boat is not truly complete until you are using it. So finish up the outfitting of your kayak with seats and back-rests, and get it in the water.

The First Scratch

The first scratch will come with a mixture of pain and relief. After all the effort you've put into the kayak, you will not want to damage its pristine finish. But once that scratch is there, you'll be released of that responsibility. Don't dishonor your effort and your boat by failing to put it in the water for fear of that first scratch.

Carry it to the water and carefully lay the kayak in. Paddle it from the shore with great care, avoiding any potential hazard. Do this every time you paddle until, eventually, the day will come when, thanks to a lapse of attention, you will hit a rock or stump that you didn't see. The boat is now scratched. Your kayak is now complete.

One day, while I was stripping one of my early kayaks, I picked up a piece of mahogany. It was a nice piece with good color, about 2 inches wide and 2 feet long. It didn't match any of the wood I had already used in the boat, but I liked it and I wanted to use it somehow. The problem was fitting it in. It was too short to run lengthwise anywhere, and it was too wide to fit in line with any other strips. I held it up to the boat, looking at it in different locations. I then laid it diagonally across the deck behind the cockpit. That was it! It looked cool!

I glued it in place and just stripped around it normally. With this inspiration I came to the realization that the strips do not need to go straight. There is no reason for them to follow the sheer or the centerline. They can be diagonal, twisted, wavy, tapered, short, multicolored, or if you must, straight.

For me, this freedom to lay strips any way that strikes my fancy is a large part of the fun of building with strips. Some people may find laying one strip after another boring. I'll admit I do, but I get over this by making life difficult for myself. I don't necessarily put the strip where it's easiest. I look for patterns that enhance the original shape of the boat or emphasize the natural contrast of the wood.

The reason why you can be creative with the strips is that the boat doesn't get its strength from the orientation of the strips. The strength is primarily a result of the separation of the inside and outside layers of fiberglass created by the wood in the middle, therefore the strips need not be oriented in any particular direction. This is not an earth-shaking revelation, but it does open up ever-more artistic possibilities for boatbuilding.

Artistry with the strips does not require great skill in woodworking. What is required is some imagination, some willingness to experiment, and some patience. An artistic pattern of wood does not need to be a complicated pattern. Some of the most striking designs are the simplest.

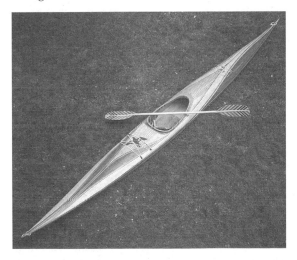

Figure 8-1. *To make a strip-built boat, your only goal is to cover all the forms with wood. This simple purpose gives you an extraordinary degree of freedom to progress beyond the simple task of assembling strips into the world of art. The only limit is your imagination. Here, the author incorporated pine, redwood, and western cedar in an asymmetrical curving design on his Guillemot Expedition Single.*

Patterns from Strips

To create a pattern with your strips, you need wood of contrasting colors. Sometimes a variety of colors is available in a single board of wood. Western red cedar, for example, can vary from a light white through a pale tan to a deep, rich chocolate-brown. By sorting though the pile at the lumberyard you can sometimes find enough different colors for a beautiful pattern. Otherwise choose several varieties of wood with contrasting colors.

Redwood is a dark wood that looks good with a light-colored wood such as Atlantic white cedar or pine. A third intermediate tone, such as Western red cedar, will give you additional possibilities.

The patterns you can make will naturally depend on the wood you have available but you can help things along by looking for transitions in color in the individual strips. Some strips will change color along their length, others may vary across their width. Look through your selection of strips as you develop ideas for a pattern.

Figure 8-2. The general rule of thumb, "Don't put all your joints next to each other," can be broken. If you like the look of an abrupt transition in color, you can align a series of scarfs without severely weakening the boat.

Simple Variations

The simplest pattern is a single stripe of contrasting wood. This stripe can just be one strip of redwood following the sheerline, with the rest of the boat built in white cedar. The stripe could also be a wide band of dark-red cedar from the cockpit down to the waterline while the remainder of the boat is in light-red cedar.

The stripe does not need to run the full length of the boat. A length of contrasting wood cut with a diagonal scarf can change the look of the boat. In my prototype for the Guillemot I started out with the basic concept of two wide bands, one band following the sheerline and the other following the deck centerline. I then modified the sheer band by cutting off the strips at an angle and changing from redwood to red cedar. I cut off the center strip at the same angle and finished it with the pine I used for the rest of the boat. I then did each side a little differently by changing where I made the transition between redwood and cedar. None of this required doing anything different from the standard stripping technique. I just picked up different-colored woods at different times. The result is a pattern that is more visually interesting than it would have been if I'd just used one color of wood or a single stripe of contrasting wood—and it wasn't harder to make.

Figure 8-3. This stripping pattern is the same as the one shown in Figure 6-33(a), Chapter 6. All I did differently was to change woods at a 45-degree butt joint. I used redwood on one side, western red cedar on the other, and the light color is pine. Creating a pattern like this is no more difficult than stripping the whole boat with wood of one color.

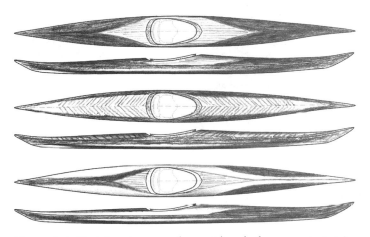

Figure 8-4. Sketch out some of your ideas before you start stripping the boat. This will let you work out how your strips will go without wasting any wood.

Obviously, my idea of what looks nice may not coincide with yours, so you need to do what pleases you. That's easier to determine if you make some sketches first. I draw a bunch of plan views of a boat and scribble for a while.

Get some colored pencils and experiment with color. Try patterns in which the strips follow the natural curves of the boat, and think of different ways to make transitions between strips. I also find that some contrast in the width of the stripes looks good. By the way, I spend more time getting fancy with the deck than I do with the hull because the deck's more visible.

Dealing with Curves

If you tire of following the lines of the boat, you can set the strips free to flow anywhere. They needn't run parallel with the sheerline or centerline. They can be bent diagonally to the centerline or cross from the deck to the hull. For these curved patterns I generally have one or two strips that lay out the borders of the pattern. In between the borders I do straight stripping with different-colored woods. Again, it's easiest to start with some sketches, even

though they're often hard to reproduce exactly on the actual boat.

Start by laying out the border strips. Clamp the strips in place initially and try to achieve fair curves. The full ¾-inch strips can take some pretty radical curves, but they are hard to deal with and can introduce other problems if you bend them too much. They may break and may create an uneven surface between the forms. It is easier to use some narrow strips to lay out the borders. When you have settled on an interesting pattern, with all the curves looking clean and fair, secure the strips with staples. If you want wider borders, use multiple strips to build them up.

You will get fair curves and better fits if you follow the general principle of laying the longest strips first. This means that if you're creating a "Y" intersection, you should lay one strip to create both the base and one arm of the Y. Then you can either lay another long strip that starts parallel to the base and then separates for the other arm, or you can lay a temporary strip to help you fit the second strip (Figure 8-7).

After you lay out the borders you can use the standard stripping techniques to fill in the areas between the borders. You can either lay the filling strips parallel to the borders or you

Figure 8-5. If the pattern you are making consists of a series of long stripes, lay those strips first.

Figure 8-6. *After you have defined the edges of your pattern with long strips, fill in the gaps as you see fit.*

can choose to follow the sheerline, or the centerline, or some other feature line. If you're using cove-and-bead strips, plan the layout of the coves and beads. You need to be able to assemble everything, and filling small gaps with coves all the way around may be impossible without taking extreme measures. It may be easier to remove the coves and beads from all the border strips. This will simplify the joints where any filler strip ends on a border strip.

Dealing with Diagonals

You can also lay strips diagonally, although it can be tricky because a short diagonal strip may not touch any form. If you have a bunch

Figure 8-8. *You generally want each strip to touch at least two forms and sometimes three. When you are making a pattern of short diagonal strips you need to install some stringers that will act as forms for each end of the strips. This boat has a flat deck. If it had more curvature, the chevron pattern (see Figure 8-9) my brother is making would require another pair of stringers to bend the strips over.*

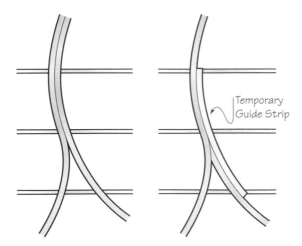

Temporary
Guide Strip

Figure 8-7. *It's easier to make a fair curve if you use long strips, left. On the right, a temporary strip is laid in place so another strip can be fitted in behind it. When the temporary strip is removed, the curve made by the two remaining strips will stay fair.*

Figure 8-9. *Here is the result of the forms in Figure 8-8. Each end of the diagonal strip lands on one of the stringers. The author's brother, Eric Schade, built this boat to Jay Babina's Outer Islander design.*

of diagonal strips together, the whole bunch may not have any reference to the desired shape of the boat. Where the surface of the boat is curving, the strips need guidance to end up in the right place. If you are laying up a large region of diagonal strips you need to install some longitudinal stringers as forms. For surfaces that are flat in the section view, you will need a stringer at each end of the strips, and if the surface is curved in the section view you may need another stringer to support the middle elevation of the curve.

Cut stringers of pine measuring at least $\frac{1}{2}$ inch by $\frac{1}{2}$ inch and lay them out to define the border of the diagonal region. Mark where they cross the forms. Cut a notch in the forms to fit the stringer and inset the stringer flush with the forms. For regions with a lot of curvature in the section view install another stringer down the middle. You now have forms to mount the diagonal strips on. Be sure to put tape on your new stringers so the strips don't stick.

You can now lay strips diagonally across the stringers, leaving

the ends rough. After you have filled the area defined by the stringers, use the stringers as guides to trim off the excess. Staple or clamp a strip on top of the edge to define a fair curve and serve as a guide for trimming. Saw close to the edge and use a plane to clean it up. You can now strip the surrounding area any way you choose.

Dotted Lines

Another striking pattern can be made with really short strips. The simplest example of this is a dotted line. The first way to do this is to lay out a long strip that defines one side of the line. Then, with two basketfuls of short strips of contrasting colors, glue alternating colors to the side of the long strip. The short strips can be any length you want and they can be cut at any angle you choose. After you glue on all the short pieces, glue another long piece on the other side (Figure 8-14, top).

Figure 8-10. *If you are making some kind of a repeating pattern or "dotted line," you need some way to make a lot of identical pieces. The author's brother set up his bandsaw to make parallelograms by tilting the table and installing a fence.*

Figure 8-11. *A repeating pattern will require a lot of pieces. Here is a bucketful of the parallelograms being made in Figure 8-10.*

There is a risk of the little strips falling off before the glue dries. One way around this is to use hot-melt glue, which cools quickly enough to keep the pieces in place. Otherwise, you can pre-assemble a stripe on your workbench. Start with the long strip laid on edge. Glue the edge of the short strips to the long strip. Do not glue between the short strips. When the glue dries, the strip can be carefully laid in place. It will stay flexible because the short pieces are not glued together.

Figure 8-13. *Bruce Wolfrom created two distinctive patterns incorporating dotted lines on his Guillemot Expedition Singles. The boat on the left has round light dots.*

Figure 8-12. *By combining redwood parallelograms with white cedar triangles you can create a striking detail.*

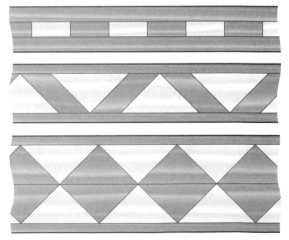

Figure 8-14. *The dotted-line detail can be as simple or as complicated as you choose. Try varying the width of the strips, the shapes of the pieces, and the colors of wood.*

You can also stack several layers of short strips to make more complicated patterns. The short strips do not all need to be the same shape. There is an infinite variety of possible patterns if you are committed enough.

Make a jig to cut the short pieces. You can use the miter fence of a chop saw or bandsaw in conjunction with a length stop. For the multi-layered patterns it is important that the pieces have uniform dimensions. Cut them carefully.

Dressing Up the Surface

All this marquetry may sound like too much work. Don't worry, there are other ways to jazz up your boat a little. I like to put some artwork on top of the strips in the form of veneer. I've tried to find the right word to describe this technique. Someone suggested "intarsia." Intarsia is a technique where you inlay patterns into a background of wood. However, I cheat and don't inlay the wood, so I thought the word decoupage might be closer. With decoupage you glue paper to a background then varnish over it. I can't find any reference to using wood, but it's close enough so I'll go with it.

Decoupage with Paper

Before you try wood, be aware that there's no reason you can't do traditional decoupage. Artwork on paper is an easy way to add a distinctive detail to your boat. You can draw or print a picture, pattern or logo on thin tracing paper or rice paper and fiberglass over it. The resin will make the paper virtually disappear, leaving just the black of the printing visible.

You can do a drawing with non-fading ink or make a photocopy of a suitable drawing. Although it will be protected from the sun by the resin and varnish, there is still some chance that the artwork will fade if you use the wrong ink. Also, be sure to test a sample drawing to see how well your paper disappears and to make sure the resin doesn't make the ink run.

Figure 8-15. A simple decoration can be created with artwork on paper. In this case I printed a guillemot on lightweight tracing paper using my laser printer, and cut around the outside of the picture. Rice paper works even better because it virtually disappears in the resin.

Remember that paper isn't as flexible as glass cloth, so you can't apply a paper picture to a surface that's a compound curve. Choose a place that's relatively flat and try spreading the drawing out. If you can't make it lie flat, don't attempt to apply it there.

Apply the picture just before glassing. Trim the paper just bigger than the artwork so the edge will be less noticeable, and spread a coat of resin on the boat where you want it to go. Carefully apply the picture at one side and roll it on slowly, avoiding trapping air under the paper. Once it's in place, use your gloved fingers or a squeegee to move any trapped air to the edges. You can then lay the fiberglass over it, proceeding with care so that you don't move the paper.

Feathers and Ferns

The decoupage technique offers a lot of options for experimentation. I have seen feathers, ferns, and leaves laid under the fiberglass. Any object that is thin and flat is a potential decorative element. Remember that any thickness or 3-D relief that the object has will be "telegraphed" through the fiberglass and may create a bump on the finished surface. There's nothing wrong with this: just realize that it will happen, and that it may make that area hard to sand.

Working with Veneer

A picture or pattern made of wood looks very classy. Using the thin paper-backed veneers available today, you can glue your artwork right to the surface of the boat without inlaying. You will be able to feel the veneer when under the fiberglass when you run your hand over it, but that's all right. The bump will be small and barely visible. One of the beauties of this technique is that it looks much harder to do than it really is.

Another advantage of this thin paper-backed veneer is that it can be cut with scissors or an X-Acto knife. I draw the outline of the pattern I want on the paper backing (make sure you reverse the drawing when you draw on the back) and then sit down in front of the TV while I cut out along the lines. The design can be as simple or complex as you want. It can be a bird such as the guillemot I have put on some of my kayaks or it can be an abstract pattern.

If you come up with a design that requires one color of veneer within, or right next to, another, you will need to do some careful fitting. For a piece that fits in a hole in another, cut the outer piece first. Use the hole as a pattern to trace on the back of the inner piece. You can now cut out the inner piece following the line.

A nail file is good for sanding back the edge for a close fit. Alternatively, you can use a knife to trace through the hole of the bigger piece directly onto the smaller piece—just make sure you don't ruin the first piece.

Once you have all the pieces cut out, assemble them to make sure everything fits the way you expected. You are now ready to glue the artwork to the boat. There are two ways: ironing on is quick and easy, but may not be as strong, it is best suited for small pieces; epoxying on requires more care, but is stronger and better suited for large pieces.

Iron-On Veneer

Common yellow carpenter's glue (aliphatic resin) can be used as a hot-melt glue. It can be applied to a piece, let dry, then heated to create a bond. This means you can make your own iron-on veneer. For large areas, you should really apply glue to both surfaces, but with small pieces this is not necessary.

Thin down a small amount of glue with a few drops of water and paint a layer on the whole back surface of the veneer. If you are gluing on pieces that are wider than about $1/2$ inch, you should also paint glue on the boat. Keep the glue line a little away from the edges of the veneer, because any glue that squeezes out will be visible in the finished product. Don't worry about the edge not being glued down. When you apply the epoxy over it, capillary attraction will pull resin under the edge, assuring a good bond.

After the glue dries, paint on another coat to increase the thickness. Let all the glue dry completely, then hold the veneer in place and tack it down with a firm press of a hot iron. Arrange all the pieces on the boat. When everything is in place, go over the whole artwork with the hot iron. As you press, you'll hear the crackling as it melts.

Figure 8-16. A wooden "inlay" of a guillemot looks even more impressive than decoupage in paper (Figure 8-15). Here, the veneer is so thin that it did not need to be inlaid into the strips. It was just laminated to the surface and glassed over.

Use firm pressure to push the melting glue into the wood of the boat. Don't overheat the veneer, though, as it may scorch.

The heat of the iron may also shrink the veneer, so if you have pieces fitting inside each other where the tolerances are close, you should pre-shrink the wood by running a hot iron over it before you cut out your pattern.

After the veneer is firmly in place, you can proceed with a sealer coat of epoxy and fiberglass, as usual. A potential problem with this method is that since the glue can be activated by heat, it may soften and cause a bubble on a hot, sunny day. This should not be a problem with small pieces, but a large piece of veneer may need more care.

Figure 8-17. *Plastic wrap stretched around an intricate veneer holds it in place while the epoxy sets. See text under Epoxied Veneer.*

Epoxied Veneer

With large pieces of veneer, which need a stronger bond to the boat, you'd be better off using epoxy to glue down your artwork. It's more complicated to get right, though, and if you do it wrong you can make a real mess.

It's easier if you apply a sealer coat on the boat before applying the veneer. Without the sealer coat you may get some splotchiness around the veneer where the boat has epoxy on it.

Assemble the veneer artwork and hold it together with masking tape on the front face. Use one of the "long-term" types of masking tape that are easier to remove. Paint a coat of epoxy on the boat and the veneer. Do not put on too much epoxy because it will only cause drips. Lay the artwork in place and press it down. Now, to hold it in place and clamp it down, I stretch plastic wrap around it and the boat (Figure 8-17). Pull the plastic wrap as tight as you can and go around the boat enough times to completely cover the artwork. Use a roller or your hands to press down more. You can apply a little more pressure by following the first layers of plastic wrap with a layer of something springy like foam or bubble wrap, followed by a couple more turns of plastic wrap.

When the epoxy has set, remove the plastic wrap. If you have to remove the tape you used to hold the artwork together before gluing, you don't want to let the epoxy get too hard. Carefully remove the tape. There will be wrinkles in the epoxy caused by the plastic wrap. They're hard to avoid, so just try not to use too much glue, and remove any resulting wrinkles with a scraper and sandpaper. Be careful not to damage the veneer as you clean up the epoxy. Clean out any dust that collects in bubbles so the bubbles don't show up later.

Now you can glass the boat normally. There is no need to put a sealer coat on the veneer as it is so thin that it doesn't absorb much epoxy. Whichever method you use for gluing down the veneer, since it is not inlaid there will be a bump around the edge of the artwork after you glass it. Be careful sanding this area. You do not want to sand through the fiberglass. This can be hard to avoid if you are using power tools, and it's probably best if you leave this area to sand by hand.

You can avoid the bump around the artwork if you actually go through the effort of inlaying it, which means carving out a depression for the veneer. I wouldn't advise you to use the thin veneer if you're doing this. It will be easier with thicker veneer. I don't feel the effort is worth it, but for the real perfectionist it may be the way to go.

Painted Finishes

The last way to dress up your boat I will discuss only briefly. You can paint the boat. You can paint all of it, part of it, or just some artistic pattern. There is actually a good reason for painting all of it: You don't need to be so careful with your stripping. You can leave gaps between the strips and just fill them with fairing compound, which lets you finish the boat faster and use lesser-quality wood. If you don't want to be quite that drastic, you can just paint on some artwork.

Painting the whole boat. Even though I've spent a lot of time in this book describing how to make the wood look good, there is really no reason for you to give your kayak a brightwork finish. Don't be embarrassed to paint the whole thing, or maybe just the hull.

Fill big gaps with putty. Apply fairing compound to fill any small hollows before glassing, and sand the compound fair. Glass the boat normally and then apply a high-build primer, suited to the fiberglass and the paint you're using, to fill any small imperfections. Sand the primer smooth and paint away. Just be aware that uneven spots will show up more on a painted surface than they will on wood finished bright.

Painting artwork. Some bright spots of color may be just the ticket to personalizing your boat. Maybe you want a bigger pattern than you can produce on a sheet of paper. Whatever your reason, paint is perfectly reasonable.

If you paint your pattern before glassing, it will be protected from scratches. You will also be able to sand and revarnish the outside of the boat without worrying about damaging your artwork.

It may be, though, that you want to be able to remove the artwork, in which case you should put it on last. If you plan to paint before glassing, first apply a sealer coat of resin.

Be aware that the resin may have problems bonding to some paints. Epoxy-based paints should be all right, as should water-based stains and dies. Gloss paints should be carefully sanded to provide a good mechanical bond. Also remember that the color of the resin and varnish over the paint will affect the color somewhat.

Be Creative

There are innumerable ways of personalizing your kayak, but one of the best ways is to just get out and paddle it. After all, it takes time to decorate your boat artistically, and if what you really want to do is get out on the water, don't bother getting fancy. Just make the boat and put it in the water. The real beauty of a kayak is not what it looks like, but how it handles on the water.

With that said, let me urge you to be creative. If you have an idea you want to try, go for it. If you have a set of wood-burning tools and an inspiration, give it a try. If you think you can do something cool with stain, give it a try. Don't be put off because you don't know if it has been done before; give it a try. You will either be pleased with your work or you will learn a good lesson. Both are valuable. If you are nervous about attempting something new, try it on a smaller project: maybe a strip-built mailbox.

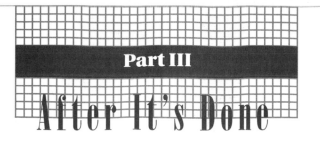

Part III

After It's Done

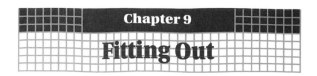

uch of the safety and performance of a kayak depends on how well it fits the paddler. To handle a kayak at its best, you don't sit in it. You wear it. For some, this immediately brings on visions of being trapped in a boat that fits like a pair of fine leather gloves, gloves that take 10 minutes to remove. A kayak should indeed fit like a glove, but there's no need for it to trap you. You want a boat that fits well but also lets you move freely.

When I described stability earlier in the book, I mentioned leaning and how it contributes to stability. You cannot lean a boat properly if you're flopping around in it. Your butt needs to stay in place and you must be able to apply pressure to the boat with your feet and knees, or thighs.

For comfort you need back support that comes from two places. The obvious one is the backrest, but less obvious is the support you get from bracing your thighs. Proper thigh braces take strain off your stomach muscles and leg muscles as you lean back. The backrest should support your back without restricting your movement.

The Seat

The seat is your primary connection to the boat. The first thing you notice when you sit in the boat is whether the seat is comfortable or not. If you don't get the seat right, you'll never be comfortable.

Much of the power you put into the paddle gets transferred to the boat through the seat, so you don't want to move around in it. It should fit so well that you don't *need* to move around in it to get and stay comfortable.

Comfort comes less from soft material than good shape. That's why one of the most com-

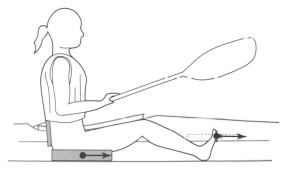

Figure 9-1. *The force of your paddling forward is transferred to the boat through the points where you touch it. The primary points are your seat and, importantly, your feet. If you do not have firm footbraces, your legs and stomach will soon get tired and the boat will feel uncomfortable. The backrest provides support to counteract the force of your feet pushing against the footbraces.*

fortable things I ever sat in was a old cast-iron tractor seat. It provided absolutely no cushioning but was well contoured to fit my bottom. A comfortable seat will match your anatomy. It will rise up in the back, wrap around you, and support you under the thighs. And that's important because holding your legs up in the air can be tiring. Extending the seat forward, and angling the front upward to support your legs, will help keep them from falling asleep.

For stability you usually want the seat as low as possible, to keep your center of gravity low. A difference of half an inch can make a real difference in stability. But it also depends on how you're built. Smaller, lighter paddlers may prefer a higher seat because it gets them up out of the boat more, and the higher center of gravity also works to their advantage when they try to lean the boat.

Some of the most comfortable kayak seats are hard fiberglass molds. This is one way to make a good seat. You can either take a mold off a kayak you find comfortable or you can sculpt your own mold from plaster. You can then glue this seat to the bottom or hang it from the cheek plates. And while a hard seat can be comfortable, as I've noted, the same seat made of a cushioning material will be even more comfortable.

I sculpt my own seats from a material popularly called "minicell" foam. You can buy seats made of this material, but for a better fit you may want to construct your own. My starting point for a seat is a 14-inch by 16-inch by 3-inch block of minicell. Ethafoam is another material you can use, but it has larger cells than minicell and thus absorbs more water.

The typical tool for sculpting the foam is popularly known as "dragon skin," a piece of metal with small sharp perforations in it, similar to a cheese grater. You can also use a coarse disk sander in your drill to shape the foam. I use a high-speed right-angle grinder. It can do a lot of damage quickly and it will catch and dive if you're not careful, creating a divot in the foam. But once you get used to it, the grinder works great, as long as you remember to wear a dust mask. All the material you remove from the seat will make it into the air.

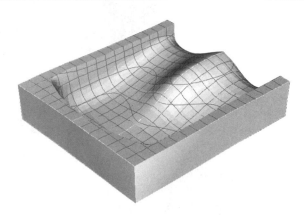

Figure 9-3. The foam seat should be low in the back and sloping upwards to the front. Leave a ridge between your legs but do not extend this back to the bottom of the seat. Leave the foam at full height all the way around the sides and behind the back. Round over the front edge so it does not cut into your legs. This seat will be comfortable and provide good support for your thighs.

Use a loop of tape under the seat to secure it to the floor or workbench while you grind. Cutting with the top edge of the grinder, start near the back of the seat and pull toward the front. Start by cutting a couple of troughs for your legs. Lift as you pull to the front. Leave the front at almost the full height of the foam. Next join the two troughs by cutting across near the back. Leave the full height of foam all the way around the back and along the sides. You want a ridge down the middle between your legs but no ridge under your bottom. Sit in the seat well before you think it's finished, to feel what pokes. The bottom thickness at the lowest point should be $1/2$ inch or less. Round off the front end of the leg area so there is no sharp edge to cut off circulation.

When I have finished the seat I turn it over and cut a groove lengthwise down the centerline. This limber hole allows water to pass under the seat, along the floor of the kayak, so the boat is easier to sponge dry.

Figure 9-2. You can sculpt your own custom seat from a piece of foam. A high-speed grinder with coarse sandpaper and a delicate touch will quickly make a lot of dust and a comfortable seat. Always move the grinder so the disk is spinning in opposition to the direction you are cutting.

Ideally, the seat location will put your center of gravity right at the designed center of buoyancy of the kayak. But as a practical matter you want the seat where it's most comfortable and in a place from which you can handle the boat best. In a well-designed boat, these three points will be in the same place. The best practice is to paddle the boat for a while with the seat temporarily held in place with tape or small spots of glue. Move the seat forward or back a few times to see where you like it best. Mark the front edge of the seat on the bottom so you can return it to the right place.

Apply some contact cement (the stuff that's marked "Highly flammable") in stripes down either side of the bottom, following the manufacturer's instructions. You don't need to mess the whole bottom up, narrow stripes will do the job and make the seat a little easier to remove if you make a mistake. The glue grabs as soon as it touches, so align your seat carefully before committing yourself.

The Cheek Plates

The cheek plates fit on either side of the seat and hold your body centered in the kayak while you are leaning. If you do not want to make my hanging wooden cheek plates, you can build this support from chunks of foam. The hanging version is easier to attach a backrest to, and permits you to store a sponge behind them where you won't lose it. A deep, well-contoured seat may virtually eliminate the need for the cheek plates, but for a proper fit in the kayak it's important that you don't move from side to side. Some paddlers may want to install foam spacers on their cheek plates to make a tighter fit.

The Backrest

There was a time when a backrest was frowned upon in a kayak. Some kayaks still do not come with one. There is a reason for that, but it's not good enough now that you can make a backrest that avoids the problem.

Many times when you're handling a kayak you want to be able to lean back. For strong paddling it's also important that your torso is free to move and rotate. But a poorly designed backrest will not let your back move.

As you sit in a kayak with your feet up against the footbraces, you push back with your toes. This pressure can push you backward in the kayak. Your back and legs will get very tired trying to maintain a balance between pushing too much and not enough. To counter this you need something to push against, and a well-contoured seat that wraps around behind your butt is part of the solution. A backrest is the complete solution. It just needs to be able to provide the support without restricting your back's movement.

This paradox can be solved by making the backrest flexible. The backrest system I use moves from side to side and reclines backward,

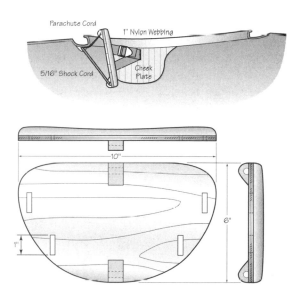

Figure 9-4. A comfortable, articulated backrest is constructed from 1/4-inch marine plywood or a panel of fiberglass-covered strips. It's held in place by webbing attached to the cheek plates and threaded through slots. A shock cord from the back of the cockpit to the bottom of the backrest holds it up at the correct height and a light piece of cord at the top counteracts the shock cord's tendency to flip the whole system over. This backrest will move with the paddler, while still providing back support.

but it always provides solid support to the lumbar area. It's adjustable and can be customized to fit most paddlers.

Cut the backrest out of plywood or a strip-built panel measuring about 10 inches by 6 inches by ¼ inch, and cut some 1-inch slots for webbing to thread through (Figure 9-4). If you use a strip-built panel, make the slots oversized and fill them with epoxy before cutting the correct-sized slot. This will make it stronger. You can either attach some pad-eyes to the top and bottom of the backrest or drill some holes through which you can loop some rope.

The backrest is attached to the boat with webbing. Use two pieces of 1-inch-wide nylon webbing about 30 inches long. Attach the female side of a nylon buckle, such as those made by Fastex, to one end of the webbing. Double over the webbing so that the side with the buckle is about 4 inches long. Sew the two halves together to form a loop that will accept a ½-inch dowel.

You will need slots drilled through the cheek plates to accept the webbing, but be careful that you don't drill straight through the side of the boat after you've drilled through the cheek plate. You might want to slide a piece of sheet metal up behind the cheek plate to stop the drill.

Place the slot as high up on the cheek plate as you can without drilling into the fillet at the top. This is usually about ½ inch down from the top. Drill a series of ½-inch holes to make an oversized slot. Use a file to clean up the slot. Stick some tape behind the slot and pour some resin thickened with silica into the hole to fill it in again. Now drill a series of ¼-inch holes to create the slot the webbing will go through. Rock the drill up and down to even up the width, and use a file to clean up any remaining roughness.

Slide the loop you made in the webbing through the slot and insert a ½-inch dowel (1¼ inches long) into the loop on the back side of

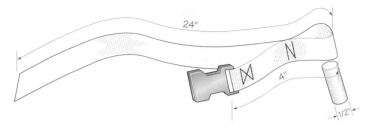

Figure 9-5. *Sew the female side of the plastic buckle onto one end of the webbing, and sew a loop big enough to hold a ½-inch dowel. This loop will be inserted through a ¼-inch-wide slot in the cheek plates. Inserting the dowel into the loop will trap the webbing in the slot. The long end of the webbing is threaded through the backrest and the male end of the buckle is threaded onto the webbing. The backrest can be adjusted by moving the male buckle.*

the cheek plate. When you pull the webbing tight, the dowel will be locked in place. If you want a little more security use a short piece of PVC pipe instead of the dowel and loop some string through the pipe to tie it in place. Install the other piece of webbing on the other side so you have one buckle on each side and one long strap on each side.

Thread the long straps through the slots on the backrest. Thread the male side of the buckle onto the remaining long end of the webbing and connect the buckles.

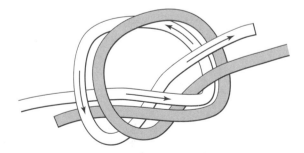

Figure 9-6. *Shock cord does not like to stay tied. This is the only knot I have found that works. Make an overhand knot in one end (gray) then thread the other end (white) backward through the knot, parallel to the other line, and pull both lines tight. This knot is used on the backrest and can be used on deck lines as well.*

Figure 9-8. *You can save a lot of time by purchasing one of several available makes of ready-made footbraces. On the left are machined aluminum rails with one of the aluminum-and-plastic footbraces. The pair on the right is all plastic. Across the back is one of the aluminum rails in a plastic track for a rudder system. These are all strong, corrosion-resistant, fully adjustable, and easy to install.*

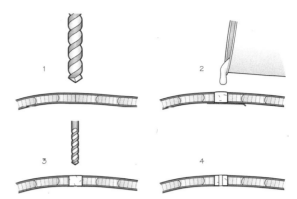

Figure 9-9. *Any time you penetrate the skin of the kayak to install hardware, such as the footbraces in Figure 9-8, you should drill the hole oversized, fill the hole with resin, and then re-drill the hole to size. This will seal the wood completely and distribute the force of the hardware on the strips.*

unthickened epoxy into the hole to soak into the bare wood. Finally, fill the hole with epoxy mixed with chopped fiberglass. When these plugs have cured, you can drill the correct-sized holes through them to install the footbraces. The extra work makes a stronger joint and seals the wood strips against moisture. See Figure 9-9.

Figure 9-10 shows an adjustable bulkhead-style footbrace you can make yourself from ¼-inch marine plywood. The angle and lean of the wings makes this system very comfortable. Mount the bottom on the support after rounding the peg at the back of the support with a file to fit in the hole in the bottom. Glue the brace on the top of the support. After the glue has dried,

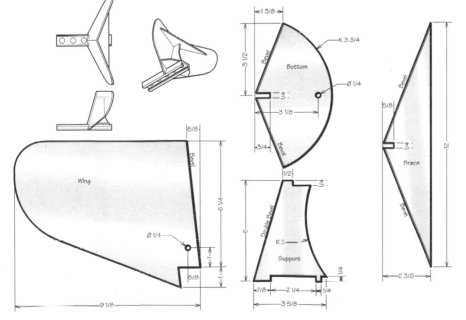

Figure 9-10. *Dimensions for a home-made footbrace. A bulkhead-type footbrace like this is probably the most comfortable. Install the "Support" into the "Bottom," place the "Brace" on top and glue two "Wings" to the front. This assembly then gets glued to the top of the "Slider" shown in Figure 9-11. The angle of the wings lets you sit with your toes pointed forward. Use ¼-inch marine plywood throughout.*

Loop a 12-inch piece of ⁵/₁₆-inch shock cord through the loop at the bottom of the backrest to the loop installed at the back of the cockpit. Tie the ends of the shock cord together so the loop is snug. Shock cord is amazingly hard to tie. Most knots just slip out, and I've found only one knot that works. Unfortunately I don't know the name of it, so I'll call it the "shock-cord knot." See Figure 9-6. When you pull this knot tight it's very secure, yet I have always been able to untie it when I needed to.

The tight shock cord will tend to flip the backrest over, so I tie a piece of light nylon cord (such as parachute cord) from the top of the backrest back to the loop under the deck to keep the backrest aligned properly (Figure 9-7). This cord does not need to be very strong because it doesn't really get much force on it when you are sitting. It's just there to keep the backrest upright.

This backrest has a lot of adjustments, which can make it difficult to set up, but once you've got it all right it should be very comfortable. You can control how far back it is by adjusting the webbing straps. By taking up on the top or bottom webbing you can set the angle of the backrest. Tightening up on the shock cord will raise the backrest. The shock cord permits the backrest to move up and down and lean back, but people who are more comfortable with a more rigid backrest may want to use thicker shock cord or rope that doesn't stretch much.

Footbraces

When you're paddling, the force from the paddle is transferred from you to the boat in two places. The first is your seat, and the other is your footbraces. Without footbraces, all the force must go through the seat. This will soon tire most people. One excellent solution for a footbrace is to place the forward bulkhead right at your feet. This makes efficient use of space and can be very comfortable.

A bulkhead footbrace is most comfortable if you can angle it to match your feet. When sitting down, with your legs out front, your toes naturally want to point to the side and forward. Tilt the bulkhead slightly forward and have it slope back to the sides to match the natural angle of your toes. The easiest way to do this is not actually to tilt the bulkhead but to add foam to create the shape on the face of the bulkhead. You will need to reinforce the bulkhead to withstand the pressure from your feet pushing on it.

A bulkhead can make a comfortable footbrace but it's often more convenient to have the footbraces adjustable. This lets you lend the boat to different-sized people. It can also be nice to change your foot position during long paddles. The easiest method is to just buy a plastic or aluminum adjustable footbrace and bolt it through the sides of the boat.

Plan it so that the center position on the footbraces approximately matches your setting. Sit in the boat to figure this out. Measure a couple of times before drilling any holes. Drill the holes oversized—about ¹/₂ inch diameter is appropriate—then seal the inside end of the hole with tape, and brush

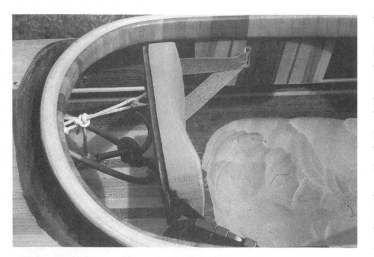

Figure 9-7. *The backrest is suspended away from the back of the coaming. Instead of pad-eyes on the backrest, I used loops of cord to attach the shock cord. The buckle, visible at the bottom of the picture, allows access to the space behind the seat.*

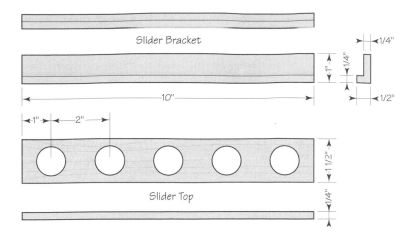

Slider Bracket

Slider Top

Figure 9-11. This slider is mounted on the bottom of the footbrace shown in Figure 9-10. The slider will slip onto the rail in Figure 9-12.

file a bevel on the edge of the bottom and brace to match the angle of the support. Also bevel the edge of the wings to a miter so they will fit together tightly. Drill a ¼-inch hole near the bottom of the wings through which to thread a rope. Glue the wings to the front of the support assembly with the top of the notch on the wings in line with the bottom of the support assembly.

Cut an L-shaped piece of hardwood such as ash, mahogany, or oak for the slider brackets.

Glue the brackets to the sides of the slider top. The slider top can be of plywood or hardwood. The holes in the slider top are not functional—they're there to save weight. Glue the footbrace wing assembly onto the slider, with the back of the bottom aligned with the back of the slider.

Make the rail out of hardwood. Use a ⅜-inch drill to make a series of holes along the length of the rail. Countersink both sides of the holes to break the sharp corners before cutting

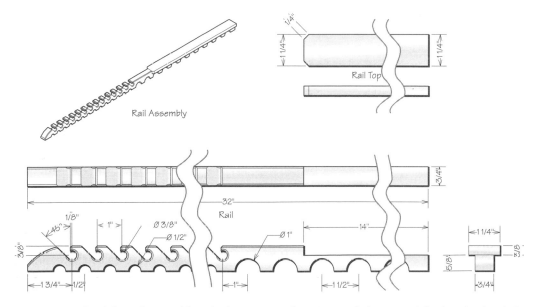

Rail Assembly

Rail Top

Rail

Figure 9-12. Details of the rail assembly, which is mounted on the inside bottom of the kayak. The slider and footbrace assembly shown in Figures 9-10 and 9-11 fits over the "Rail Top." The hooks will hold a rope that loops through the wings of the footbrace.

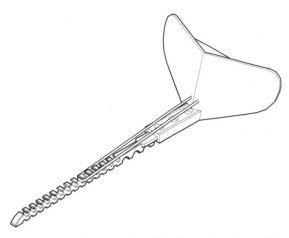

Figure 9-13. The completed footbrace is adjusted by moving the loop of rope to different hooks. Mount the rail so the range of adjustments will serve the likely users of the kayak.

free the holes to create a hook. The half holes on the bottom of the rail are again to save weight and are not required. Cut back the height of the rail to accept the rail top. Glue the hardwood rail top onto the rail.

The rail is glued lengthwise down the centerline on the bottom of the boat. A circle of rope strung through the holes in the wings is looped onto the hooks to adjust the footbraces, which slide on the rail. The dimensions of the wings may need to be adjusted to fit your boat. As drawn, they will fit the Great Auk and Guillemot Double. They may need to be changed to fit the Guillemot.

Knee and Thigh Braces

As I've already mentioned, an important aspect of the stability of a kayak is the paddler's ability to lean. This is not merely a matter of shifting weight from side to side. In a poorly outfitted kayak this will cause your position to move, and when you've finished leaning you may find yourself unable to regain your balance. While your seat does much of the work of keeping you in place, it's your knees that control the boat. Without proper knee or thigh braces, the boat may feel unstable, you won't be able to lean

well, and you certainly will have a hard time performing an Eskimo roll.

Paddlers need to be able to apply pressure to the boat by pushing their legs toward the middle of the boat, so boats with smaller cockpits can be fitted with thigh braces. These are "hooks" that wrap a little bit around the inside of the thigh.

But sea kayaks tend to have larger cockpits, and the most convenient place to get some purchase on the boat is at the knees. Here, some cups can be fashioned of foam to cushion the knee (Figure 9-14).

Cut some wedges of minicell or Ethafoam. Sand a hollow that fits the contour of your knee. Sit comfortably in the boat. Bring your knees up toward the deck. Put the foam wedge between your knee and the deck. Inspect how it fits your knees and the deck and shape it more, to fit snugly. Take some time to make your wedges comfortable.

When you are done shaping the knee braces, carefully mark their position under the deck. Apply contact cement to the deck and foam. Carefully place the foam when the cement is dry to the touch.

Figure 9-14. A comfortable fit in a kayak depends on the paddler's contact points with the boat. Many of the techniques used by skilled kayakers depend on leaning the boat. Comfortable leaning requires a good seat that does not let your bottom move, rigid footbraces that let you press against them, and finally solid contact with the upper part of the leg, which can be accomplished with knee braces, as shown in this figure, or thigh braces. I recommend carving blocks of foam to cup your knees. (See Figure 7-20.)

Bulkheads

The best way to keep a boat from sinking is to keep the water out. This obvious statement is easier said than done when you need a hole in the boat in order to sit in it. The next choice is to limit how much water can get in. This can be done in several ways: air bags, a sea sock, bulkheads, or a combination of all three.

Air bags are essentially balloons you stuff in the ends of the kayak to provide flotation. Sea-kayak air bags can be purchased shaped to fit into the ends, with filling tubes attached. A sea sock is secured to the cockpit coaming and pushed inside the cockpit. The paddler sits inside the sock. The amount of water that can get into the cockpit then is limited to the volume of the sock minus the volume of the occupant.

Bulkheads are watertight walls that separate one section of the boat from another. In a kayak they perform the same function as the sea sock: they limit the amount of water that can enter the boat. They also offer the secondary advantage of creating a dry-storage compartment.

It's never a bad idea to have some redundancy. Bulkheads plus air bags will make sure that if, for some reason, the integrity of the bulkhead is compromised (a hole through the hull from a violent collision with a rock, for example), you will still be able to paddle home safely. Topping this off with a sea sock is not out of the question.

Install your bulkheads so the cockpit is as small as possible, but don't fix them in place until you have installed your footbraces, otherwise you might find them too close to your feet.

I only install bulkheads if I'm installing a hatch. If I don't want a forehatch, I'll use an air bag in the bow instead.

There are several ways to make a bulkhead. You can strip-build a panel and cover it with glass on both sides. Or you can cut a piece of marine plywood to fit, or you can use a panel of foam.

A purist will probably want to go with wood because it seems so much more solid than a piece of foam. It is. And strangely enough, that's a potential problem. You see, if you slide over a rock, the boat is going to flex slightly, creating a bump inside the boat (Figure 9-15). The bump moves down the boat as the rock scratches its way down the length of your new varnish, until it comes to the bulkhead. Here, the rigid wood bulkhead does not let the boat flex to absorb the abuse. The rock and the bulkhead may act like a pair of scissors. Potentially, you will get a hole from something you could have slid right over with no more damage than a big ugly scratch on the bottom. The foam bulkhead lets the boat flex, so all you get is that ugly scratch.

Having said that, I must point out that the skin of the average strip-built kayak is already so rigid that a stiff bulkhead may not make that significant a difference. So, even if you use a wooden bulkhead, your boat is not going to implode with the first rock you hit. The foam bulkhead will only make a difference in the hardest collisions. Still, foam has one great advantage over wood. A foam bulkhead is easier to install.

If your planned bulkhead happens to fall right where one of the building forms was located, then simply use the form as a pattern. Cut a piece of 3-inch-thick minicell foam 1/4-inch bigger than the form.

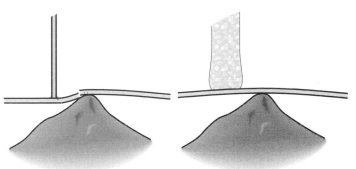

Figure 9-15. *A rigid plywood bulkhead (left) stiffens the boat but does not permit it to flex over obstacles. The foam bulkhead (right) compresses upon impact and distributes the force of the collision over a wider area, making it less likely that the rock will penetrate the kayak's skin.*

If the bulkhead does not lie right on a form, use the forms on either side to estimate the shape. Cut it oversized because the foam will compress as you squeeze it into position. If you can't force it in, trim off ⅛ inch or less, and try again. The press-fit foam will provide a pretty good initial seal. Use RTV (silicone caulk) or a boat caulk to assure a watertight seal. Poke the end of the tube between the bulkhead and the skin and inject the caulk. A little will ooze out. Clean this up by smoothing it out with a gloved finger.

A wooden bulkhead needs to fit better. Use nearby forms as a pattern to cut out a pattern from cardboard. Get the cardboard pattern right before committing it to wood. After you transfer the pattern to the wood, cut it out with a jigsaw or bandsaw. Pre-coat the bulkhead with resin before installing it. Tack the bulkhead in place with a few dots of hot-melt glue. Mix up some filler with epoxy, sawdust, and silica. Create a fillet around the edge of the bulkhead. Let it cure. You might need to do some light sanding to remove any sharp points.

Deck Lines

Deck lines serve two purposes. They can be used to secure charts, water bottles, spare paddles, and other cargo to the deck They are also safety devices. If you fall overboard, they give you something to grab onto as you climb back in.

The deck lines are attached with some sort of pad-eye. The pad-eye can be a purchased item of plastic or corrosion-resistant metal. Both are good. The plastic pad-eyes are strong enough and will never corrode.

You can also make your own pad-eyes from wood, but don't use the same wood you built the kayak with. You need a stronger hardwood, such as mahogany, teak, or oak. Cut out the pad-eye roughly to shape and drill a suitably large hole for your rope or shock cord. It's easiest if you drill the hole while the piece is still attached to a big piece of wood. Cut the pieces out after drilling, sand them to a smooth shape, and contour the bottom to fit the deck if necessary.

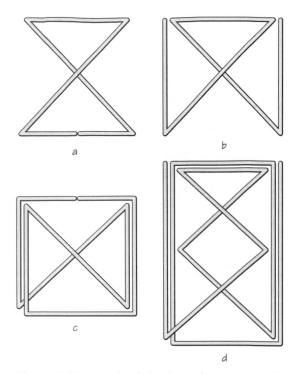

Figure 9-16. *A web of shock cord or rope on the deck provides a place to hold down charts, water bottles, and the occasional candy bar. Patterns (a), (b), and (c) use four pad-eyes set up in a square pattern and provide progressively more options for holding things down. Pattern (d) requires six pad-eyes and is what I use on expedition boats where I might want to carry several items on deck. I generally use pattern (a) for holding down hatches—see Figure 9-18.*

When the pad-eyes are done, paint them completely with resin to seal the wood and let it cure. Clean up any drips and thoroughly sand the location on the deck where you will mount them. Mix up some resin, some milled fiberglass, and a little silica to glue down the pad-eyes. Apply the glue to both the pad-eye and the deck. Press it into place and clean up the extra glue. Hold the part in place with some tape until the resin cures.

Wooden pad-eyes look the best, but may be prone to splitting if abused. The plastic pad-eyes are stronger and if you bolt them through the skin there is no chance that they will peel off. Use stainless steel or bronze hardware for all the bolts, nuts, and washers to prevent cor-

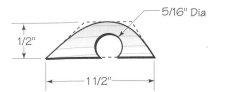

Figure 9-17. A simple wooden loop or pad-eye can be made to mount deck lines. Adjust the size of the hole to accommodate the size of the line you're using. You will probably have to contour the bottom to conform to the shape of the deck. Silica-thickened resin is usually all that is required to attach the pad-eye.

Figure 9-19. You can also use webbing and buckles to hold down the hatch. Here, on the Great Auk, I installed wooden risers so the webbing could push down on the sides of the hatch.

rosion problems. Make sure you use a washer on the inside to ensure that the bolt does not rip through or crush the skin. Seal the exposed wood in the hole with resin. Apply a little varnish to the bolt before putting the nut on to keep the nut from coming loose.

If you are putting pad-eyes in places you won't be able to reach from a hatch or the cockpit, you won't be able to put a nut on the bolt, of course, so plan ahead. Install all your pad-eyes before you attach the deck to the hull. Put a drop of epoxy on all the nuts so that they will bond to the deck. Put a little wax on the bolts so they are removable. Now you will be

able to remove the pad-eyes to sand the deck. Make sure you clean out the holes after sanding and don't let any varnish drip into them. The epoxy does not bond well to the metal, so it's possible for the nut to break loose if you have to force it. Sanding the hardware slightly will create a better bond.

Securing Hatch Covers

I use shock cord to hold down the hatch because it's quick, reliable, and easy to replace. Put a loop on either side of one end of the hatch. Put two hooks at the other end. Now you can string some ³/₈-inch shock cord through the pad-eyes. By crossing the shock cord and looping it over the hooks you can securely hold down the hatch.

You can also use nylon webbing with plastic buckles to secure the hatch. Although it can be hard to get these straps really tight, and even though they tend to stretch when they get wet, you can assure a tight seal by mounting pieces of wood on the hatch cover for the straps to bridge over. Also, wet the straps before you tighten them (Figure 9-19).

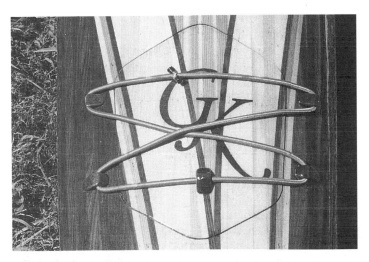

Figure 9-18. A simple crossed loop of shock cord is all that is required to hold down the hatch cover. The loop runs through pad-eyes on the deck near one end of the hatch and attaches to wooden hooks near the other end. The pad-eye in the middle of the hatch cover attaches it to the shock cord so you don't lose it.

Some people have used a "dog" system consisting of a wooden toggle long enough to reach across the hatch and beyond. A threaded nut is mounted in the center. A knob with threaded rod is mounted through the hatch and threaded to the toggle. Rubber gaskets, made from a tire inner tube, seal the hole. In use, the toggle is hooked under the deck and the knob is tightened to hold the cover in place and put pressure on the gasket.

Hatch Gaskets

The best material I have found for gaskets is neoprene foam weather-stripping. This is available in $\frac{3}{4}$-inch by $\frac{1}{4}$-inch self-adhesive rolls. Start by cutting one end horizontally to a wedge shape with a razor blade (Figure 9-20). Peel back the protective paper and stick the end down close to the outer edge of the hatch cover. In the corners, just push it into the angle and hold it with one finger as you bend it in the desired direction. Work all the way around, ride the strip up the wedge you made at the beginning, and cut it off level with the razor blade. You should wait to do this until most of your varnishing and sanding is done. Make sure the surface is clean before sticking down the gasket.

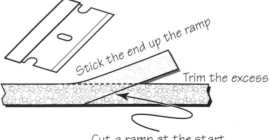
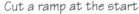

Figure 9-20. Neoprene foam from wet-suit material or self-adhesive weather-stripping makes a fairly watertight seal for your hatches. Start off your strip of closed-cell foam with a ramp, or wedge, cut in the end. After you've stuck the foam down all the way around, glue it down over the wedge and cut it off flush with a razor blade (left). Use contact cement to glue down gaskets made from wet-suit material.

Grab-Loops

The easiest place to grab the boat, if you fall out of it or need to drag it, is at one end or the other so it pays to have some good grab-loops there. The boat will also be much more secure on your car roof if you tie the ends down to the bumper.

The easiest grab-loop is a ring of rope tied through a hole drilled crosswise in the end of the boat (Figure 9-21). This isn't the whole reason behind the end-pours you did, but they do come in handy here. So try to drill though the end-pour, and if you miss, just pour more material in and try again. A $\frac{1}{2}$-inch-diameter hole is about right. Round over the edge of the hole with a large countersink or a rasp. Seal the exposed wood with several coats of epoxy and varnish.

Rudders

Rudders are optional. They can be helpful in a tandem kayak and they can make some conditions easier to handle in a single, but on the other hand a rudder has moving parts that are prone to breakage. Incidentally, you control a kayak rudder with your feet, but the pedals must not interfere with your ability to brace yourself.

You can either buy a complete rudder, or make your own. There are good commercial rudders made of aluminum with several different mounting styles, so shop around. For most

Figure 9-21. A rope through the end-pour provides a strong place to lift the boat and tie it down to the bumper of your car.

people the commercial rudder systems are the way to go because building one of your own requires more tools than are available in the average garage workshop.

Mounting a Rudder

There are several different systems for mounting rudders. Some mount to a flat crosswise face at the stern, called a transom. I'll call them "transom-mount" rudders. Others mount on a pin that's set vertically into the deck at the stern. I'll call these "pin-mount" rudders.

Designs like the Great Auk and the Guillemot Double have sterns with enough meat in them for pin-mount rudders but on designs like the Guillemot, where the stern is small, you may need to cut off the last few inches of the stern. If you cut off your end-pour in the process, you'll need to tape off the end, do another small end-pour, and apply some fiberglass over the end. You can attach a transom-mount rudder to this.

Making Your Own Rudder

You can make a good rudder out of ¼-inch marine plywood. Cut out three pieces, each a little bit bigger than 6 inches by 3¾ inches, and laminate them together with resin to make a piece of ¾-inch plywood. Following the drawing in Figure 9-23, drill out the various holes and cut out the shape of the "T." The pivot hole should be drilled oversized, filled with resin, and drilled to fit your mounting hardware. Do the same for the blade support and rudder pivot holes.

The rudder blade also can be made out of ¼-inch plywood (Figure 9-24). The rudder will work most efficiently if it is shaped into an airfoil with a sander or a rasp. Don't thin the upper part, just the blade that will be in the water. A layer of fiberglass over the whole rudder blade will make it very strong.

Be sure to seal any exposed wood with resin. If you don't like the looks of the plywood, give everything a couple coats of spray enamel.

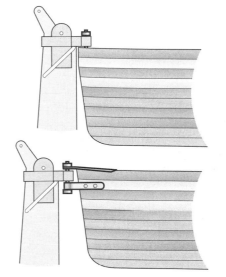

Figure 9-22. *Methods of attaching a rudder to the stern. In the upper example, a hole is drilled down through the deck into the end pour to accept a stainless steel bolt, which is then mounted vertically as a pivot. A locknut on top secures the rudder in place. In the lower example, stainless steel brackets support a vertical bolt dropped down through them.*

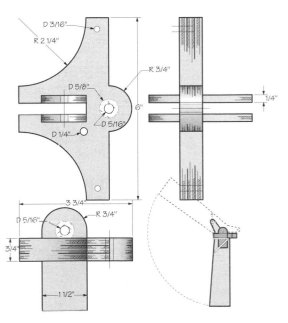

Figure 9-23. *Make the "T" of the rudder assembly from marine plywood. Use three layers of ¼-inch, or one layer of ¾-inch, plywood for the main body, and drill out the pivot holes in the manner shown in Figure 9-9.*

Use a ¼-inch stainless steel bolt through the blade support and blade for a pivot. A length of ¼-inch shock cord through the hole in the T and the blade will pull the blade down when you release the rudder lift-rope.

You can install a pin at the very back of the kayak for a pin-mount rudder system by drilling a 5/16-inch hole straight down about 2 inches into the deck. Cut the head off a ¼-inch diameter stainless steel bolt 3½ inches long. Use the kind of bolt that is threaded only on the last inch. File grooves and generally rough up the bottom 2 inches of the bolt to give the resin a good hold. Paint some epoxy on the bolt and in the hole and insert the bolt into the hole. The rudder can then be fitted down over this pin. Put a washer on the bottom and another on top and hold everything in place with a locking nut. Use stainless steel hardware throughout.

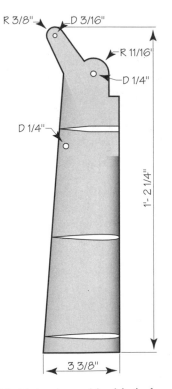

Figure 9-24. *Make the rudder blade from ¼-inch marine plywood covered with light fiberglass, or by laminating multiple layers of fiberglass and epoxy. Shape the lower part of the blade into an airfoil as shown in the cross sections.*

For a transom-mount rudder get some stainless-steel sheet about ¾ inch wide by 3 inches long. Round over the ends and bend 1 inch on each end to 90 degrees. Drill 5/16-inch holes through the center of both of these tabs, and drill two ⅛-inch holes in the middle part. This U-shaped piece can then be screwed to the transom of the kayak.

Rudder Control Cables

To enable the pedal control cables to exit the cockpit, I run some tubing through the rear bulkhead and out through the skin of the boat near the stern. The control cables run inside these tubes of soft copper tubing or plastic, both of which are available at most hardware stores. The plastic tubing is lighter and easier to handle, but use the smallest diameter that will hold your control cables.

Drill some holes through the bulkhead as close to the side of the boat as you can get. If you have minicell foam bulkheads you can make a nice clean hole by twisting a drinking straw through the foam.

The hole through the skin of the kayak requires some care, so first decide where you want the holes. The cables can come up through the deck, or out through the sides. For a pin-mount rudder, up through the deck may make more sense, whereas transom-mount rudders might need the cables to come through the sides. Even if you go through the deck, you still want the holes out toward the side. The cables should come out at a straight line toward the ends of the T of the rudder.

Using a drill bit the size of your tubing, start by drilling straight down. When you have the start of a hole, lean the drill back towards the rudder. Keep the drill buried by only leaning as far back as the bit will go while staying in the wood. The goal is to have the rudder cable come up through the deck at a very shallow angle. Once you are through the skin, you can continue to lean the drill to carve the hole.

Seal the wood grain with epoxy and let it cure before running the tubing through the hole. You will need to run all the tubing in from outside the hole in the skin. When the tubing is almost all the way in, rough up the outside of the tubing so resin will have some surface to grip on. Smear some dookie schmutz around the end of the tubing and into the hole. Slide the tubing the rest of the way in and fill any gaps with dookie schmutz. Leave a couple of inches of tubing sticking out. You may need to use some tape to hold the tubing in place while everything cures. After it has cured, trim off the excess tubing flush with the deck. Sand the surface smooth and remove any excess dookie schmutz.

The tubing should be long enough that it can run up forward of the seat. You may want to glue down the loose end of the tubing or secure it under a pad-eye. In any case, it should stay out of the way and let your control pedals work freely.

For most rudders you will need a lift-control rope as well. This is generally mounted on the deck. This permits the rudder to be lifted out of the water when you don't need it or when you are coming ashore. The rope can run through a few pad-eyes to keep it in place and should end up with a cleat mount just behind the cockpit on one side of the boat. On the rudder described above, the lift-rope is tied to the tab at the top of the rudder. The first pad-eye should be mounted on the centerline 3 or 4 inches in front of the rudder. The steering control cables are tied to the arms of the T.

Rudder Control Pedals

The standard, commercially available rudder pedals are mounted in much the same way as the adjustable footbraces I described previously. In fact they are often the same footbraces mounted in a track that lets them slide forward and back. This system works by transferring all the pressure from pushing on the pedals back through the control cables to the rudder. This works well except for two problems: Since all the force on the pedals goes through the cables, the cables are under a lot of stress and may break; and if the control cable breaks, there's nothing to hold the pedals, so you can no longer brace properly.

You can get around this problem if you use a bulkhead-type footbrace like the one I describe how to make. The difference is the bulkhead must pivot (Figure 9-25). Use the same track and slider as the adjustable bulkhead footbrace described previously. Make the support out of $3/4$-inch marine plywood. Drill a $5/16$-inch hole down the front from the top for the axle, which will be a $1/4$-inch-diameter stainless steel bolt, $4^1/2$ inches long. Like other places where metal comes in contact with wood, a stronger hole can be made by drilling the hole oversized, refilling with resin, and then re-drilling to the proper size. Round over the front face of the brace and bevel back inside the slots so the footbrace can pivot freely.

Make two mirror-image wings from $1/4$-inch plywood. Drill a hole out near the edge for the control rope to lace through. The large hole through the wings is just to lighten it. Cut out the braces and make the axle hole through them. Glue the braces to the back of one of the wings and let the glue cure, then attach the other wing. Make sure the axle holes in the braces are lined up. It may help to insert a bolt or dowel through the holes while the glue sets up. Glue a small pad-eye at the top of the footbrace.

The support is screwed and glued to the slider. Build a good fillet of resin around the joint between the slider and support. The footbrace is attached to the support by threading the axle bolt down through the support and braces at the back of the foot support. Use a locking nut to hold the axle in place (Figure 9-26).

Mount the rail on the floor of the hull and double-check the positioning with the footbrace in place to make sure you will be able to sit comfortably.

The control cables for this system are nylon parachute cord. This is a small, lightweight, braided rope. The cables do not need to be super-strong because this system does not put a lot of stress on them. Measure the length from the front bulkhead back to the rudder. Add 2 inches to this length then multiply by two to estimate how much rope you need. Divide the

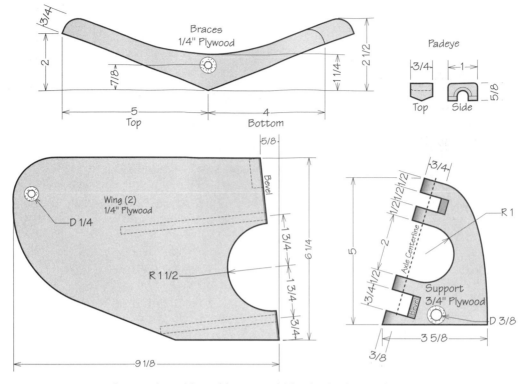

Figure 9-25. *You can make an adjustable rudder control like the footbrace shown in Figure 9-10. Make the top and bottom braces the same, except that the bottom brace is 8 inches long overall instead of 10 inches. Drill a long hole down the middle of the support, following the axle centerline. The support is made of ³/₄-inch plywood and is mounted to the slider shown in Figure 9-11. Mount the small pad-eye near the top of the joint between the two wings.*

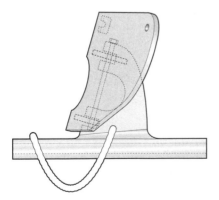

Figure 9-26. *The completed rudder control will slide onto the same rail as the footbrace (see Figures 9-12 and 9-13). Build a good fillet of dookie schmutz between the support and the slider. Make the rope long enough that you can reach it to adjust the location while you're sitting in the boat.*

rope in half and tie the middle to the center of the forward bulkhead (Figure 9-27). To do this you will either need a pad-eye mounted to the bulkhead or a small hole through it. If you have a foam bulkhead, poke a hole through the foam and cut a 6-inch disk of plywood with a hole in the middle. Place the disk on the forward face of the bulkhead. Thread the control ropes through the bulkhead and disk and tie a knot in the end of the loop. Your foam bulkhead will need to be securely glued to the kayak.

Run the ropes to the pad-eye on the back of the footbrace. Run one rope through the left side of the pad-eye and over to the hole on the edge of the right wing, and vice versa with the other rope. You then need to insert the ends of the rope into the tubing going back to the rudder. You

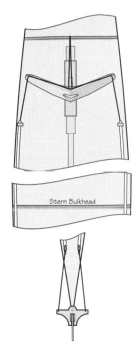

may need to run a piece of thin wire down from the stern to snake the rope up the tubing.

Center the control pedals and the rudder and tie the ropes snugly and securely to the arms of the rudder. The ropes don't need to be too tight. Because of the way the control ropes are threaded through the control pedals, the pedals can move forward and back without re-tying the ropes. Rub the ropes with candle wax where they go through the pedals to make them slide more easily. Like the adjustable footbraces, a loop of rope through the support keeps the control-pedal assembly in place.

Stern Bulkhead

Figure 9-27. *The control cables lead from the rudder "T" at the back of the boat, up through tubes to the outer hole on the wings of the rudder control, to the pad-eye in the middle of the control, up to the bulkhead forward of the control. Drill a hole through the top of the bulkhead so you can tie and tighten the control ropes easily. If the hole is small enough it will not leak fast enough to matter. Despite what I say in Figure 9-15, you should probably use a plywood bulkhead for this setup.*

Figure 9-28. *A rudder similar to the one described in this book. Note the rope going to the top of the rudder to lift it out of the way. The control cable for this uphaul runs on deck to a cleat just behind the cockpit. You should lift the rudder whenever you come ashore.*

I t would be a pity to go through all the effort of making a fine wooden boat and then have to propel it with a paddle made of plastic. Building a paddle is a relatively short and easy project for you. It's also a good project for you to practice on before you commit yourself to building a kayak.

I personally prefer a feathered paddle with a fairly large blade. A feathered paddle has the blades at each end set at an angle to each other, which makes going into a head wind easier because the upper blade is turned to slice easily into the wind. Formerly, this angle would have been 90 degrees but the problem with such a large angle is that it can be hard on the wrists, because they must bend a lot to turn the paddle with each stroke, and this gives some people a repetitive strain injury. Now, feathered paddles are made with a smaller angle of about 60 to 70 degrees. The paddle we're building here has a 70-degree feather, but you can change the angle if you wish.

Figure 10-1. *Making a paddle is good practice for working with wood and fiberglass. It's a relatively small project that doesn't require the commitment building a boat calls for. The feather pattern on the left looks good but is harder to make.*

A larger blade is more efficient for transferring power to the water than is a smaller blade, but it takes more strength at a slower stroke rate. Some people are more comfortable using a smaller blade and a faster cadence. Before you make your paddle, you may want to borrow a few different paddles and see what you prefer. While you are at it, try paddles of varying lengths, too. The most comfortable length is an individual choice, and there's no set formula for determining it. The building instructions given here will give you about a 90-inch paddle. In general, though, a wider boat will require a longer paddle and a shorter-than-average person may need a shorter paddle.

Using a longer paddle will have some of the effect of using a bigger blade. The longer lever-arm will result in more strength and slower cadence being required to propel the boat at the same speed that a shorter paddle does. Human physiology seems to be such that the body works best putting out a low level of power fast instead of a lot of power slowly. It's like shifting to a lower gear on a bicycle to climb a hill, which keeps your legs moving fast but with less effort.

The two means of achieving this with a paddle are to make the shaft shorter or the blade smaller. I prefer to keep the blade large and make the paddle short because it maintains the efficiency of the blade and lets me paddle a faster cadence. I can do this because I prefer paddling a narrow boat. Someone with a wider boat will need a longer paddle with a smaller blade to have the same effect.

Another consideration is the shaft diameter. The size that puts the least strain on your hand is the one that will fit into your hand when it's totally relaxed. It's the position your hand takes when you just let it hang by your side. You'll probably find that you haven't handled a shaft that big before. In fact, most paddle manufactures make thinner shafts to save weight and material, but I'd suggest you make the shaft the size given in these instructions, and try it out. I think you'll be pleasantly surprised, but if you really do find it too big, you can always shave more off. If you are concerned about weight, consider making a hollow shaft.

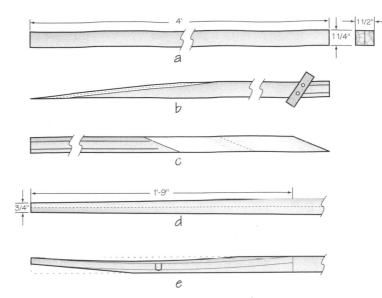

Figure 10-2. How the paddle shaft is made: (a) Laminate two blanks. (b) Cut a scarf in each blank (left) and mark the "octagon" (right). (c) Scarf one half shaft so the laminations run across. On the other half shaft, they run lengthwise. (d) Taper the blade end of the shafts. (e) Rough out the shape of the end. Note the "U" to indicate the direction of spooning.

Making the Shaft

You need a strong, light wood such as Sitka spruce for the shaft of the paddle. I laminate several pieces together for strength and durability, and I find that lamination is a good way to compensate for poor grain. Ideally, the grain should run straight up and down the shaft, but it can be hard to find good-quality wood like this.

I usually only laminate two pieces to make the shaft, but if the grain in your wood is bad, use more laminations and shuffle the pieces so the grain does not line up when you glue it back together. I also scarf the shaft in the middle so that the grain better matches the angle of the paddle blade, so the pieces you laminate need only be about half the length of the finished paddle.

Cutting the Wood

From a piece of 1¼-inch rough-cut spruce, cut four pieces ¾ inch wide by 4 feet long. This will make a paddle about 7 feet 6 inches long. If you don't want a feathered paddle, however, you should use full-length pieces for the shaft. Otherwise, the directions are the same—you just don't need to create the scarf joint that the feathered paddle requires.

Gluing It Together

Flip two of the pieces end-for-end so that the grain does not line up with the other two pieces. Glue together two pieces to make a 1½-inch by 1¼-inch shaft, double-checking that the grain of the two pieces does not align for greater strength. You can use either epoxy mixed with some thickener or another waterproof glue. Clamp the pieces together.

If you want to make a hollow-shafted paddle you can use a router to cut a ½-inch-diameter half-round groove down the middle of the two halves. Do not cut down into the area of the blade because the hollow may become exposed as you shape the blade. Seal the inside of the grooves with epoxy before gluing the halves together. You will end up with a cylindrical hole down the middle of the shaft.

After the glue has cured, scrape off the excess drips of epoxy. Plane all four sides. If you used rough 1¼-inch spruce, plane enough to get smooth wood. You'll end up with a shaft measuring about 1⅜ inches by 1⅛ inches.

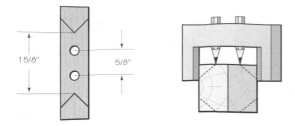

Figure 10-3. An octagoning tool helps you to round the shaft accurately.

Mark the Octagon

Before making more cuts, mark the guidelines for "octagoning" the shaft. Make the marking tool from some scrap lumber and pencil stubs (Figure 10-3). Use it to mark two guidelines on each side of the shaft that will help you when you start rounding it.

Cut the Scarf

If you're not making a feathered paddle, skip this step altogether and go straight to the section dealing with the tapering of the ends.

Make a jig to cut the scarfs on a table saw. Attach a strip of wood that fits the slot on your

Figure 10-4. The octagoning tool is placed over the shaft with its tabs touching the sides of the shaft. Slide it up and down the length of the shaft so that the pencils mark parallel lines.

Figure 10-5. The jig for the shaft scarf fits on a table saw. A strip tacked to the bottom of the jig slides in the slot of the saw. A fence mounted to the top of the jig at an angle to the saw controls the taper of the scarf. An 8-inch to 1-inch taper will suffice. In this picture to the left of the shaft, I have a long, thin, 10-degree wedge that will tip the shaft to get a 70-degree feather.

saw to a piece of plywood. This jig should ride on the right-hand side of the blade (Figure 10-5). Attach a fence to the top at a shallow angle to the direction of travel. My jig cuts about a 7.5 to 1 scarf. Set it up so you pull the shaft through the saw. Tilt the blade toward the shaft by 10 degrees. With the glue line on the shaft running horizontal, cut off the end of one shaft.

Cut the other shaft with the glue joint vertical. Turning the shaft like this makes a 90-degree feather. The tilt of the saw blade makes a feather of 90 degrees, less 10 degrees, less another 10 degrees, which equals 70 degrees. This is confusing, but it works. To make a left-handed paddle, you must tilt the blade away from the shaft. In that case, 90 degrees plus 10 degrees, plus another 10 degrees equals 110 degrees, which is 180 degrees minus 70 degrees. If you can't tilt the saw blade properly, make a long 10-degree wedge that will tilt the shaft instead of the blade. You can plane a strip to fit. Tilt the shaft towards the blade for

Figure 10-6. *The two scarfs. Notice that the glue line goes the length of the scarf in one, and across the scarf in the other.*

Figure 10-7. *After being glued together, the scarfs result in some strange angles. Sight down the length of the shaft to be sure everything is straight.*

a right-handed paddle or away for a left-handed paddle.

Glue It Together

If you need to, clean up the saw cut with a block plane to make a tight joint. Liberally apply glue to the scarf faces. Let the end-grain absorb some glue for a few minutes, then apply some more thickened glue. Clamp the joint together with one clamp in the middle—spring clamps are easiest to use. Sight down the length of the shaft to see if it's straight. If it isn't, adjust it until it is.

Put another clamp at one end of the scarf, and sight for straightness again. Put on another clamp at the other end of the scarf. Sight again. Be obsessive about straightening the shaft. If you don't do it now, you will either have to cut

the scarf and do it again or paddle with a crooked shaft. Make sure the joint is securely clamped before leaving it to dry. You don't want it to slip.

Incidentally, use epoxy filled with some chopped glass fibers and silica to create a catsup-consistency glue. You can also use one of the waterproof carpenter's glues such as Tight-Bond II, one of the urethane glues, such as Gorilla, or you can use the old standby, resorcinol. Each has its own gluing characteristics, so read the directions on your choice.

Taper the Ends

After the glue dries, it's time to taper the ends where the blade goes. This taper is for cosmetic purposes only, so you can skip this step if you choose. You should be planing the faces that show the glue line. This is the face you will glue the blades on.

Check the Orientation

To check the orientation of the blades, put a ∩ mark on one of the recently planed faces. Holding the shaft in front of you, with the mark on your right, face the open mouth of the ∩ backward, that is, pointing behind you. When you cock your right hand backward, toward you, the recently planed face on the left-hand end of the shaft should be facing up. Place a similar ∩ facing backward on that face. In other words, when you go through a paddling motion, the ∩ marks should represent the spooning of the blades, always facing backward. If you're making a left-handed paddle, perform the mirror image of these instructions.

Making the Blades

This is a chance to get creative. You can use a wide variety of woods in the blades, including cedar, fir, spruce, mahogany, ash, basswood, black walnut, teak, cherry, and maple. I usually dig through my scrap pile to see what's available. You want it to be fairly light, so the spruce you got for the shaft is a good primary source. Use dark woods such as walnut and mahogany for contrast. A piece of ash for the outer piece provides increased durability. In the end, you want a stack 3¾ inches tall of 2½-inch by 21-inch planks (Figure 10-8). Five ¾-inch pieces will create the correct-sized blank.

Paint epoxy on all mating surfaces and let the glue soak in for a few minutes. Stack the pieces together and clamp. When cured, clean off the drips with a scraper. This blank is thick enough for four blade halves.

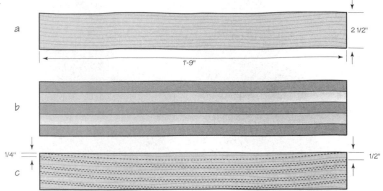

Figure 10-8. The blades start out as a large block of several layers of wood. Cut pieces of wood to the dimensions shown in (a) and stack them to a height of 3¾ inches. Glue them together (b), and cut them out of the block with a bandsaw. Use a template that curves ½ inch deep over 21 inches to mark out each cut, and alternate the direction of the taper (c) so one end is ½ inch thick and the other end is ¼ inch thick.

Cut Out the Blades

Cut a template out of cardboard or plywood. This template has a smooth curve about ½ inch deep and 21 inches long, defining the amount of spooning for the blades (Figure 10-8c). Mark four blades on the blank with the blade thickness tapering from ½ inch at one end to ¼ inch at the other. Alternate the tapers and cut along the lines with a bandsaw (Figure 10-9).

Rough-Cut the Ends

It saves some effort if you cut the excess off the ends of the shaft. Pay attention to the ∩ marks you made earlier. With the spoon template curved the same direction as the ∩ mark, place the template even with the outer end of the shaft and tilt somewhat forward on the inboard end to leave a good rib down the center. Cut a little off the back at the outer end.

Attaching the Blades

Again apply glue and let it soak in for a few minutes. Glue the blades on either side of the shaft. Clamp securely, using three or four pipe

Figure 10-9. *Two paddle blades newly cut from the block. This task requires a bandsaw.*

clamps (Figure 10-10). Glue only one end at a time because it's easier.

Grinding the Blade

You can do all the shaping with hand tools such as a block plane, a spokeshave, gouges, and a rasp. The hardest part is the concave face of the paddle, and the best tool for this may be the spokeshave. One technique to make this job easier is to smooth the blade pieces before gluing them to the shaft. Pre-smoothing permits you to get right up to the edge of the piece. A block plane can smooth the back face of the blade quickly. Form the fillet between the blade and the shaft using a 1/2-inch-radius gouge (Figure 10-11). Be sure to use sharp tools.

I use a 5-inch, high-speed, right-angle grinder to sculpt the blade, and it's a powerful tool. With a 36-grit sandpaper disk it will remove wood at a horrific rate, and 80-grit is merely terrifying. I rough it out with 36 and work further with 80. You can grind a beautiful paddle in a couple of hours or you can make a complete mess in a matter of seconds. The prospect of the first makes me risk the possibility of the second. I also use chisels, gouges, a block plane, and a spokeshave for fine-tuning the shape.

If you use a grinder, never let it stand still. Be moving when the sandpaper touches the wood. Sweep down the length of the blade with smooth, even, fast strokes. To create a fillet where the blade meets the shaft, press down at the side of the shaft and pull toward yourself across the blade. Don't sand to the final thickness yet. If the grinder frightens you, practice on some scrap, or just use hand tools. Sharp sandpaper, while scarier, will produce smoother results when dealing with woods of different hardnesses.

The primary goal of the shaping is to make the paddle smooth. You want a smooth transition from the shaft to the blade. There should be no sharp steps because these tend to concentrate the stress on the paddle, which may cause it to break. Remove as little wood as possible while still achieving a flowing shape. This sculpting requires a little art, but if you work carefully you will get nice results.

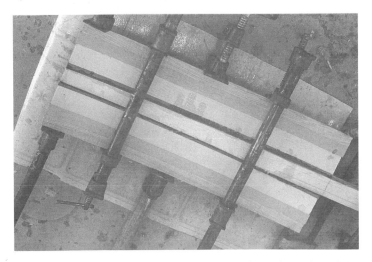

Figure 10-10. *The blades are glued directly to the sides of the shafts. The thick end of the blade is oriented toward the middle of the paddle.*

Figure 10-11. *Use a disk sander, gouge, and plane to blend the blade into the shaft. Try to remove as little wood from the shaft as possible.*

Cut the blade pattern out of paper, marking the centerline at each end. Trace the pattern onto one blade. Flip the pattern over to mark the other blade. This should ensure that the two blades are mirror images of each other. Cut them out with a bandsaw or coping saw. Do not cut into the shaft.

At this point I use the grinder a little bit more to even up the thickness around the edge of the blade. I then go to it with a hand sander. Knock off any remaining high spots. The final

thickness of the edge should be about ⅛ inch to ³⁄₁₆ inch.

Rounding the Shaft

Plane off the corners of the shaft to create an octagon shape, using as guides the lines you marked earlier. Use a spokeshave and chisel to get up close to the blade. On the back side, continue the shaping as far along the shaft as it will go. On the front side, fillet into the end of the blade.

Next, knock the corners off the octagon to make a 16-sided shape and start rounding it out. Use a block plane set shallow to shave off high spots. If the slot of your block plane is adjustable, close it up a bit, this will reduce snagging when planing against the grain. Again, sharp tools will produce the best results. The final shape should be slightly oval with the long axis of the oval perpendicular to the face of the blade. Some people may find a slight egg shape more comfortable. The pointy end of the egg should fit under the knuckles.

Note that the dimensions given in the drawing result in a large-diameter shaft. If you want

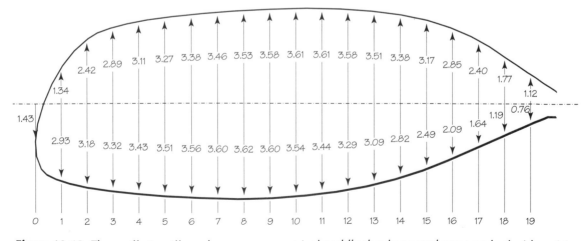

Figure 10-12. *These offsets will produce an asymmetrical paddle that has equal areas on both sides of the centerline.*

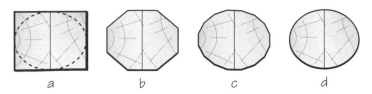

a   b   c   d

Figure 10-13. Four steps to convert a rectangular paddle shaft (a) into an oval (d). First shave the shaft back to the lines made with the octagoning tool then remove the corners to make a 16-sided shaft (c). Carefully remove the remaining corners. The best tool for this is a spokeshave.

a smaller shaft, first make it to the indicated dimensions then reduce it to fit.

Around the scarf area, the shape may get a little "squirrelly" because of the dimensions of the two halves meeting at a strange angle. This is the part of the shaft that experiences the least force, and therefore may be the thinnest. If you want a nice round shape, don't be too worried about planing away too much material. If you get nervous, leave it out-of-round; your hand will not often feel this area when you're paddling.

Final-finish sanding may now proceed. Starting with 80-grit, proceed through 120 to 220. Sand the transition from the shaft to the blade to a nice smooth fillet. Do not round over the edge of the blade yet; leave it square.

Fiberglassing the Paddle

The edge of the blade may be toughened with fiberglass. I use strands pulled from a piece of 24-ounce woven roving. Two or three of these strands wrapped along the edge will provide an $\frac{1}{8}$-inch perimeter of glass to absorb some of the abuse from rocks. A few extra at the tip will provide added protection. If you don't have any roving, yarns from lighter-weight glass will work; you just need more. Twist them together to make them easier to deal with.

Make a shelf of tape all around the edge of the blade to hold the roving while the epoxy dries. Paint some epoxy around the edge and then lay strands of fiberglass in it. Paint in more epoxy to wet the glass out. You want to build up $\frac{1}{8}$ inch to $\frac{1}{4}$ inch of glass to provide good edge protection.

The paddle as described above probably does not need glass over the whole face for strength. A 2-inch-wide strip at the tip will increase the durability. Apply it on both sides. While you're at it, coat the whole paddle with epoxy resin. If you're going to abuse your paddle, apply glass over the whole blade, first on the front, then additionally on the back if desired. A couple of strands of roving run down the center spine will increase the strength with very little weight.

Sand the glass lightly to reduce the texture and apply another coat of resin. Do not sand so deeply into the glass that you cut through the glass fibers.

Use a good-quality spar varnish for durable ultra-violet protection. Apply three coats, minimum, sanding between coats. Six coats is about optimum.

Variations on a Theme

What we've done so far could be called the basic process for making a kayak paddle, but there are many possible variations on the theme once you've learned the basics.

Sometimes, for example, I make a feather-pattern paddle. The reason I haven't already described how to make one is because, while they look good, they can be weaker. Because the grain does not run parallel to the length of the blade, the blade is more flexible—a problem I solve by applying reinforcement to the back of the blade.

The process for making diagonal striping is similar to the method for a normal blade. The difference is that the blank you make has the wood set diagonally. Cut pieces of wood measuring 1½ inches by 12 inches. Mark a 45-degree angle on one end of all the pieces and assemble all the pieces so the marks line up. Use enough pieces so that the length of one side is 21 inches. Although it saves wood to cut the pieces to length with a 45-degree angle, if

Figure 10-14. *The feather-pattern blade shown in Figure 10-1 requires a laminated block with diagonally oriented wood, like this one. Use 10-inch-long pieces of wood staggered back at a 45-degree angle. And be aware that this block can be hard to clamp.*

form. Cut a piece of 2 × 4 to match the curve. Clamp to this, with a piece of wax paper between the blade and the form.

After the glue cures, clean up the edge to be glued to the shaft. Glue and clamp the blades to the shaft and proceed to grind and shape as you would the normal blade.

The cause of most broken paddles is compression failure. When the wood gets compressed on the inside of a bend it causes a chain reaction in which splits occur and the paddle breaks. Compression occurs on the back face of the blade, near your hands on the side facing

you leave the ends square you'll leave a place to give your pipe clamps a purchase.

After gluing up, saw off the ends on one side and clean it up with a plane. Using this side as a guide, saw off the ends on the other side to create a parallelogram about 8 inches across. Leave as much width as you can. Now cut the blank in half to make two parallelograms, each about 4 inches wide.

Previously, we've cut out all the blade pieces from one blank, but with the diagonal blades you have to use two blanks to make the blades symmetrical. Cut off square the end that will be the tip of the blade. Mark out the blade-cutting lines on the long face with a constant thickness of about 3/8 inch. Make sure you mark the curves going in opposite directions on each blank to be sure you will get matching sets of blades.

To reduce the flexibility of the blades, I glue thin strips of wood to the back of the blade with the grain running parallel to the shaft. I use a hardwood such as ash, cut about 1/8 inch thick. Glue two 1 1/2-inch to 2-inch-wide strips on the back side, next to what will be the inner edge of each blade (Figure 10-15). Be careful about how you clamp them on, because just clamping on the blade will tend to straighten it out. To keep this from happening, clamp them on a

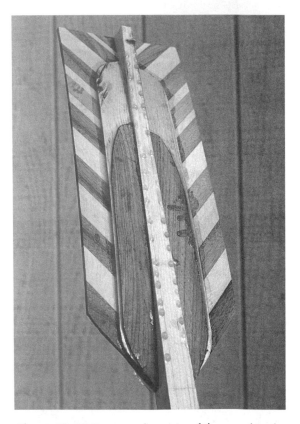

Figure 10-15. *Because the grain of the wood in the feather pattern is not oriented for optimum strength, you will need to laminate additional wood to the back of the blades before gluing them to the shaft.*

away from you, by your knuckles. Hardwoods such as ash endure compression better than softwoods. If you want to incorporate hardwood for cosmetic reasons or for strength, the best place for it is on the back side of the blade and up the shaft.

Finally, let me remind you that you can be a lot more efficient with your time and materials if you make several paddles at the same time. By making thicker blanks for the blades, you can produce the raw materials for several paddles with little additional effort and a lot less waste.

Figure 10-16. *These are the tools that work best for this project. The high-speed right-angle grinder can be used to sculpt the blades. Gouges are easy to control when you're blending the blades into the shaft. The spokeshave is designed to fair round objects such as the shaft.*

Tools for Paddles

These are the tools you need to make the paddles described above:

- Table saw
- Bandsaw
- Right-angle grinder (optional)
- Block plane
- Spokeshave
- Sanding block
- Gouge (optional)

Materials for Paddles

These are the materials you need for the paddles described above:

- One paddle can be made from a 3/4-inch by 6-inch by 10-foot plank.
- Spruce is the first choice for the majority of the paddle.
- Mahogany, cedar, ash, fir, walnut, basswood, and cherry can all be used to beautify, lighten, or strengthen as desired.
- Fiberglass cloth.
- Epoxy resin, resorcinol glue, or waterproof or water-resistant resin glues.

Figure 10-17. *The finshed paddle.*

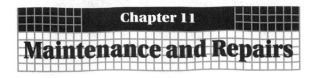

Compared with most wooden boats, strip-built kayaks don't need much maintenance. I typically do no more than put on a new coat of varnish before each kayaking season. Well, that's what I tell myself I will do. In actuality I don't usually get to it every year.

I do try to inspect the boat fairly frequently, however, looking for major scratches that may have reached the glass. If I hear a loud noise when I'm paddling over rocks I'll take a look to make sure there was no damage that reached the wood.

Yearly Wear and Tear

Abrasion from pulling the boat up the beach will eventually sand off all the varnish. It should be renewed about once a year. Wash the boat off and sand the area to be varnished. Paint on the varnish normally. Don't worry about getting a perfect finish on the bottom. If you're like me, the bottom will be scratched up again before you know it, so why bother trying for perfection?

The deck is another matter, though. Eventually, the inevitable mistakes are going to take their toll on the finish of the deck, which may signal that it's time to give the kayak a complete refinishing. Here's how:

Remove all the hardware and lines mounted on the deck, and sand the boat until the gloss is gone everywhere. You will notice a change in tone of the surface as you sand through the varnish into the epoxy, and this is useful because you should avoid sanding too far into the epoxy. There is no need to remove all the varnish. Re-varnish as if you were working on a new boat. The results will probably look like new.

Bad Scratches

Some of the worst scratches will gouge through the varnish into the epoxy and fiberglass, but they're not of immediate concern. As long as they don't let water get to the wood, they don't need immediate attention. When you get a chance, you can paint some varnish onto the scratch to protect the epoxy. Rinse off the boat and scrub the scratch clean before varnishing. If it looks as though the fibers of the glass are separated from the epoxy, you may need to clean a little deeper. Wet down the scratch with a solvent such as lacquer thinner or acetone and scrub it clean, then varnish.

Dealing with Bruises

The boat is strong and will survive a lot of abuse with nothing more than cosmetic damage, but worse things happen sometimes. For example, you misjudge the timing of a wave as you pass over a rock and so, instead of passing over it, you're left teetering on the rock. If this is enough to cause a bruise that goes into the wood, you should do a little extra work to prevent water damage.

A quick fix is to slap some varnish over the bruise to keep the water out for a while. Eventually you will need to do something more permanent.

Start by removing the damaged glass. Sand the damaged region and remove any loose glass. Feather the edges of the fiberglass so there is no sudden change in thickness. If the wood got wet, let it dry. If it got wet with salt water, rinse it off with fresh water first.

Cut out a piece of fiberglass the size of the sanded area and another slightly bigger than the area of exposed wood. If the area had more than one layer of glass on it, cut out another patch of intermediate size. Spread epoxy on the damaged area and lay on the patches starting with the largest and progressing to the smallest. Wet out each layer as you apply it. After the patch has cured, sand it smooth and re-varnish it.

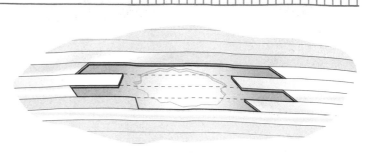

Figure 11-1. To patch a hole, cut back the wooden strips to differing lengths, then glue in new strips, sand everything smooth, and fiberglass over them, inside and outside. See text.

Patching Holes

You really did it this time. You misjudged a wave and got dropped on top of a sharp rock, and now you have a hole in the boat. This will take more effort to fix, but it's possible. Luckily this is most likely to happen near the center of mass of the boat. The reason this is lucky is because you need to be able to reach inside.

Start by cutting out all the damaged wood. You could just fit strips into the resulting hole, but the problem with this is that your repair will be pretty obvious. If, however, you give the hole a ragged edge by cutting back every other strip a few inches, it won't show as much.

Use a razor saw to cut along the joints between strips and cut the ends off at different angles (Figure 11-1). Now you can fit and glue strips into these gaps.

After the glue dries, sand the patch smooth and fair. Now sand the glass off the original wood surrounding the patch and fiberglass it in the manner I recommended above for the bruise patch, laying down the pieces of fiberglass in order, largest to smallest.

You now need to glass the inside. Do your best to sand and fair out the new strips, and sand the glass surrounding the patch to prepare it for fiberglassing. Lay glass over the patch.

If you still have some of the original wood you used to build the kayak, you should be able to make a good match. With a little care, you will be the only one able to see the damage.

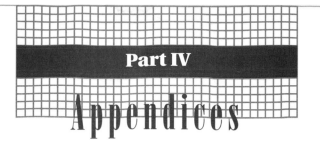

Part IV

Appendices

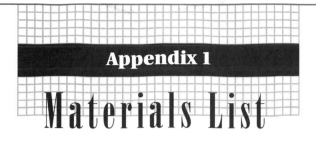

Appendix 1

Materials List

Primary Material Requirements

	Great Auk	Guillemot	Double	
Length	17	17	20	ft
Surface Area	58	47	80	sq ft
Total Cockpit Perimeter	85	76	153	in
Coaming Strips (2" long)	122	109	218	
Surface Area w/ Coaming	8,552	7,030	11,885	sq in
3/4" Square Edge Strips	1,140	937	1,585	ft
18' Strips	60	49	83	
3/4" Cove & Bead Strips	1,222	1,004	1,698	ft
18' Strips	64	53	89	
Coaming Lip (1/8x1/2 Ash)	51	46	92	ft
2x4 strongback	14 ft 11 in	14 ft 11 in	17 ft 11 in	
Glass (yds)[1]	27	27	32	yds
1 in tape	82	82	96	ft
2 in tape	41	41	48	ft
Epoxy (gal)	1.4	1.1	1.9	gal

All above materials amounts include 20% increase for mistakes and other waste.
[1]   This estimate for glass includes 20% fudge-factor above and assumes no care is taken cutting out the glass, i.e. each layer is cut with no overlap. You can get by with much less.

Figure A1-1. *Use this table as a guide for your material needs. Note that it takes more cove-and-bead strips than it does square-edged strips because the bead fits into the cove and makes the effective width narrower.*

Epoxy Usage Estimates

Fiberglass	Coverage (sq ft/gallon)	
	First Coat	Subsequent
4 ounce	150	300
6 ounce	130	250
10 ounce	100	170

Density of mixed epoxy nominally: 8.8 lbs/Gallon

Figure A1-2. *The amount of epoxy you need depends on the thickness of the fiberglass you're using and how much resin the wood absorbs. The first coat uses more resin because the wood absorbs it. Subsequent coats just need to wet out the fiberglass. An amount of 150 square feet per gallon translates to about 1 fluid ounce per square foot.*

Softwood:	You'll need straight-grained, knot-free softwood for strips. Calculate the amount required by looking up the surface area of the boat in square inches in the table above and dividing that by the width of the strips. This will tell you how many inches of strips are required. Be sure to deduct $1/8$ inch from the width of cove-and-bead strips, to account for the cove. If you are cutting your own strips, this usually requires the equivalent of two 12-inch by $3/4$-inch boards 1 foot longer than the boat.
	You'll also need a 2 × 4 about 2 feet shorter than the boat. I usually do not have the strongback go through the last forms so I deduct 1 inch to account for the thickness of the form.
Plywood:	$1/4$-inch marine ply: 10 inches by 6 inches for the backrest, 10 inches by 12 inches for the cheek plates. $1/2$-inch, low-grade ply for the forms—one sheet. Particleboard or chipboard also works.
Hardwood:	6 inches by $3/4$ inch by 3 feet for coaming lip, hatches, and assorted hardware. Ash is good.
Fiberglass:	Two complete layers for a 17-foot boat can be cut from a 10-yard package if they are cut diagonally. With careful cutting, a 20-yard length will provide enough for a whole boat. Avoid piecing together scraps unless you really don't mind sanding.
Fiberglass tape:	1 inch wide: 4 times the length of boat. 2 inches wide: 2 times the length of boat.
Resin:	I recommend epoxy. One gallon of epoxy will cover about 150 square feet of 6-ounce cloth on bare wood. Subsequent layers go twice as far. With 4-ounce cloth you can cover about 15 percent more. For some reason, polyester resin never seems to cover as much per gallon.
Contact cement:	Use the kind with a label that says "Warning: Highly Flammable" or something similar. It's for gluing down foam seats. One bottle should suffice.
Webbing:	4 feet of 1-inch webbing, plus two sets of buckles and sliders for the backrest.
Foam:	14 inches by 16 inches for the seat. Check your bulkhead dimensions if you choose to use foam for the backrest (10 inches by 6 inches). Ethafoam is good, Minicell is better.
Varnish:	1 quart of glossy marine spar varnish.
Fiber packing tape:	2 rolls.
Staples:	About 2 boxes of $9/16$-inch "ceiling tile" staples. If you are not using cove-and-bead strips, you may need another box.
Sealant:	Silicone RTV or a boating sealant for the foam bulkheads.
Sundries:	Plastic squeegees, sandpaper, cheap brushes, acid brushes, foam brushes, rubber gloves, measuring cups, free time, a paddle, a spray skirt, a PFD, and more free time.

Material & Tool Sources

Some materials, such as wood, are relatively easy to find, but many tools and supplies such as epoxy can be hard to track down if you don't know where to look. Once you're pointed in the right direction, however, you'll find you can easily buy all the tools and materials required. Here are some of the sources for materials.

Wood

■   M. L. Condon Co.
260 Ferris Avenue
White Plains, NY 10603
Carries a large selection of boatbuilding woods
Tel: 914-946-4111

■   EdenSaw Wood, Ltd.
211 Seton Road
Port Townsend, WA 98368
Wood and pre-cut strip
Tel: 800-745-3336
http://www.olympus.net/edensaw/

■   Flounder Bay Boat Lumber
1019 3rd Street
Anacortes, WA 98221
Wood, pre-cut strips, and epoxy
Tel: 800-228-4691
http://www.flounderbay.com/

■   Newfound Woodworks
RFD #2 Box 850
Bristol, NH 03222
Complete kits with all the materials and forms required for all of the designs in this book as well as other designs by the author and others. Pre-cut cove-and-bead strips, computer-cut forms, fiberglass, epoxy, seats, and other accessories
Tel: 603-744-6872
info@newfound.com
http://www.newfound.com/

■   The Woodworkers' Store
4365 Willow Drive
Medina, MN 55340
Veneer and woodworking tools
Tel: 800-279-4441

■   Your local lumber yard
Pine, western red cedar, redwood, etc.

Look for advertisers in *WoodenBoat, Messing About in Boats,* and *Canoe and Kayak* magazines.

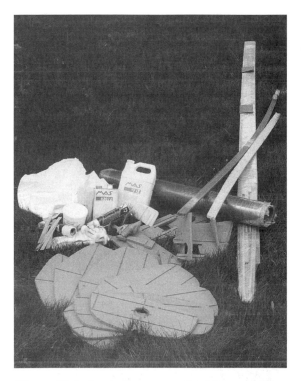

Figure A2-1. *Several sources offer kits containing everything you need to make a strip-built kayak. Here's one from the Newfound Woodworks for my Little Auk design (Figure A3-1, Appendix 3). The kit includes the forms, cove-and-bead strips, fiberglass, and epoxy resin. Newfound Woodworks offers similar kits for all the designs in this book.*

Glass and Resin

- Defender Industries, Inc.
  42 Great Neck Road
  Waterford, CT 06385
  Fiberglass, resin, boating supplies
  Tel:800-420-7766
  http://www.defenderus.com/

- Fibre Glast Developments Corp.
  1944 Neva Drive
  Dayton, OH 45414
  Fiberglass, resins, respirators, and tools
  Tel: 800-821-3283
  http://www.fibreglast.com/

- MAS–Phoenix Resins
  1501 Sherman Avenue
  Pennsauken, NJ 08110
  Epoxy and some tools
  Tel: 800-398-7556
  http://www.masepoxies.com/

- Raka Marine
  2755 S. U.S. Highway 1
  Boynton Beach, FL 33435
  Epoxy and fiberglass
  Tel: 561-364-8086
  http://www.magg.net/~raka-inc/

- System Three Resins Inc.
  P.O. Box 70436
  Seattle, WA 98107
  Epoxy, fiberglass, and tools
  Tel: 206-782-7976
  http://www.systemthree.com/

- John R. Sweet
  U.S. 220 South
  Mustoe, VA 24468
  Fiberglass, exotic cloths, polyester resin, minicell foam, and PVA mold release
  Tel: 540-468-222
  Please call 9:30 a.m. to 6:00 p.m. Monday through Friday.

- West System, Gougeon Brothers Inc.
  P.O. Box 908
  Bay City, MI 48707-0908
  Epoxy, fiberglass, and tools
  Tel: 517-684-7286
  http://www.cris.com/~gougeon/

Outfitting and Tools

- Aquaterra
  1110 Powdersville Road
  P.O. Box 8002
  Easley, SC 29640
  Foot braces and spray skirts
  Tel: 803-855-1987

- Caretta Kayaks
  P.O. Box 478
  Tybee Island
  GA 31328
  Footbraces, foam, seats, and paddles
  Tel: 912-231-0793

- Jesada Tools
  310 Mears Blvd.
  Oldsmar, FL 34677
  Cove-and-bead router bits and other tools
  Tel: 800-531-5559
  http://jesada.com/catalog/

- Colorado Kayak Supply
  P.O. Box 3059
  Buena Vista, CO 81211
  Spray skirts, foam, float bags, and PFDs
  Tel: 800-535-3565

- Nantahala Outdoor Center
  13077 Highway 19 West
  Bryson City, NC 28713-9114
  Spray skirts, foam, float bags, PFDs
  Tel: 800-367-3521
  http://www.nocweb.com/

- Trend Lines
  375 Beacham Street
  Chelsea, MA 02150
  Woodworking tools
  Tel: 800-877-7899.

- Your local boatyard
  Padeyes, varnish, rope, etc.

- Your local hardware store
  Sandpaper, tools, sealants, varnish, shock cord, etc.

Books

- Amazon Books
  http://www.amazon.com/

- The WoodenBoat Store
  WoodenBoat Magazine
  Tel: 800-225-5205
  http://www.woodenboat.com/

- International Marine/Ragged Mountain Press
  The McGraw-Hill Companies
  P.O. Box 220
  Camden, ME 04843
  Tel: 800-262-4729
  http://www.books.mcgraw-hill.com

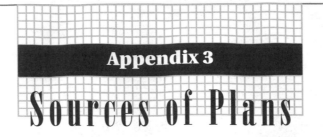

Sources of Plans

Plans of the kayak designs in this book are available from the author. The drawings provide full-sized patterns of all the forms and avoid the need for lofting. Kits with computer-cut forms and all the required materials can also be purchased through the author. For more information please write to: Nick Schade, Guillemot Kayaks, 10 Ash Swamp Road, Apt. N, Glastonbury, CT 06033. Tel: 860-659-8847. Web address: http://www.guillemot-kayaks.com/ E-mail address: Info@Guillemot-Kayaks.com.

Here are some other designs available from the author:

Guillemot Expedition Single

- Length: 19 feet (5.80 meters)
- Beam: 21 inches (53 centimeters)
- Weight: About 45 pounds (20.4 kilograms)
- Design goal: Extended expeditions

This is a longer version of the Guillemot, designed to provide better tracking, more volume, and greater speed for camping and touring. Although this kayak is long for a single, it is not unwieldy in handling. With a hard chine to help it carve a turn, it's very responsive. It is quite stable for its width and has a smooth transition from initial to final stability. I'm very pleased with the design, and everyone who has tried this boat is amazed at how easily it handles. It does not feel like a 19-foot boat. Novices have been very comfortable with its stability and ease of handling, and experienced paddlers are pleased with its performance. See figure 8-1.

Guillemot Play

- Length: 16½ feet (5.0 meters)
- Beam: 22 inches (56 centimeters)
- Weight: About 38 pounds (17.2 kilograms)
- Design goals: Playing, day trips

This is a low-volume, exciting "play" boat. It turns easily with a steering stroke like a white-water boat, yet tracks much better than a white-water kayak. This boat is probably best suited for a small paddler because there is very little knee room. My brother is 6 feet 2 inches tall and has a lot of fun with this boat, so I know a large paddler can fit in it. All the Guillemots roll well but this design is the easiest to roll. The low aft deck permits paddlers to lean way back and easily touch their heads to the aft deck. This is a good boat for surfing.

Little Auk

- Length: 11 feet (3.35 meters)
- Beam: 28 inches (71 centimeters)
- Weight: About 25 pounds (11.3 kilograms)
- Design goal: A stable, fun boat for sheltered exploring

This is shrunken version of the Great Auk, designed for someone who wants a light, easy-to-handle paddle-boat of distinctive character. Its small size makes it easy to put on the roof of a car or on the deck of a yacht and transport it to explore your favorite lake or harbor. Once there, you will be able to gunkhole into places inaccessible to most other

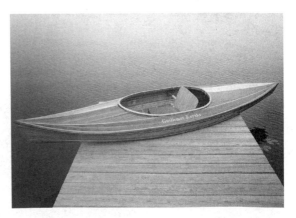

Figure A3-1. *The Little Auk design is intended as a fun, lightweight boat for exploring sheltered coves and lakes.*

boats. Its stability ensures that just sitting in it does-n't turn into an adventure in its own right. You could derive a similar boat by respacing the forms of the Great Auk, but this design eliminates the distortion created by such a radical change in length.

Guillemot Fast Double

- Length: 25½ feet (7.80 meters)
- Beam: 21 inches (53 centimeters)
- Weight: About 65 pounds (29.5 kilograms)
- Design goals: Fast touring and camping

Many double kayaks, the Guillemot Double includ-ed, are compromises between the length necessary to hold two paddlers and a length that is practical for storage and transportation. Typically, doubles should be a little longer for better performance, so the Guillemot Fast Double is intended to favor per-formance. It is a fast, fun boat, if you can deal with a boat 25 feet long. The width is the same as the Guillemot's at 21 inches. Although this boat may appear a little unstable, its length gives it good sta-bility. This is a boat for a pair of experienced paddlers who want to paddle together but don't want the com-promises of a shorter and wider double. This is not intended as a racing boat; it's a high-performance touring kayak.

Other Sources of Plans

- The Bear Mountain Boat Shop
  275 John Street, Peterborough
  Ontario, K9J 5E8, Canada
  Tel: 705-740-0470
  http://www.ptbo.igs.net/~bearmountain/

- Laughing Loon Canoes and Kayaks
  Rob Macks
  833 N. Colrain Road
  Greenfield, MA 01301
  Tel: 413-773-5375
  http://www.shaysnet.com/~robm/

- Loon Kayaks
  HCR 32 Box 253
  Sebasco Estates, ME 04565
  Tel: 207-389-1565

- Newfound Woodworks
  67 Danforth Brook Rd.
  Bristol, NH 03222
  Tel: 603-744-6872
  http://www.newfound.com/

- Outer Island, c/o Jason Designs
  7 Jeffrey Lane
  N. Branford, CT 06471
  Tel: 203-481-3221.

- Red Wing Designs
  John Winters, Box 283, Burk's Falls,
  Ontario P0A 1C0, Canada
  Tel: 705-382-2057.
  http://home.ican.net/~735769

Figure A3-2. *The Outer Island, designed by Jay Babina, is a strip-built kayak based on traditional Inuit designs.*

Appendix 4

Custom Designing

The designs in this book provide a good range of kayaks to choose from, and if you add to this the other sources of plans listed in Appendix 3, you can probably find a kayak for just about any need. But everyone is different, and most designers either design for themselves or for an "average" paddler.

Kayaks work best when they fit the paddler like a glove, and chances are good that any given design is not perfect for any given paddler. For the ideal fit, you need a custom-designed boat. There are several ways to get a custom design: hire a designer, design your own, or modify an existing design. The latter two choices are fun and satisfying. I urge you to give it a try.

Designing Your Own Boat

Many boatbuilders out there are not satisfied with the easy way. They want to build a boat, but they want it to be *their* boat. For those of you who think it's cheating to build someone else's design, I urge you to go ahead and design your own. It is immensely satisfying and, at the risk of losing business, I have to say that it's not all that hard to design a decent kayak. As long as you don't try anything too radical without good reason, chances are you can come up with a good boat.

Historical Designs

One very satisfying endeavor is to recreate a historic boat. By this I mean one of the original Eskimo designs that can be found in museums. While some would protest that making a strip-built version of what was originally a skin-on-frame design verges on sacrilege, this is your boat, so you get to do what you want. The bibliography lists several sources of historical designs. If you are lucky, the design you want to build will have a table of offsets. If it does, you can just use these offsets to create forms for your own boat.

Before trying to build from the offsets, you should determine whether they've been faired. In the interest of accuracy, some offset tables are tran-scribed directly from the boat as it hangs in the museum. But the 100 years of hanging have often taken their toll. You may need to redraw the boat to fair out the ravages of time.

If the book does not include offsets, it will generally have a study drawing, with sectional lines drawn in the end view. These small drawings can be scaled up on a photocopy machine until they are a usable size, and converted into patterns for forms. Again the result may not be fair. Distortion will be introduced by the enlargement. It would pay to redraw the boat based on these forms and fair it out.

If the offset table or drawing does not provide enough stations to make closely spaced forms, you may need to interpolate some more. One good way is to string the forms you have on a strongback and bend some strips around them. You can now make measurements directly where you need forms. Offset tables do not usually include all the information required to make the end forms. You will have to scale the drawings to get them.

Stealing Designs

As a guy trying to make some money designing kayaks, I cannot advocate stealing lines off another boat that you want to copy. However, if you want to use another design as a starting point, taking some measurements is a good way to start. There are several resources that talk about taking lines off a boat. I'll leave it to you to research this task.

Starting from Scratch

Even if you are taking lines from an historical boat or stealing lines from a design you like, you may still have a lot of work ahead of you. To fair out an old design you will need to be able to connect between profile, plan, and sectional views of the kayak. This can be an involved process when designing by hand.

The design cycle. Like choosing a kayak, the first step in designing one is determining what you want to do with it. From this, you will make a decision about overall length, waterline length, breadth, depth, and midsection shape.

I often start by drawing a profile view, plan view, and a middle cross-sectional shape. These drawings need to be compared to make sure they relate correctly to each other. From there, a waterline may be drawn. The points on this waterline are used to start planning more sections, and the fairness of these sections may be checked with more waterlines or buttock lines.

Where errors are encountered, changes are made. After flipping between the three drawings until you're bored silly, you will finally have a design. Some time during this process you may want to double-check the particulars, such as displacement, stability, hull-form coefficients, wetted surface, etc. If you don't like them, you tweak and redo until everything is about the way you want it.

Computer-aided design (CAD). In a standard CAD package this design cycle is still complicated. A package with 3-D capability is a help. The best solution is a CAD package intended for naval architecture.

A good naval architecture package will manipulate a 3-D model of the boat. It will automatically draw sections, buttocks, and waterlines. No error-prone transfer of dimensions from one view to the next is required. The software will probably have tools for calculating the particulars. On the whole, if you're going to be doing much boat design, a good naval architecture program will help a lot.

Typically, a naval architecture CAD package will let you manipulate a "surface" as if it were a rectangular rubber sheet. The shape of the sheet is changed by using a grid of control points, which may be visualized as magnets pulling on the rubber sheet. As you move the control point, the region of the sheet nearest the control gets pulled along with the control. The closer the sheet is to the control point the more influence the control point has. The result is the sheet will bend smoothly between the control points. By arranging the grid of the control point into something that resembles a boat, the rubber sheet will produce a smooth boat shape.

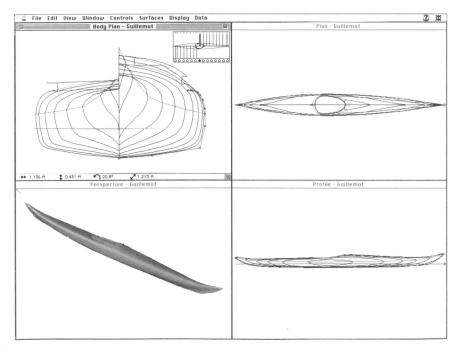

Figure A4-1. *Designing a kayak on a computer is most easily done using software designed for the task. This figure shows some of the design windows available in MaxSurf. The body plan window (upper left) lets you see the stations of the kayak. The square dots visible on the right side of the body plan are control points for the surface of the boat. Moving these control points will change the shape of the sections.*

The most sophisticated type of surface used in CAD is a non-uniform rational B-spline (NURB), which is a mathematical representation of a curve. The spline referred to harks back to the wooden splines formerly used by naval architects to draw fair curves. The difference between a non-uniform and a uniform rational B-spline is that the "non-" kind can be used to represent circles, cylinders, or spheres by changing the weighting or "power of the magnet" in each control point. NURB capability is usually not required to design a kayak.

The mathematical control points of a NURB and other surfaces do not lie on the surface. Some CAD packages do additional mathematical manipulations to force the surface through the control points because it's easier to understand what you're doing when the control points lie on the surface. The trade-off is less control. Because of the additional math required by the software, the control points on the surface have a less direct influence on the surface. A change of one control point on the surface will move the surface locally but it may also make large changes to a part of the surface far away from the control. This can make it difficult to achieve a desired shape.

The price of a naval architecture CAD package usually depends on how many surfaces it lets you use. A kayak needs at least two surfaces: the hull and the deck. An additional surface can be used to define the cockpit, but it's not required, and you may even be able to get away with a single surface if you plan a simple deck shape. When you're looking for a CAD package, consider the number of surfaces you need, whether you want control points on the surface, and the types of calculations you want to be able perform. Most packages will calculate "upright" properties such as displacement, wetted surface, center of gravity, hull form coefficients, and so on. Others will generate stability curves and more sophisticated calculations. You should be able to find a relatively inexpensive package that fulfills the requirements for designing a kayak.

Modifying a Design

Most designers would prefer you didn't mess with their designs. I am one of those designers. I drew up my designs the way I wanted them and I think they are right the way they are; but I know

many people cannot leave well enough alone. I am one of those people.

If someone handed me a design and said, "Build this, it's good" the first thing I would do is "improve" it. Maybe it isn't really an improvement, but with luck maybe it is. I am not going to fight this aspect of human nature. If you want to change the designs in this book or others, here are some ways to do so.

The simplest way to modify a strip design is just to change the form spacing. Making the spacing 11 inches instead of 12 inches will turn a 17-foot kayak into a kayak 15 feet 7 inches long. With a design like the Great Auk, this will probably be a decent boat. However, that much change can cause some problems.

For example, the end forms are still the same. Again, with the Great Auk, you can just cut a little off the inboard end of the forms as defined by the offsets and move the sectional forms accordingly. This will probably work fine. The alternative is to change the length measurements of the offsets accordingly. For example if you multiply all the length measurements by $^{11}/_{12}$ the forms will be scaled correctly for the 11-inch form spacing.

A simple multiplication will accurately scale down a dimension—but other factors change as well, such as the displacement. As you scale down the length, the weight-carrying capacity is also reduced. This might actually be why you want to do the scaling in the first place. If you weigh 100 pounds, a kayak designed for someone weighting 180 pounds probably is not ideally suited to you. A simple linear

Figure A4-2. My brother used my forms for the Great Auk to make a double. He added a center form to make the boat longer and redesigned the deck to accommodate two cockpits.

scaling may be sufficient for you, but what if you want to change the length yet keep some volume? Then you may want to close up the spacing at the ends while maintaining it in the middle. Since there is less volume in the ends anyway, this will have less effect on the overall volume.

You need to be careful when changing the form spacing because you don't want to make the hull unfair. Having all the forms spaced at 12 inches and changing just one to 9 inches will undoubtedly cause a weird curve in the shape. You must change the spacing gradually. For example, you can make all the spacing, moving out from the center, 1/8 inch less than the previous, that is 11 7/8, 11 3/4, 11 5/8 and so on. This will keep the transition smooth.

But once again you run into the problem of the end forms not being scaled. Since the scaling is not linear, you need a more complicated equation to modify the offset table. Modify the long position (LP) by the following equations:

$$NewLP = CenterLP - \text{SIGN}[CenterLP]\frac{(SF\ CenterLP^2)}{24}$$

Where:

CenterLP is the long position in **feet** with the zero point at the longitudinal center of the boat

If originally the zero point is at the end then
CenterLP = F(*Length*,2) − *EndLP*

EndLP is the old long position in **feet** where the zero point for the offsets table is at the bow or stern

Length is the length of the original boat in **feet**

SF is the Spacing Factor, or the reduction in form spacing in **inches** as the forms move away from the center

New LP is the new long position in **feet**, and

SIGN[*x*] is a function that returns +1 for all positive values of *x* and -1 for all negative values of *x*. (This is a standard spreadsheet function.)

If you want to build a boat of a specific length, use the following formula to determine the Spacing Factor in **inches**:

$$Spacing\ Factor = \frac{48\ (OldLength - NewLength)}{OldLength^3}$$

Where:

OldLength is the length of the design you are modifying in **feet**, and

NewLength is the desired length in **feet**.

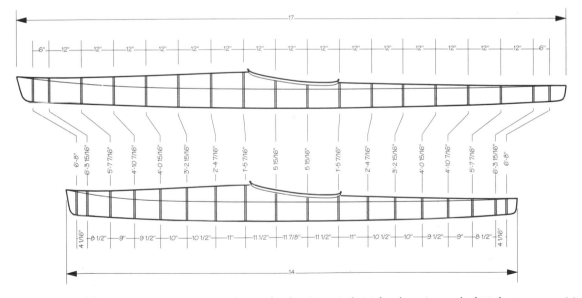

Figure A4-3. *If for some reason you wanted to make the Great Auk 14 feet long instead of 17 feet, you could just shrink the spacing of the forms proportionally to 9⅓ inches or you could gradually reduce the spacing by ½ inch for each form as in this example. This would keep more volume than proportional scaling, which may be an advantage for some people. Note that you may need to scale the end forms as well.*

Plug the resulting **Spacing Factor** in the first equation.

For example, to convert a 17-foot design to a 14-foot design:

From the second equation : $\dfrac{48\,(17'-14')}{17'^2} - 0.5''$

Given forms located at {½', 1', 2', 3', 4', 5', 6', 7', 8', 9', 10', 11', 12', 13', 14', 15', 16', 16½'} the first equation will give the form locations:

{6' 8", 6' 3¹⁵/₁₆", 5' 7⁷/₁₆", 4' 10⁷/₁₆", 4' 0¹⁵/₁₆", 3' 2¹⁵/₁₆", 2' 4⁷/₁₆", 1' 5⁷/₁₆", 5¹⁵/₁₆", -5¹⁵/₁₆", -1' 5⁷/₁₆", -2' 4⁷/₁₆", -3' 2¹⁵/₁₆", -4' 0¹⁵/₁₆", -4' 10⁷/₁₆", -5' 7⁷/₁₆", -6' 3¹⁵/₁₆", -6' 8"}

Notice that the zero point is at the center. If you want to move it to the bow, add half the new length (7 feet). While the fractions are confusing, you will see that each space between forms gets ½ inch smaller as you move toward the ends, except at the center and the ends themselves. The center spacing doesn't follow the ½-inch rule because it is less than 1 foot away from the zero point. The ends don't follow because they started out with less than 1-foot spacing.

One other method to modify length is to repeat a center form or delete a center form. Repeating a center form is a good start for making a tandem from a single design. Deleting a form is riskier, but may successfully shorten a tandem.

If you want to adjust the width of the kayak, it's best to just do a linear scaling. For example if you want change a 24-inch wide boat to a 22-inch design, multiply all the offsets by ²²/₂₄ = 0.92. I do not recommend that you make large changes in the width of a design unless you are willing to risk severe changes in stability.

You can change the height using a linear scaling like the width adjustment if you feel you want more volume. One change you can make without affecting the performance is to scale the deck only. To accomplish this you must not change the sheer dimensions. All scaling must be performed relative to the sheerline, that is, subtract the height of the sheer from all the points, perform the scaling, then add the height back on.

The final possible change is a variation in rocker. This is accomplished by varying the elevation of the forms. By gradually raising the forms toward the

ends, you'll add more rocker to the keel. Once again, the end forms may need to be modified, either by tilting them upward or performing a calculation on the offset table. A small change on a simple design might not require a modification of the end forms.

All this scaling is best done on a computer spreadsheet. There are a lot of potential points of entry for errors. The spreadsheet will ensure that you use the same formula everywhere and let you catch data-entry errors. Plot out the points using the graphing function to double-check the results.

Moving the Cockpit

A less drastic modification that you might want to make is just to move the cockpit. This is useful in a tandem if you have paddlers of different weights in each cockpit. You may want to adjust the location of the seats to balance the boat. If the design of the boat does not give the center of buoyancy, you will have to calculate it. Then the mass of each paddler, times their distance from the center of buoyancy, must be equal. The distance to measure is from the center of buoyancy to the center of mass of the paddler.

Find your center of mass this way: Sit on the floor and attempt to lift yourself with your hands. When your hands are in front of your CM, you will tip backward. If they're behind your CM, you will lift you butt, but your feet will not lift. When your hands are aligned with your CM, you'll be trying to lift your whole body. If you can lift yourself, try out for the Olympic gymnastics team. Afterward, customize your cockpit location to match your CM. You want enough room behind you to lean back comfortably (4 to 6 inches). This usually means the your CM is about 14 to 16 inches in front of the back of the cockpit.

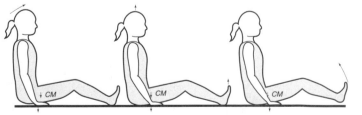

Figure A4-4. *Your center of mass (CM) should align with the center of buoyancy (CB) of the boat. The location of the cockpits in the designs in this book should be good, but if you want to determine where your CM is, you can attempt to lift yourself with your hands. See text.*

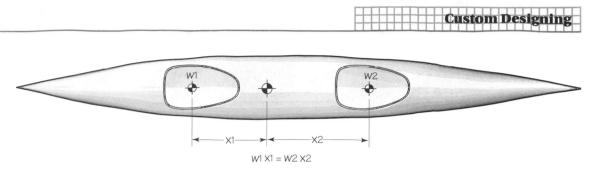

Figure A4-5. *A double kayak should be tailored to its passengers. The combined center of mass (CM) of the passengers should be located at the center of buoyancy (CB) of the boat. To customize the boat, locate the cockpits so that the weights of the paddlers are correctly balanced. See text. Usually, the back of the cockpit should be 14 to 16 inches behind the CM of the paddler.*

With a double kayak, the relative weight of the paddlers can make a big difference in how the boat floats. The Guillemot Double is designed for two paddlers of about the same weight. If the bow paddler is much lighter than the stern paddler you may need to adjust the position of the cockpits. In general, the weight of the paddler, times his or her distance from the center of buoyancy, must be equal for each paddler. You can adjust the position of each cockpit to make the boat balance.

Last Warning

Again, be careful when modifying a design. The designer went to a lot of trouble to get the design right. In an effort to "improve" a design you may make an unusable kayak. Do some calculations of displacement and stability as a sanity check. However, modification of a proven design may be safer than designing from scratch and provides a good way to learn how changing parameters affects performance. It's your boat; do what you want.

English and Metric Conversion Factors

he measurements used in this book are English units. The following conversions can be used:

- Multiply English units by the given factor to get metric units.
- Divide metric units by the given factor to get English units.

English Units	Factor	Metric Units
inches	2.54	centimeters
feet	30.48	centimeters
yards	0.9144	meters
pounds	0.454	kilograms
ounces	28.34	grams
fluid ounces	28.41	milliliters

Appendix 6

Safety

There are a variety of risks attached to building and paddling a kayak. Dust and fumes can cause long-term damage to your health, tools can remove your appendages, and the sea can drown you in your finished boat. Your safety depends on your good judgment. Recognize the risks, and act within your abilities. It is impossible to anticipate all the dangers, but with proper care the risks can be minimized.

Dangers in the Shop

Wood Dust

Wood dust caused by sawing may seem pretty benign because it's a natural product, but be careful. Trees have had millions of years of evolution devoted to keeping bugs out of their hearts. In that time, they've developed some potent toxins. You should always wear a dust mask while sawing and sanding.

Do as much of the cutting and smoothing as you can outdoors. If you are buying new tools, look for tools with built-in dust collection.

Wearing a dust mask is often inconvenient, and some woods, such as cedar, smell very nice—but there's a good reason why cedar chests are used to store sweaters. It is not because they smell nice, nor is it because moths just don't like the smell. Cedar is toxic and moths know to keep their distance when they smell it. Wear a dust mask.

Epoxy

Epoxy is relatively safe to work with, although as a petrochemical it can be dangerous when concentrated. Unlike polyester resin, it doesn't smell too bad, and it isn't as dangerous, but the fact that it doesn't stink doesn't mean it isn't a health hazard. Work in a well-ventilated space and wear a respirator. Read the manufacturer's Material Safety Data Sheet (MSDS). This should be available upon request

from the manufacturer. The respirator should be designed to protect you from fumes. A dust mask should also be worn when sanding epoxy.

Epoxy sensitivity. Many former users of epoxy had to give up working with the stuff because they became sensitized to it. These people are subject to severe reactions, including death, if they come in contact with uncured epoxy. You should not let uncured epoxy touch your bare skin. Wear long-sleeved shirts or a coverall such as a disposable paper "poopie suit." Use disposable gloves, and if they develop a hole, replace them. Instead of gloves you can get a barrier cream that provides some protection, but do not put barrier cream on under gloves because it contains zinc oxide that combines with sweat to create a sensitizing agent. Resist testing new epoxy with your bare finger to determine whether it has cured yet.

Polyester Resin

Polyester resin smells really bad and this is almost an advantage. It is hard to stand working with the stuff without a respirator, in fact you'll find it more comfortable to work with a respirator than without.

Solvents

Powerful solvents such as acetone and toluol can be useful to have around. They can be used to thin epoxy or polyester resin. However, they are very dangerous. Their highly volatile fumes should not be breathed. Never use a solvent to clean your skin. The solvents can easily enter your body through your skin and they make it easier for the resin to enter your skin. Never use a solvent as a hand cleaner.

Wash your hands with soap and water or a waterless hand cleaner intended for cleaning up resin. Tools can be washed with white vinegar. Common white vinegar is very effective for softening and cleaning uncured epoxy. It is cheap, easy to get, and safe enough to eat. You should not use it to wash your hands. Unless you really need them, don't bother with any of the more powerful solvents for cleaning.

Fiberglass Dust

Fiberglass cloth is safe to work with. It is no more toxic than a soda bottle. It's when you're sanding it that problems start, although the long-term effects of breathing fiberglass dust are still uncertain. In my book (and this is my book) this means avoid it. Once again, wear a dust mask. There is certainly no harm in added protection.

The more obvious problem with sanding fiberglass is itching. The dust will cause a severe rash in some people. The rash goes away after a while with no apparent long-term effects. Until it goes away, it itches. Again, you should wear full-length clothing and work with good ventilation.

Your Uniform

A good uniform for working with epoxy and fiberglass is a Tyvek painter's suit with rubber bands holding the sleeves closed, rubber gloves on your hands, safety glasses, and a respirator or dust mask on your face. If you are putting your head anywhere near the wet epoxy (as when taping the interior seam) you should wrap your head and hair in a plastic bag. I am always a little afraid to let the neighbors see me dressed like this. I look like a science-fiction spaceman in this attire, but I stay clean and (I hope) healthy.

Hazardous Tools

Power tools have the ability to remove digits and limbs at worst, and draw blood at best. They should be treated with the utmost respect. Never put your fingers anywhere near the moving cutter. Use feather boards where possible. Move deliberately when using something that can cause such severe damage so quickly. Wear safety glasses whenever you use a tool with moving parts.

Edge tools such as planes and chisels can damage a body pretty quickly as well, especially when they're sharp, but you are less likely to make a mistake with a sharp tool because less force is required to get the job done. Know where you're going with a tool at all times and know where it will go if you slip. If the very idea of having to use a tool this way makes you wince, keep a first-aid kit handy for common cuts.

On the Water

Sea kayaking is a potentially deadly sport. Going out on the water is not an excursion that should be taken lightly, no matter how well you think you know it. However, this is not the place to cover all the safety aspects of sea kayaking. There are other good books which can do the job much better than I can in the short space available. I will, however, cover several rules that should limit the damage you can do to yourself.

Always wear a PFD (personal flotation device, or life jacket). Wear it. Don't tie it down behind you. It might get swept away by the same thing that tipped you over, and it does no good if it is not on. I am a strong swimmer, but the ocean doesn't care. I wear my life jacket even on the safest water because I want the habit to be so ingrained that I will feel naked without it. This way, if I forget my life jacket in a place where I might need it, I will turn around and get it.

Dress for the coldest temperature. If the air is 90°F and the water is 45°F, dress for 45°. This means a wet suit, or a dry suit with insulation under it. You will be uncomfortable for the air temperature, but this is good excuse to learn how to roll. A little rotary cooling does wonders.

Don't go out in conditions beyond your abilities. If you don't know if you can handle the conditions, play it safe. The weather out on the water can change quickly. Listen to the weather report. Know your abilities and use sound judgment.

Have flotation in the boat. Bulkheads will stop water getting into the rest of the boat from the cockpit, and sinking it. A strip-built kayak will not sink completely, but it may float so low that you cannot pump it out. Bulkheads are the first line of defense. You should also use float bags, even if you have bulkheads. A bulkhead or hatch may fail, letting water in the ends. You may also get a hole in the hull. Playing in the surf one day, my brother got a hole all the way through the bow compartment of his kayak. He would not have been able to paddle home if he hadn't had float bags.

Learn self-rescue techniques. The best, most reliable technique is the Eskimo roll. With a good roll you never need to leave your kayak, and the effects of exposure to cold water are minimized. It is worth taking lessons from a good teacher to learn how to roll. Although it's difficult to learn, and although you can hurt yourself doing a roll incorrectly, once you learn, rolling is easy and fun. It doesn't take strength, it takes practice. Knowing how to roll is not a require-

ment for kayaking safely, but the skill will extend the range of weather and water conditions in which you can safely paddle.

Whether you roll or not, you should learn and practice other rescue techniques. A paddle float or inflatable sponsons can provide a means of steadying the kayak after you fall out. For beginners, inflatable sponsons can be used like training wheels on a bike. They will let you paddle a more stable platform until you become used to handling a kayak. But no system is infallible, so learn as many ways of helping yourself as possible.

Many people who have never paddled a kayak before put their newly built boat in the water, paddle out 100 yards, and flip over. It probably isn't inten-

tional, but it's a good idea. Float out to waist deep water, deliberately flip over, and get out of the kayak so you know what it feels like. Don't try this alone. Have someone standing next to you, to help you out if you have problems. You will not be trapped in the boat, but if you flip by mistake you don't want to panic. You should know how it feels before it happens. When you flip, put your hands on either side of the cockpit. Push away from the boat as you roll forward.

Like any boat, a kayak can be dangerous. In skilled hands, a kayak is as seaworthy a boat as has ever been made. If you have not kayaked before, try to get lessons. You will be happier with your boat if you know how to use it correctly, and there's no substitute for a good teacher.

Glossary

Beam. The width of the boat at the widest point. Can be measured at the waterline or at the sheerline.

Bias-cut cloth. Cloth cut at a 45-degree angle to the warp and weft of the weave.

Block coefficient. The displacement of the boat divided by the displacement of an imaginary block-shaped hull of the same length, width, and depth. Used for design analysis.

Bows. The front of a boat. In the navy this is referred to as "the pointy end," but this description does not work well for most kayaks.

Brace. Using your paddle and body English to maintain balance.

Bulkhead. Watertight separating wall between cockpit area and storage areas in the bow and stern.

Buttocks. Lines defining the hull of a boat. They cut the hull around a vertical plane parallel to the centerline.

Cheek plates. Plates hanging from the coaming on either side of the seat.

Chine. The corner or curve in the hull where it changes from the sides to the bottom. Also turn-of-the-bilge. A "soft" chine is rounded, a "hard" chine is angular.

Coaming. The raised section around the cockpit, over which you secure the spray skirt. "Combing" is an alternate spelling.

Cockpit. The hole in which you sit.

Cove-and-bead. A type of wood strip with a hollow in one edge and a matching bulge on the other edge, which permits the strips to fit snugly even when they are placed at an angle to each other.

Deck lines. Rope or shock cord on the deck used to hold down cargo, or as a safety line.

Displacement. The weight of water displaced by the boat. This is equal to the weight of the boat, passenger(s), and cargo.

Dookie schmutz. I'm not sure this is a real term, but I heard it once and it seemed so descriptive that I adopted it. I use it to describe any thickened resin that is used to fill cracks or as a glue. It is usually the consistency of peanut butter or mayonnaise.

Draft or Draught. Depth of the deepest part of the boat from the waterline.

DWL. Datum waterline or design waterline.

End-pour. A puddle of filled resin poured in the very end of the kayak. This provides strength and a place to mount grab-loops.

Eskimo roll. A maneuver for righting a capsized kayak without leaving the boat. Good fun!

Fair. A description of the smoothness of a curve. A fair curve will not have any abrupt changes in curvature. Also used as a verb.

Fillet. A smoothly curved fill in what would otherwise be a sharply angled joint.

Footbraces. A place to push your feet against. This makes sitting in the kayak much more comfortable and secure.

Forms. Solid cross-sectional shapes upon which the boat is built.

Hatch. A hole with a watertight cover, giving access to storage in the ends of the kayak.

Heeling or Tipping. A heeling moment is the force attempting to tip the boat over.

Hull Speed. A theoretical limit to how fast a boat can go, dependent on its waterline length.

Keel. The very bottom centerline of a boat.

LCB. Longitudinal center of buoyancy. The lengthwise location of the center of buoyancy.

LCF. Longitudinal center of flotation. The lengthwise location of the geometric center of the shape described by the waterline.

LOA. Length over all. The full length of the boat, including overhangs.

LWL. Length at the waterline. The length of the boat actually in the water.

Monocoque. A structure in which the outer skin supports stresses. There are few or no internal frames.

NURBS. Non-uniform rational B-splines. A mathematical representation of a curve or surface, used in some boat-design CAD software.

Offsets. A table of numbers describing the shape of the boat.

Overhang. The section of the bow or stern that extends out beyond the end of the waterline.

Plumb. Vertical. A plumb bow runs straight up and down, and has little or no overhang.

Prismatic coefficient. The displacement of the boat divided by the displacement of an imaginary hull the same shape as the widest part of the real hull for the full length of the imaginary hull. Used for design analysis.

Resin. Either epoxy or polyester. A liquid plastic used with fiberglass which, when cured, makes the boat strong.

Righting moment. The force trying to keep a boat upright. This is counteracted by the heeling moment trying to tip a boat over.

Rocker. The slight upward curvature in a boat's keel from amidships toward each end.

Roving. An unspun yarn. In this context, a bundle of glass fibers about $1/4$ inch wide.

Rudder. A steering device.

Scarf. A means of joining two pieces of wood lengthwise with a minimum loss in strength.

Sections. Lines depicting the hull of a boat. They run vertically in a plane perpendicular to the longitudinal centerline. For a kayak, these are made into building forms.

Sheer or sheerline. The line separating the deck from the hull.

Skeg. An extension of the keel, or a rudder-like fin toward the back that helps the boat go straight. A skeg may be retractable.

Skin. The surface of the boat. In the case of a strip-built boat, the wood-glass-epoxy laminate.

Sponson. An additional source of flotation attached to the side of a boat for increased stability. In kayaking, this is usually an inflatable bag.

Spray skirt. A fabric skirt worn around the waist and secured over a lip on the coaming to keep water from entering the kayak. I prefer neoprene material.

Stability. The tendency for the boat to stay upright. This is a function of the heeling moment and the righting moment. As long as the righting moment is greater, the boat will return to the upright position.

Stem. The section of the bow or stern coming up from the keel to the very front of the boat.

Stern. The back end of a boat.

Strongback. The supporting structure that holds the forms while the boat is being assembled. For my kayaks, this is a 2×4.

Thixotropic. The property of some materials to become fluid when disturbed and stiffening up when left alone. Quicksand is thixotropic. When resin is thixotropic, it can be spread in place and stay there without sagging.

Tracking. The ability to go straight.

V. The angle the hull makes upward from either side of the keel. Also called deadrise.

VCB. Vertical center of buoyancy. This is the elevation of the center of buoyancy and it will always be under water.

Waterline(s). The waterline is the line at the surface of the water of the floating boat (often called the datum waterline). Waterlines are a series of lines depicting the hull of the boat at various elevations that run parallel to the surface of the water, like contour lines on a map.

Wetted-surface area. The area of the hull surface below the waterline.

Appendix 8

Bibliography

Guillemot kayaks home page.
http://www.Guillemot-Kayaks.com/
The author's worldwide-web home page. The best place to get the latest updates and ideas about strip-building kayaks. It contains a wide variety of kayak-building information, a bulletin board, a catalog of the author's Guillemot Kayaks designs and other sea kayak information. The bulletin board is a good place to post questions when you run into trouble, or to share your ideas and experiences with other readers of this book.

Some of these books might be out of print; check with your library or secondhand bookseller.

Adney, Edwin T., and Howard I. Chappelle. 1983.
The Bark Canoes and Skin Boats of North America.
Washington, DC: Smithsonian Institution Press.
Primarily about birchbark canoes, but some good information about traditional kayaks.

Arima, Eugene Y. 1992.
Contributions to Kayak Studies.
Ottawa, Canada: National Museums of Canada.
An assortment of information investigating the construction and performance of traditional kayaks.

Arima, Eugene Y. 1987.
Inuit Kayaks in Canada: A Review of Historical Records and Construction.
Ottawa, Canada: National Museums of Canada.
A review of historical records with much information about Inuit kayaks, their design and construction.

Dutky, Paul. 1993.
The Bombproof Roll and Beyond.
Birmingham, Ala.: Menasha Ridge Press.

A well-illustrated manual for learning to do the Eskimo roll. This is a good resource for teaching yourself to roll or to study before taking a class. Rolling is not a required skill for sea kayaking but a damned useful one.

Dyson, George. 1986.
Baidarka.
Seattle, Wash.: Alaska Northwest Books.
A richly illustrated book covering the history of Aleut kayak development. George Dyson's adventures and philosophy, and his method of building kayaks using aluminum tubing and nylon.

The Forest Products Laboratory. 1987.
The Encyclopedia of Wood (revised edition).
New York, N.Y.: Sterling Publishing Co. Inc.
The name just about says it all. This book contains all the technical information you will ever want about wood.

Gilpatrick, Gil. 1985.
Building a Strip Canoe (revised edition).
Freeport, Maine: DeLorme Publishing Co.
This is the book that taught me strip-building. A good no-nonsense introduction to strip-building.

Gougeon Bros., Inc. 1985.
The Gougeon Brothers on Boat Construction: wood & West Systems Materials.
Bay City, Mich.: Gougeon Bros., Inc.
Written by the makers of West Systems epoxy with their products in mind. This a large reference with a lot of information about building boats with wood and epoxy.

Hazen, David. 1994.
The Stripper's Guide to Canoe Building.
Larkspur, Calif.: Tamal Vista Publications.
An older strip-built instruction book with some information about building kayaks. Good for a second or third opinion.

Hutchinson, Derek. 1988.
Eskimo Rolling.
Camden, Maine: International Marine.
For those of you who can't stop at learning just one way to roll, this book includes descriptions of some of the more exotic techniques.

Hutchinson, Derek. 1985.
Guide to Sea Kayaking. Old Saybrook, Conn.: Globe Pequot Press.
A good description of some of the skills require to sea kayak safely. Not a substitute for lessons, but a good supplement.

Kulczyki, Chris. 1993.
The Kayak Shop.
Camden, Maine: Ragged Mountain Press.
Instructions on how to build a stitch-and-glue plywood kayak. Some information here may be transferable to a stripper.

Lewis, Edward V., ed. 1988.
The Principles of Naval Architecture,
(three volumes).
Jersey City, N.J.: The Society of Naval Architects and Marine Engineers.
A comprehensive text of naval architecture for boats of all sizes.

Moores, Ted, and Merilyn Mohr. 1983.
Canoecraft.
North York, Ontario, Canada: Camden House Publishing.
A book about strip-building canoes. Provides a different perspective on the building process.

Richert, Chad.
Kayaks—Stripper Style: How to Build Them.
Kirkland, Wash.: Canoe and Kayak Magazine.
A small book trying to do the same thing as the one you are now reading.

System Three Resins, Inc. 1992.
The Epoxy Book.
Seattle, Wash.: System Three Resins, Inc.
System Three is a manufacturer of epoxy. This book is written with their resins in mind, but it's still a very good source of epoxy knowledge. If you have not used epoxy or fiberglass before, this book is worthwhile.

Walbridge, Charles, ed. 1986.
Boatbuilder's Manual.
Birmingham, Ala: Menasha Ridge Press.
This book was written for builders of fiberglass whitewater kayaks, but it contains a lot of good information about fiberglassing, materials, and resins that is applicable to strip-built kayaks.

Watson, Aldren A. 1982.
Hand Tools: Their Ways and Workings.
New York, N.Y.: Lyons & Burford.
A good reference for how to use and care for hand tools.

Winters, John. 1997.
The Shape of the Canoe.
Burk's Falls, Ontario, Canada: Redwind Design.
A well-written technical discussion of canoe and kayak design.

Zimmerly, David W. 1986.
Qajaq: Kayaks of Siberia and Alaska.
Juneau, Alaska: Alaska State Museums.
This book was written to accompany an exhibition of traditional kayaks. Provides a good background about Alaskan and Siberian kayaks.

Index

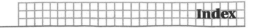